W9-DDK-885

1/4·26

WEINGARTNER ON

MUSIC & CONDUCTING

Three Essays by Felix Weingartner

ON CONDUCTING
Translated by Ernest Newman

ON THE PERFORMANCE OF
BEETHOVEN'S SYMPHONIES
Translated by Jessie Crosland

THE SYMPHONY SINCE BEETHOVEN
Translated by H. M. Schott

Dover Publications, Inc., New York

Published in Canada by General Publishing Company, Ltd.,
30 Lesmill Road, Don Mills, Toronto, Ontario.

The present volume, first published by Dover Publications, Inc.,
in 1969, contains the following material:
The unabridged and unaltered text of *On Conducting* (Ernest
Newman's translation of the third German edition of Weingartner's
Über das Dirigieren), originally published by Breitkopf & Härtel,
Leipzig (second edition, 1925). All passages altered or added by
Weingartner in the fourth German edition have been newly
translated specially for the present Dover edition and appear in an
Appendix to *On Conducting*.
On the Performance of Beethoven's Symphonies (Jessie Crosland's
translation of the first German edition of Weingartner's *Ratschläge
für Aufführungen der Symphonien Beethovens*), originally published
by Breitkopf & Härtel, Leipzig, in 1907. This text has been corrected and revised to conform entirely with the third German
edition; all such alterations have been prepared specially for the
present edition.
The Symphony Since Beethoven, a completely new unabridged
translation of the fourth German edition of Weingartner's *Die
Symphonie nach Beethoven*, prepared specially for the present
edition by H. M. Schott. Mr. Schott has also furnished several
new notes and a new Translator's Preface.
See the Publisher's Note on the facing page for the bibliography
of the various German editions and for more specific information
on the preparation of the present volume.

Standard Book Number: 486-22106-7
Library of Congress Catalog Card Number: 68-31129

MANUFACTURED IN THE UNITED STATES OF AMERICA

Dover Publications, Inc.
180 Varick Street
New York, N.Y. 10014

Publisher's Note

The present volume contains English translations of three important literary works of the conductor Felix Weingartner (1863–1942).
The translations given here take fully into account the revisions
undertaken by the author at various times.

On Conducting first appeared in German (as *Über das Dirigieren*)
in 1895. A second, unchanged German edition was published the
following year. The translation by Ernest Newman (second edition,
1925) which is the basis of the present text was made from the
heavily revised third German edition of 1905. In order to show the
reader the definitive form of the work, as established by the fourth
German edition of 1913 (a fifth German edition, 1920, introduced no
changes), while still preserving Newman's text intact, we have added
in an Appendix to *On Conducting* new translations (specially prepared for this edition) of material rewritten or added by Weingartner
in the fourth German edition, and we have placed within brackets
those passages in Newman's text which correspond to passages
omitted in the fourth German edition.

On the Performance of Beethoven's Symphonies first appeared in
German in 1906 with the title *Ratschläge für Aufführungen der
Symphonien Beethovens*. A very lightly altered second edition
was published in 1916. When the third edition appeared in 1928
(with a few more changes), it had become Volume (*Band*) I,
Beethoven, of a series known as *Ratschläge für Aufführungen klassischer Symphonien* (the series now included a volume on Schubert
and Schumann and one on Mozart, both of which had also originally
been published separately). The only English translation of this work
on Beethoven, by Jessie Crosland, appeared in 1907, and was thus
prepared from the first German edition. The present text is basically
the Crosland translation, but we have incorporated directly into it
new translations of those sections rewritten or added in later
editions by Weingartner and we have completely omitted what he

v

later omitted, so that the reader will have before him here a full translation of the definitive form of the work. In addition, we have replaced Weingartner's system of references to pages in the complete Breitkopf & Härtel Beethoven with references to bars numbered consecutively throughout each movement, since many more readers today will have access to scores numbered consecutively than to the Breitkopf edition. Finally, we have reviewed the entire text of this Crosland translation, overhauling the peculiar punctuation and styling of the original edition, correcting the numerous typographical and other errors and occasionally making improvements in the diction.

The Symphony Since Beethoven first appeared in German (as *Die Symphonie nach Beethoven*) in 1897; second edition *ca.* 1901. The third edition, 1909, was a thorough revision amounting practically to a new book, while the fourth and final edition of 1926 introduced even more changes. Two independent English translations already in existence were both prepared from the now altogether obsolete second German edition. Therefore, the present volume includes an all new translation, written specially for Dover by H. M. Schott, of the complete German fourth edition. Mr. Schott has added a few explanatory notes of his own, as well as a very welcome Translator's Preface to which we refer the reader for further information on Weingartner and his era.

General Table of Contents

ON CONDUCTING

Translated by Ernest Newman

Translator's Note*

Herr Weingartner's "On Conducting" first appeared in the *Neue Deutsche Rundschau*, Berlin, and then in book form in 1895. A second edition, not differing from the first, appeared in 1896. The third edition, from which the present translation is made, was issued in 1905; it omits so much that was in the first edition, and contains so much that did not appear there, as to be practically an entirely new treatise. I have added a few notes in order to make a point here and there clearer to the English reader.

E. N.

* For a translation of the Preface to the Fourth German Edition, see Appendix, p. 49. For an explanation of this Appendix and what it contains, see Publisher's Note, p. v.

On Conducting

Under the same title as that of the present volume, Richard Wagner published in 1869 his well-known *brochure*,* which, assailing as it did with uncompromising candour the most famous conductors of that epoch, drew upon him the furious enmity of the persons he attacked. In spite, however, of the hatred, open or concealed, of the music-popes whose infallibility was assailed, Wagner's book laid the foundation for a new understanding of the function of the conductor, in whom we now recognise not only the external factor that holds together an orchestral, choral or operatic performance, but above all the spiritualising internal factor that gives the performance its very soul. Wagner was certainly not the first to realise how much depends on the way a piece of music is rendered. He opines that the reason Bach rarely marked tempi in his scores was because he said to himself, as it were, "If anyone does not understand my theme and my figuration, has no feeling for their character and their expression, of what use will an Italian tempo-indication be to him?" I maintain, on the contrary, that the vigorous old master would have been incapable of looking at art in this resigned way. I believe rather that he so rarely indicated the tempo or gave any dynamic marks only because he always had in view his own presence at the performances. If we picture to ourselves a Bach performance in his own lifetime we must think of himself at the organ with his little band of musicians round him. [How many of his innumerable cantatas, now assured of immortality, must in his own day have been sung just once, on the Feast-day for which they were composed, whereupon the manuscript went into the drawer "with the others," and for the next Feast-day

* *Über das Dirigieren.* The book was translated into English in 1887 by Mr. Edward Dannreuther. Mr. Ashton Ellis's version appears in Volume IV of his translation of Wagner's complete *Prose Works*. [Tr.]

the inexhaustible Cantor wrote a new one!]* His Suites and Concertos, again, are to be regarded as chamber-music works at whose production he himself or a privileged pupil sat at the clavicembalo; the "Well-tempered Clavier" and the Sonatas were intended as studies. Why should he waste time in noting down instructions for execution? It always rested with him to give the correct tempo, and to explain to the musicians the interpretation he wanted. The mighty teacher of the Thomas-School certainly never anticipated a collected edition of his works, [in preparing which the editors were often greatly puzzled by the careless figuring of the bass—which again shows that he knew the execution of the *continuo*† to be in trusty hands; nor did he anticipate concert productions of them with large orchestras and choruses.]

How‡ much Mozart considered the question of interpretation is to be seen in the careful way he has marked his works (especially his latest), and from many passages in his letters. It is not improbable that in Mannheim he heard for the first time an orchestra that could really play *crescendo* and *diminuendo*. Even our best orchestras of to-day need to be constantly told that the increase and decrease of tone is to be done evenly and gradually, not suddenly; and the difficulty of doing this increases with the number of bars over which these variations in volume have to be extended. "*Diminuendo* signifies *forte*, *crescendo* signifies *piano*," said Bülow. This is only a seeming contradiction, since to play *forte* at the beginning of a *crescendo*, and *piano* at the beginning of a *diminuendo*, really means the negation of *crescendo* and *diminuendo*. We know that not only Mozart, but Weber, Mendelssohn and Spohr were excellent conductors, and that each of them, from his own artistic standpoint, fought energetically against abuses and errors of taste. How Wagner did this is shown among other things in the book of his I have mentioned. This, however, with all its perfect outspokenness, seems quite mild when we read the flaming words with which Berlioz opens his treatise on "The theory of the conductor's art." He says:

* The passages within square brackets throughout *On Conducting* correspond to passages omitted by Weingartner in the fourth German edition of the work. See Publisher's Note, p. v.

† The "continuo" or "basso continuo" is the equivalent of the English thorough bass. [Tr.]

‡ Passage rewritten in fourth German edition. See Appendix, p. 49.

Singers have often been reproached with being the most dangerous of the factors concerned in the production of music; but, I think, unjustly. The most formidable intermediary is in my opinion the conductor. A bad singer can spoil only his own part, while an incompetent or malicious conductor can spoil everything. The composer must indeed count himself fortunate when the conductor into whose hands he has fallen is not both incompetent *and* malicious; for against the destructive influence of such a man nothing can avail. The most excellent orchestra is crippled by him; the finest singers are perplexed and exhausted; there is no longer any ardour or precision in the rendering. Under conducting of this kind the composer's finest audacities become mere oddities; enthusiasm is killed; inspiration comes precipitately to earth; the angel's wings are clipped; a genius is made to look like an eccentric or a madman; the godlike statue is thrown from its pedestal and dragged in the mud. The worst of it is that the public, no matter how good its musical education may be, is not in a position, at the first performance of a new work, to detect the mutilations, stupidities, errors and sins against art that such a conductor has on his conscience.

What experiences Berlioz must have had for this wild cry to be drawn from him can be estimated from the single fact that a conductor who in the first half of the nineteenth century occupied a really foremost position, and of whom both Wagner and Berlioz spoke with the warmest acknowledgment—that Habeneck of Paris, as Berlioz tells us, conducted not from the score but from *a violin part*, a custom to-day confined to beer-garden concerts with their waltzes and pot-pourris. Yet Habeneck, by means of diligent rehearsals with the orchestra of the Conservatoire, must have given performances of a technical perfection that as a rule could not be met with in Germany at the same time; Wagner confesses that it was from Habeneck's rendering that he first really understood Beethoven's Ninth Symphony, after having received at the Leipzig Gewandhaus such confused impressions of it that for a time he "had his doubts" even about Beethoven himself.* Like so many things in Wagner's writings, these "doubts" must not be taken

---

* See Mr. Ellis's translation of Wagner's *Prose Works*, Vol. IV, pp. 300–302. [Tr.]

literally, for a musician of his rank must have been able to judge from his knowledge of the score—of which indeed he had made a manuscript copy for himself—how much of the confused impression was due to the work and how much to the rendering. The fact remains, however, that a bad interpretation can not only completely deceive the uninstructed but also prevent the instructed from listening with full sympathy. I still remember in the early eighties, when I was a pupil at the Leipzig Conservatoire, to have heard some performances by the splendid Gewandhaus orchestra, which, through the fault of its half solid, half elegant conductor, answered so little to the ideas I had formed for myself of the works in question, that I preferred not to stay to the end of many of the performances, so as not to have my precious picture marred. Of course I did not "have doubts" about any of our masters. Only my longing increased to be able at some time to render the works as I felt them. As I gave imprudently outspoken expression to this desire and to my dissatisfaction with what I heard, it was looked upon as unwarrantable self-glorification on my part. However, as Bülow soon afterwards appeared with the Meiningen orchestra, people then realised what was meant by a finely-balanced *ensemble*; and I heard much agreement expressed with what I had previously maintained. The impression of Bülow's interpretations must have kindled in our Leipzig conductor a spark of that temperament that had been long extinguished under the ashes of convention, for at one of the concerts given after the visit of the Meiningen band he played the great "Leonora" overture in a quite surprising way. It was especially noticeable, however, that he did not imitate Bülow's arbitrarinesses —of which I shall speak later—but let the work unfold itself in great-featured simplicity. And as his was the larger and better orchestra, the effect was such that the generally rather reserved audience broke out into a huge exclamation of joy, that even surpassed the storms of applause that had been given to Bülow. In a few minutes the *Zopf* ★ was blown away as by a breeze from heaven, all arbitrariness was banished, and Beethoven *spoke to us without commentary*. This experience was very instructive to me.

When Wagner, after his first Parisian sojourn, came to Dresden as conductor, he had learned from Habeneck to what perfection orchestral performances can attain under conscientious guidance;

★ The German term *Zopf*—literally "pigtail"—is used to denote a pedantic, obsolete style in art. [Tr.]

and from all we have learned of him as conductor, from himself and from others, he obviously aimed in his own performances not only at correctness but at bringing out that to which the sounds and notes are only the *means*. He sought for the unifying thread, the psychological line, the revelation of which suddenly transforms, as if by magic, a more or less indefinite sound-picture into a beautifully shaped, heart-moving vision, making people ask themselves in astonishment how it is that this work, which they had long thought they knew, should have all at once become quite another thing, and the unprejudiced mind joyfully confesses, "Yes, thus, *thus*, must it really be." Out of the garment of tone there emerges the *spirit of the art-work*; its noble countenance, formerly only confusedly visible, is now unveiled, and enraptures those who are privileged to behold it. Wagner calls this form, this quintessence, this spirit of the art-work its *melos*, which term, later on, was perverted by inability to understand Wagner's own creations into "endless melody." His desire to make this *melos* stand out clearly carried him so far that in some places in Beethoven's works where he held the evident purpose of the composer to be not fully realised in the orchestration—whether because the instruments at Beethoven's disposal were imperfect, or because his increasing deafness sometimes clouded his perception of the relations of the various orchestral timbres—he discreetly altered the orchestration, touching it up so as to bring the hitherto unclear melody into due prominence. Of course the music-popes and wretched literalists screamed anathema. It is certainly open to question whether all these retouchings were happy and deserving of imitation; there is no doubt however that he very often hit upon the right thing. I believe, for example, that nowadays no conductor who can think at all will play the Ninth Symphony without Wagner's instrumental emendations; [the vocal changes, on the contrary, I look upon as both purposeless and tasteless.*]

Added to this desire for clarity in Wagner was the passionate temperament with which, aided by a keen understanding, he threw himself into his work; he brought to it also a faculty of *immediate communication* with the players and imposition of his will on them—in a word that genius which, in spite of other acknowledgments, he

---

* See Wagner's article on "The Rendering of Beethoven's Ninth Symphony," in Vol. V of Mr. Ellis's translation of the *Prose Works*. [Tr.] N.B.: At this point in his fourth edition Weingartner adds a footnote with a general reference to *On the Performance of Beethoven's Symphonies*.

had to deny to Habeneck, but which made some of his own performances historically memorable, in spite of the perishable nature
of all reproductive art. [*There is no performance of genius possible
without temperament.* This truth must be perpetually insisted on,
notwithstanding that Schopenhauer has voiced it distinctly enough.
Temperament, however, can be given neither by education, nor
conscientiousness, nor, by the way, by favour; it must be *inborn*,
the free gift of nature. Therefore performances of genius can only
receive recognition either by another genius—just as the height and
beauty of a mountain are best appreciated from another summit—
or by that naïve instinct, often found among non-artists and the
people, that gives itself up spontaneously to the beautiful. But they
are quite incomprehensible to those "aesthetes" who consider them
as problems of the understanding and would solve them, like a
mathematical problem, by analysis—incomprehensible not only
because temperament is an endowment of the heart, not of the
understanding, but also because the curb that the artist has to put
on his temperament has to be directed by head and heart, not by
the former alone. Hence in most cases critical aesthetic and aesthetic-
ising criticism pass undeserved censure—honest as the intention
may be—on performances of genius, and only gradually attain to the
correct view when the naïve instinct to which I have referred has
given its final verdict, and disparagement would now be like
flying in the face of a *plébiscite*. Artistic truth bears a prophetic,
critical truth a posthumous character; from this comes that blind
adulation we sometimes see—especially in cases where the earlier
condemnation had been particularly strong—that will not allow the
slightest weakness to be pointed out in the idol.]

I regret that I never saw Wagner conduct. He was described to
me; the body, of no more than middle-height, with its stiff deport-
ment, the movement of the arms not immoderately great or sweep-
ing, but decisive and very much to the point; showing no
restlessness, in spite of his vivacity; usually not needing the score at
the concert; fixing his expressive glance on the players and ruling the
orchestra imperially, like the Weber he used to admire as a boy. The
old flautist Fürstenau of Dresden told me that often, when Wagner
conducted, the players had no sense of being led. Each believed
himself to be following freely his own feeling, yet they all worked
together wonderfully. It was Wagner's mighty will that powerfully
but unperceived had overborne their single wills, so that each thought

himself free, while in reality he only followed the leader, whose
artistic force lived and worked in him. "Everything went so easily
and beautifully that it was the height of enjoyment," said Fürstenau;
and the eyes of the old artist gleamed with joyful enthusiasm.

After Wagner had given up regular conducting he sought to
transfer his feeling, his insight and his power to some younger,
plastic spirits in whom they might live on. His plan of an ideal
school, where singers and conductors of the type he desired should
be trained,* was not realised owing to the indolence of his contemporaries. A few young musicians associated themselves with him,
to whom he now imparted of his spirit. Of these, the oldest is the
most significant—his intimate friend, at that time his most faithful
champion, his *alter ego*, as he himself once called him—the master-
conductor Hans von Bülow. After a comparatively short co-operation they had to part company, and Bülow's star first shone brilliantly
again when in 1880 he became chief of the Meiningen orchestra. A
year later the Duke, whose scenic art had already effectively
influenced the dramatic theatre, sent him off with the orchestra on
a grand concert-tour through Germany, Austria and Russia.
Seldom has such a victory of mind over matter been seen. A rather
poorly-appointed orchestra, by no means absolutely excellent in its
proportions, conquered everywhere the large orchestras, famous
the whole world over as possessing the best artists; this was the
work of the eminent conductor, who—a second Leonidas—had the
courage to defy with a small troop of admirably schooled players the
big musical armies that were mostly led by ordinary time-beaters.
By dint of diligent, indefatigable practice he had so infused into the
orchestra his own conception of the works as to get a perfection of
ensemble at that time unknown. The most scrupulous rhythmical
exactitude was united with so artistic a balance of the various
timbres, that the question whether this or that player was the better,
or whether this or that peculiarity of the conductor was justifiable,
could scarcely be raised. The orchestra seemed to be a single
instrument, on which Bülow played as on a pianoforte.

These concert-tours of the Meiningen orchestra were of inestim-
able significance. Those whom it concerned† recognized that it

* Wagner's "Report to His Majesty King Ludwig II of Bavaria upon a
German Music-School to be founded in Munich" is translated in Mr. Ellis's
fourth volume. [Tr.]

† Addition here in fourth edition. See Appendix, p. 50.

would not do to go on simply beating time and playing away with
the old reprehensible carelessness and thoughtlessness, for that
would certainly lower them in the eyes of the public, which, after
once having nibbled dainties at the table of the great, would no
longer be content with canteen-fare. So these people first of all took
pains to cultivate the orchestra better on the technical side, held
more rehearsals, followed more conscientiously the dynamic
indications, and in general gave more attention to accurate *ensemble*.
The capability of orchestras has since then greatly increased, and
composers to-day can set problems that even a few years ago would
have seemed insoluble, while at the same time a better rendering of
the works of the old masters has been made possible. These things
represent the *gain* from Bülow's work, and make his name an
ineradicable landmark in the evolution of the art of conducting; to
him alone, after those great composers who themselves were
notable conductors, we owe the diffusion and the strengthening of
the consciousness that conducting is an art and not a handicraft.

But Bülow's work had also its harmful features, for which the
guilt lies both with himself and a number of his followers; and to
expose these and attack them is as much a duty of sincerity as to
acknowledge the gains with frank delight. In the first place, it
cannot be denied that even while he was leader of the Meiningen
orchestra there was often to be detected a *pedagogic element* in
Bülow's renderings. It was clearly seen that he wished to deal a
blow on the one side at philistine, metronomic time-beating, on the
other side at a certain elegant off-handedness. Where a modification
of the tempo was necessary to get expressive phrasing, it happened
that in order to make this modification quite clear to his hearers he
exaggerated it; indeed, he fell into a quite new tempo that was a
negation of the main one. The "Egmont" overture was a case in
point. Wagner tells us,* *à propos* of this motive—

* See "About Conducting," pp. 332, 333, in Mr. Ellis's fourth vol. [Tr.]

—which, as he says, "is so drastic an epitome of terrific earnestness and placid self-confidence," and which, as a rule, "was tossed about like a withered leaf in the uncontrollable rush of the *allegro*"— that he induced Bülow to play it in the true sense of the composer, modifying "ever so little" the hitherto passionate tempo, "so that the orchestra might have a proper chance to accentuate this dual theme, with its rapid fluctuation between great energy and thoughtful self-content." All who have heard this overture under Bülow must agree with me that at the place in question he by no means made "ever so little" a modification, but leaped at once from the *allegro* into an *andante grave*, thereby destroying the uniform tempo that should be preserved in the *allegro* of the overture, as in general in every piece of music that has a uniform tempo-mark at the beginning. The proper expression can be obtained *without* any change of the main tempo—be it "ever so little"—if the strings, who have the first two bars of the theme, are told to bring them out energetically and very precisely by a uniform down-bowing of the crotchets, thus preventing the last quaver of the first bar from being turned, as often happens, into a semiquaver,★ whereby indeed, as Wagner says, the effect of a dance-step is given; and when we consider that the tempo of the main part of the overture is just *allegro*, not *vivace*, there can be no danger of an "uncontrollable allegro-rush" if the tempo is correct. It is a common source of trouble that introductions are taken very slowly and the main sections very fast, and the numerous gradations of these broad tempo-differences scarcely observed. We often hear the beginning of the Seventh Symphony taken *adagio*, whereas it is marked *poco sostenuto*; the finale of the Fourth Symphony is usually taken *presto*, whereas the humour of the movement only comes out when attention is given to Beethoven's marking, which is "allegro *ma non tanto*." The introduction to the "Egmont" Overture is marked *sostenuto, ma non troppo*, which does not at all signify an actually slow tempo; while the next section is marked *allegro*, that only increases to *allegro con brio* at the end—which again, however, does not imply an immoderately rapid tempo. The maintenance of an essentially easy tempo just suits the tragic weight of the work, that is completely destroyed by hurrying. The only way I can express the distinction between the introduction (that should be taken with three moderate beats) and the main portion, is that one bar of the

★ Addition here in fourth edition. See Appendix, p. 50.

3/4 section is about equivalent to a minim, and so to a third of a bar in the 3/2 section, whereby the crotchets at the entry of the allegro do not become about half what they are in the introduction. In this way any *ritenuto* at the place in question is superfluous, and the "terrific earnestness" of the

and the "calm self-confidence" of the two following bars are made perfectly clear.*

Wagner quite rightly contended against the scherzo-tempo in which it had become usual to take the third movement of the Eighth Symphony, and claimed that it should go in comfortable minuet-time. Under Bülow, however, I heard this movement played so slowly that its humorous cheerfulness was replaced by an almost disagreeable seriousness.

It certainly belies the titanic character of the "Coriolan" Overture when, as usually happens, the chief theme

---

* This passage will become clearer to the reader if he will refer to the score of the overture. If the tempi recommended by Herr Weingartner are adopted, it is evident that since one bar of the *allegro* = a third of a bar of the introduction, three crotchets in the former = one minim (or two crotchets) in the latter. The *allegro* is thus faster than the introduction in the proportion of 3 to 2. By abstaining from taking the *allegro* so fast that the proportion would be as 4 to 2, the tempo is not rapid enough to need any "holding-back" at the place Wagner discusses. [Tr.]

and all that follows it are taken in a flying *presto* instead of *allegro con brio*; but Bülow began it almost *andante* and then increased the tempo until the pause in the seventh bar, to begin again *andante* and accelerate the sequence in the same way. In the first place, taking the incredibly characteristic theme in this way robs it of its monumental strength; in the second place, I hold that if Beethoven had wanted these subtleties he would have indicated them, since he always gave his directions for performance with the greatest precision.

Bülow's *purpose* as such was always clearly recognisable and also quite correct. It was as if he said to his audience, and more especially to the players: "This extremely significant passage in the 'Egmont' Overture must not be scrambled through thoughtlessly; the comfortable, easy-going minuet of the Eighth Symphony must not be turned into a scherzo; the main theme of the 'Coriolan' Overture must be given out in a way conformable to the dignity of the work." But in the effort to be excessively clear he often went too far. His quondam hearers and admirers will recollect that often when he had worked out a passage in an especially plastic form he turned round to the public, perhaps expecting to see some astonished faces, chiefly, however, to say, "See, that's how it should be done!" But if the Venus of Melos, for example, were suddenly to begin to speak, and to give us a lecture on the laws of her conformation, we should be a good deal sobered down. Art-works and art-performances exist only for the sake of themselves and their own beauty. If they pursue a "tendentious" aim, even though this should be instructive in the best sense, the bloom goes off them. From "tendencies" of this kind Bülow's interpretations were seldom quite free. Thence came also his proneness to make details excessively prominent. In an art-work, indeed, no one part is of less significance than another, and *each* detail has its full *raison d'être*, but only in so far as it is subordinated to a homogeneous conception of the essential nature of the whole work—a continuous conception that dominates all detail.

It is this homogeneous conception of the essential nature of a musical work that constitutes what there is of specially artistic in its interpretation; it originates in a deep feeling that is not dependent on the intellect, that cannot, indeed, even be influenced by this, while it itself must dominate everything that pertains to the intellect—such as routine, technique and calculation of effects. If this feeling is not strong enough, then the intellect usurps the foremost place and leads, as was often the case with Bülow, to a propensity to ingenious analysis. In the contrary case the feeling becomes unwholesomely powerful and leads to unclearness, false sentimentality and emotional vagueness. If neither feeling nor intellect is strong enough, then we get, according to the prevailing fashion, either mere metronomic time-beating or a senseless mania for *nuance*, a mania that chiefly prompted me to write this book. Neither, however, has anything to do with art, which is at its best when that exceedingly delicate balance—more a matter of intuition than of calculation—is attained between the feeling and the intellect, which alone can give a performance true vitality and veracity.

[Here I must digress to contradict sharply an opinion that has considerable vogue. The interpreter—in our case the conductor— is *not* able to *increase* the worth of a work; he can merely diminish this occasionally, since the *best* that he can give is simply a rendering on a par with the real value of the work. He has done the best that is possible if his performance expresses just what the composer meant; anything more there is not and cannot be, since no conductor in the world can, by his interpretation, make a good work out of a bad one. What is bad remains bad, no matter how well it is played; indeed, a particularly good performance will bring out the defects of a work more clearly than an inferior one. The remark: "The work owed its success to its excellent interpretation" contains a half-truth, since the interpreter is entitled to the recognition of his undoubted deserts; but the composer has a still higher right, for it was he who made it possible for the interpreter to achieve a success with the work. If however the critic inserts in the above sentence a "solely" or "exclusively," then he either falls into an error arising from the pre-conceived opinion I have spoken of, or else he indulges in a piece of dishonesty in order to depreciate the success of composers he does not like—unless, which is indeed the more convenient course, he prefers to ignore this success altogether. How often, for example, have we heard this ludicrous phrase repeated, since some modern conductors recognised their duty and played Berlioz's works in a proper manner? The deeper impression now made by the works could of course not be denied; but the credit for the greater effect they made had to go entirely to the conductors, not to the works themselves, to which people were, and indeed in some quarter still are, as unfavourably disposed as of yore. But what had the conductors done, except by means of their interpretation brought something into the light that had really been there all the time? That of course is a great merit; but it must not be exploited to the disadvantage of the composer, who *made* what the interpreter could only *reproduce*. "Yet," it has been and perhaps will be objected, "we can listen to Beethoven and Mozart even when badly played; but Berlioz is only enjoyable when so-and-so conducts him." This, I take leave to say, is another great mistake, for in the first place Beethoven and Mozart, badly played, are likewise unenjoyable; the public however has heard these works so often and played them more or less efficiently on the piano, that it can discover the familiar beloved features even in a performance that disfigures them—can even perhaps imagine these features when they are barely recognisable; which is naturally impossible in the case of a work it does not know, such as a rarely-given composition of Berlioz or a novelty. But how feeble is the applause one usually hears after an indifferently played classical symphony, in comparison with the uncontrollable enthusiasm aroused by an artistic interpretation of the same work! Then the masterpiece appears in its true form; to be able to make this true form visible, however, is the sacred task of the conductor, and to have fulfilled it is his only honourable—nay, his *only possible*—glory. A good performance of a poor work is of no artistic consequence, and regrettable both because it furthers bad taste and because it means time and labour unprofitably squandered. The reverse case—to perform a good work badly—is inexcusable. Equally inexcusable is it, however, to set up off-hand the interpretation against the work in cases where *both* have contributed to make the artistic impression. To do this is to exhibit the conductor's function in a wholly false light, to put him, in comparison with the composer, disproportionately into the foreground, and merely serves to inflict as much harm as possible on the latter; wherefore it is generally done with that specific end in view—whether as a mere echoing of personal or partisan prejudice, or as a result of some of those sinister currents that run so strongly beneath our artist-life, and against which the individual has often a bitter fight. The effort to escape this fight, or at least to lessen it as much as possible, gives rise to the mania for founding "Unions" and "Societies," which, on the principle of *manus manum lavat*, may sometimes turn these currents to their own profit, sometimes nullify them. If Stauffacher's saying, "United, even the weak become strong," is true for those who work merely for the success of a day, yet for eternity, i.e. for the kingdom of free and progressive souls above time and space, Tell's quiet, splendid answer is always true—"The strong man is strongest when *alone*."]

The pedagogic element I have referred to in Bülow's performances became more prominent in the last years of his life; it was linked with a capriciousness that was probably increased by his physical sufferings and his consequent spiritual distemper. This capriciousness led him into eccentricities that had no object, not even a pedagogic one, and that could have been thought fine only by those who, having quite lost the capacity for thinking for themselves, fell at Bülow's feet in blind idolatry, and pocketed his insults submissively when he now and then treated them as they deserved. Through his habit of making speeches at his concerts he committed such errors of taste that it was difficult to maintain unimpaired the feeling of esteem that could in the most heartfelt way be given to the earlier Bülow. It was sad to see the public rushing to his concerts with the question, "What will he be up to to-day?"*

I would gladly spare myself the ungrateful work of enumerating some examples I myself saw of his eccentricities, if it were not necessary later on to speak of their results. In a performance of the Ninth Symphony in Berlin he began the first movement remarkably fast, and not until the entry of the main theme—

did he adopt a broader tempo. In these chords, however—

he suddenly became almost twice as slow, and remained so until he came to this passage—

* New paragraph here in fourth edition. See Appendix, p. 50.

when he just as suddenly went off again into quite a fast tempo. What was the object of these unmotived, spasmodic derangements of the tempo? In the same performance of the Ninth Symphony I heard him render the wonderful, passion-free *andante* melody of the third movement with the following *nuances*:

making it sound like some ardent love-lament out of an Italian opera. The truth is that Beethoven's markings of *espressivo* and *crescendo* are to be interpreted discreetly, in a delicate sense consistent with the nature of the whole movement; any disturbance of the tempo must be completely bad. One of those idolators I have mentioned, to whom I expressed my surprise at this downright odious treatment of the divine melody, replied to me, "Yes, yes, you are right, but Bülow is Bülow; *he may do anything.*" O blind fetish-worship and uncritical adulation, what harm have you not done!

In★ the oboe solo in the Trio of the Scherzo, he altered a C to B in the second bassoon part without any reason, whereby the rather harsh but extremely characteristic progression of the bass was made weakly chromatic. A similarly quite unmotived and enfeebling

★ The passage from here to "third 'Leonora' Overture" is a footnote in the fourth edition, preceded by the sentence: "He was also guilty of unjustified improvements, or rather changes for the worse."

substitution was that of a characterless D for the energetic C at the beginning of the great violin-passage in the third "Leonora" Overture. The Eighth Symphony he once began very quickly, took the fifth, sixth, and seventh bars quite slowly, then in the eighth bar came back to his opening tempo. And so on.

The impression given by performances of this kind was that not the work but the conductor was the chief thing, and that he wanted to divert the attention of the audience from the music to himself; so that finally there was nothing to admire but the readiness with which the orchestra followed him in his sometimes singular fancies.

One of these was the cause of a complete rupture between Bülow and myself. I made his personal acquaintance in Eisenach, where he and the Meiningen orchestra gave a concert I shall never forget, at which there was a very impressive rendering of Beethoven's C minor Symphony. Here I had the honour to be presented to him by Liszt. He interested himself in me, later on gave a little composition of mine for string orchestra, and, the post of conductor at Hanover being then vacant through the death of Ernst Frank, recommended me—without success—to his friend Bronsart, the director. When the post of second conductor in Meiningen became open through the departure of Mannstaedt, I applied for it, hoping to learn a good deal by working under Bülow. I went to see him in Berlin about it. He spoke at once of my application, and said to me literally: "I cannot make use of you; you are too independent for me. I must have some one who will do absolutely only what *I* wish. This you could not and would not do." I fully agreed with him, of course. He then advised me not to turn up my nose at the most unimportant post if only I were independent—so far as this is possible in the theatre—and above all had no other conductor over me. Thereupon we separated. Two years later we met in Hamburg. He had engaged himself to the director Pollini to conduct thirty opera-performances in the season 1887/8; I was engaged as permanent conductor there. The first opera that he took up was "Carmen." I am still convinced, and was so from the first moment, that at that time he was bent on the joke of trying what you can palm off on the public if you bear a famous name—a practice that has unfortunately found its counterpart to-day in the field of composition. He took almost all "Carmen," that is so full of passion and piquancy, in a tempo that was often intolerably slow and dragging—the beginning, for example

almost *andante*, and Escamillo's song

Auf in den Kampf To - re - ro!

downright *adagio*. He further foisted on the work so many *nuances*, "breath-pauses," and the like, that it would have greatly astonished Bizet to have heard his opera thus given. Bülow had the satisfaction of knowing that his joke succeeded completely. His admirers and the critics agreed that now for the first time the true and only right conception of "Carmen" was given to the world. This opinion indeed found some support in the fact that the *ensemble* was faultless [and the opera given without cuts,] which were unusual things at the Hamburg Stadttheater. When questioned about his remarkably slow tempi, Bülow replied that "he intended in this way to suggest the dignity of the Spaniards." This remark, that was merely a jest and not a particularly good one, also met with general admiration— except from me. I soon found an opportunity to confirm my opinion by acts. Bülow being prevented from conducting "Carmen" once, it fell to my lot to do so, and later on to alternate with him. It was absolutely impossible for me to imitate him, and, against my own convictions, to take the opera in his style. I therefore held a rehearsal of my own, and conducted as I felt was right, in accordance with the instructions of the composer, in a generally lively tempo, without any affected *nuances*, to the joy of the orchestra and of such singers as dared to express their opinion. After I had conducted two performances, Bülow ran to Pollini, complained that by my "arbitrary notions" I would spoil the opera for him, and insisted that I should not conduct it any more. Pollini told me of this in the friendliest way, and, with the excuse that he did not want to fall out with the always irritated Bülow, turned "Carmen" over to a colleague, who was very proud to take the opera "just like Bülow."

Could Bülow really not see from this much-discussed affair that he was blaming me for his own fault, since not I, who restored the unequivocal directions of Bizet, was the arbitrary one, but he, who had disregarded them? At any rate he never forgave me for having been sharp enough to see through his joke, and having dared to be "independent" with regard to him; and whereas on my arrival in Hamburg he had received me very cordially, he now lost no opportunity of showing his displeasure with me, which culminated in a public expression of his antipathy to me in full view of the audience, during some performances that I conducted. Nor was his temper towards me any more friendly when some years later in Berlin I tried to exert an influence on the Symphony Concerts; his jeering remarks, however, in which he gave free play to his wrath against me, and which his friends took good care should be spread abroad, necessarily kept me out of his company, much to my regret. Nothing could prejudice the admiration I had for what was great in him. In the present book, however, I hope that by separating the insignificant and the paltry I have shown his greatness in its true light; and while I steadfastly maintain a standpoint in many respects contrary to his, I render—what objective history will some day render to this most successful furtherer of that art of conducting that Wagner brought into new being—honour and respect.

I* once saw this aphorism in a humorous paper: "Nothing misleads us more than when a wise man does something stupid, since it is just this that we are apt to imitate in him." A true saying, true at all times and especially in the present day. It characterises in vigorous words that epigonism that is not able to comprehend a great personality as a whole, yet wants to do as it does, and believes it can attain this by imitating this or that feature of it. But it is just the significant and characteristic features that cannot be imitated, since these pertain to genius alone, and to each genius again in a particular way. So much the more zealously, however, are the seeming and often even the real weaknesses of eminent minds imitated, since it is only in these that the great man has any actual affinity with the dullard. When Wagner finally broke with the form of the so-called grand opera, that had been degraded to a mere superficial show, and built the musical drama out of poetic purposes, people

* In the fourth edition, Section II begins here.

ought to have seen that it needs a stupendous capacity to cast in one piece an entire act—in which the music flows on without a break, while not only is the dialogue replaced by recitative, but a symphonic development answering to the logic of the poem runs through the act from beginning to end—and further to bind the separate acts together in the right relation to each other—that this is surely much harder than to write a succession of arias, duets, *ensembles* and finales without any musical connection between them, so that the composer could, if he pleased, begin as the old masters did at the end or in the middle, the demand for logical development and treatment extending no further than the narrow sphere of each separate and relatively short number. What was it, however, that after Wagner had gradually become popular stimulated modern Germany to composition? Not at all the reflection whether and how the problem posed by him could be worked out to a still further solution, but the *apparent* casting of form to the winds in the Wagnerian drama. Before that time anyone who wanted to write an opera had to master thoroughly musical structure and form. *This* they could as a matter of fact all do; even the non-geniuses wrote in a quite solid style. Nowadays almost everyone who has learned to orchestrate a little, but is hardly able to put a pure four-part piece together, thinks he must write a "music-drama." That deliverance of the opera from senseless convention for which Wagner longed and worked is regarded by these people as the emancipation of their own ego from the obligations of studying seriously, practising counterpoint and being sternly critical of their own work. Wagner has sanctioned formlessness, has discarded arias and *ensembles*; therefore away with arias, away with *ensembles*; don the biretta gaily and give your fantasy free rein to declaim as it likes! Use as much brass as possible, divided strings, stopped notes and harp-glissandi, pile up the most unusual harmonies and modulations, and there you are! I am the last to deny the inevitability of a kind of Wagner-epigonism; I fell into it indeed myself in my first two attempts at opera, [about twenty years ago.] Neither do I misjudge the relative value of some of the modern music-dramas that have sprung directly from his influence. A force of such vehement revolutionary power as Wagner, at once strong and tenacious, is bound to leave deep traces behind it, and a new dramatic style in music will develop with all the more difficulty in proportion to the impossibility of eliminating from such a style the essential part of the Wagnerian reform. Wagner's world of feeling and his view of life may come to be alien to us, and later on we may also bring the most objective criticism to bear upon his work; but that he has shown the obvious gulf between the dramatic art and the form of the old opera, even in its masterpieces, this will remain his enduring service, from which no dramatic composer of the future will be able to get away, even though his own works may be quite independent. He only is *original* who remains *natural*, and to have made it possible to be natural in the musical drama is the great step signified by Wagner's achievement. But I am astonished [how little the real significance of this step has hitherto been understood, and therefore] how little influence so pregnant a phenomenon as Wagner has had on the choice of opera-poems, which lay at the very root of his reformatory work. It is really lamentable how many accomplished musicians have squandered much painful and often clever work on texts the impossibility of which could have been seen at a glance by anyone with an eye for the stage. Much better to have no more operas at all than the poetical monstrosities that are to-day set to music. So long as there is any truth in the judgment that "the music is good but the text bad," I cannot believe the style is original, or even a worthy following in Wagner's footsteps.

It must be acknowledged that in all these Wagner-imitations, even in the weakest, there is one ideal feature, namely the effort to draw close to a great exemplar. Not only the great, however, but the little and the paltry are also copied if they are successful, especially in our present industrial epoch, when the royalty has become the guardian angel of art. What was it but the plenteous royalties brought to its author by a work like "Cavalleria Rusticana"—on the quality of which I will not enlarge here—that called forth in Germany, the land of Bach and Beethoven, a veritable deluge of musical "one acts" compounded of adultery, murder and homicide? Sad as this was, one really blushed to a German Court even offer a prize for the "best" of these wretched imitations, and actually divide it between two composers. The prize should have gone by rights to the Parisian public, which, while Germany crawled on its belly to "realism," had the good taste to decline to have anything to do with it.

It almost goes without saying that the striking phenomenon of such a conductor as Hans von Bülow was bound to lead to imitations. A whole tribe of "little Bülows" sprang up, who copied the great Bülow in everything they could—his nervous movements, his

imperial pose, his stabs with the baton, his furious glances at the
audience when anything disturbed him, his half instinctive, half
demonstrative look round at some special *nuance*, and finally the
nuances themselves. His concert-speeches alone no one dared to
imitate.* I have ventured to label this kind of conductor, whose
manner was a more or less complete caricature of his master's, the
"tempo-rubato conductor." Wagner speaks of "elegant" conductors, at the head of whom—whether with justice I rather doubt—
he puts Mendelssohn—conductors who skip in the fastest possible
tempo over passages that are difficult and at first sight obscure.†
The tempo-rubato conductors were the exact opposite to these; they
sought to make the clearest passages obscure by hunting out insignificant details. Now an inner part of minor importance would be
given a significance that by no means belonged to it; now an accent
that should have been just lightly marked came out in a sharp
sforzato; often a so-called "breath-pause" would be inserted,
particularly in the case of a *crescendo* immediately followed by a
piano, as if the music were sprinkled with *fermate*. These little tricks
were helped out by continual alterations and dislocations of the
tempo. Where a gradual animation or a gentle and delicate slowing-
off is required—often however without even that pretext—a violent,
spasmodic *accelerando* or *ritenuto* was made. The latter was more
frequent than the former, since as a rule the tendency to drag—
thanks to the sport that has been for some time carried on in Bayreuth
with drawn-out tempi‡—was stronger than the passion for whipping-
up. When the tempo *was* whipped up, however, one received about
the same confused impression of the poor disheveled work that one
gets of the parts of the landscape lying nearest the railway track
when one whizzes past in an express.

[I would here insert a rule, the observance of which I hold to be
indispensable for a right apprehension of the *limits* of tempo: No

---

* Sentence rewritten in fourth edition. See Appendix, p. 50.

† See Mr. Ellis's translation of "About Conducting," in Wagner's *Prose
Works*, Vol. IV, pp. 295, 296, 306–308. Wagner says Mendelssohn himself
informed him that "a too slow tempo was the devil, and for choice he would
rather things were taken too fast," because "things might be glossed over"
by "covering the ground at a stiff pace." [Tr.]

‡ Herr Weingartner considerably annoyed the Bayreuth partisans by some
remarks in the first edition of his book, contending, for example, that if Bülow
had been given control there after the death of Wagner certain abuses would
not have been allowed to grow up.

slow tempo must be so slow that the melody of the piece is *not yet* recognisable, and no fast tempo so fast that the melody is *no longer* recognisable.]

The rhythmic distortions to which I have referred were in no way justified by any marks of the composer, but always originated with the conductor. With reference to the *sforzati* I have mentioned however, I will cite the apt remarks of Berlioz:

"A conductor often demands from his players an *exaggeration of the dynamic nuances*, either in this way to give proof of his ardour, or because he lacks fineness of musical perception. Simple shadings then become thick blurs, accents become passionate shrieks. The effects intended by the poor composer are quite distorted and coarsened, and the attempts of the conductor to be artistic, however honest they may be, remind us of the tenderness of the ass in the fable, who knocked his master down in trying to caress him."

[I would add the admonishment always to observe most precisely whether an accent comes in a *forte* or in a *piano* passage, which will determine quite different grades of strength and expression for it. It is also of the utmost importance whether a *succession* of accents occurs in a passage proceeding in uniform loudness, or during a *crescendo* or *diminuendo*, in which latter case the accents also must of course have their own gradual increase or decrease. Obvious as this may seem, it is necessary even with good orchestras to point out emphatically *where* the accents come, and so prevent their being continually hammered out in the one style.]

If many of the above-mentioned errors could be supposed to be "proofs of ardour" and of good intention, [it was in the end regrettable that by the behaviour, artistic and personal, of some "new-modish Bülows" so much attention was directed to the person of the conductor that the audience even came to regard the composers as the creatures, as it were, of their interpreters, and in conjunction with the name of a conductor people spoke of "his" Beethoven, "his" Brahms, or "his" Wagner.] Of the works played in this eccentric way, however, there was often little more left than of a plant that the professor of botany has dissected, and whose torn leaves, stamens and pistils, after being demonstrated to the students of the college, lie scattered about on the desk.

Thus I once heard the "Hebrides" Overture of Mendelssohn played with literally not one bar in the same tempo as the rest. Even the second and fourth bars, which are repetitions of the first—

and the third

were "characterised" as against these by means of a pointedly different tempo; and the same kind of thing went on to the end. All that was humanly possible in the way of the unnatural was done, with the result that the lovely work was deformed and its real character obliterated. Certainly it would be just as false to play one crotchet after another with metronomic uniformity; but the modifications of the tempo, some of which Mendelssohn himself has indicated, should be done in such a way as not to dismember the organic character of the whole thing—its "melos," the right comprehension of which, as Wagner aptly says, gives also the right tempo. At one moment the sea flows quietly round the rocks of Fingal's Cave, at another a stronger wind produces higher waves and the white foam of the breakers beats more strongly against the beach—*but the picture of the landscape remains the same*, and there is nothing in Mendelssohn's overture of an actual, formidable storm that could imprint on the scenery a radically different stamp. The atmosphere of gentle, noble melancholy that lends the Hebrides their peculiar charm is also preserved in the music. Is it then not a matter for vigorous censure when something that a master has sincerely felt and expressed in faultlessly beautiful music is distorted by the irresponsible additions of a conductor?

"To what end is all this?" I asked myself in amazement on these and many other occasions. Why this inordinate desire of some conductors to turn musical works into something other than what they really are? Whence this aversion to maintaining a uniform tempo for any length of time? Whence this rage for introducing *nuances* of which the composer never thought? The reason for these curious phenomena was mostly the personal vanity that was not satisfied with rendering a work in the spirit of its author, but must needs show the audience what it "could make out of this work." *The conductor's mania for notoriety was thus put above the spirit of the composer.* The parading of this vanity was due partly to a misconception of the better side of Bülow's work, [which founded on Wagner;] partly to a clumsy imitation of the palpable weaknesses [and uncalled-for caprices] of his later years.

The★ following instance was communicated to me by a friend. Bülow had played the G minor Symphony of Mozart with the Meiningen orchestra, and had produced a deep impression by his temperate handling of the chief theme—

that is sometimes taken thoughtlessly fast, and by his very expressive phrasing throughout the movement. The permanent conductor of the town in question—plainly stimulated by Bülow's success—having later on to conduct the same symphony, informed his acquaintances that he would now take the tempi exactly like Bülow, and at the performance, at which my friend was present, played the first movement *andante* throughout. The beautiful butterfly, fluttering gently on a summer's day over the sadly inclined campanula, was transformed into a clumsy grasshopper! This was a case of misunderstanding and an overdoing, probably well-meant, of Bülow's version. But it was otherwise with what, to

★ Addition here in fourth edition. See Appendix, p. 50.

my horror, I had to listen to in the Pastoral Symphony. In the "Scene at the Brook," for example, in the following passage—

the conductor made in the second bar a strong *ritenuto* and after the last quaver quite a "breath-pause," so that a complete interruption ensued, and the third bar, detached from the second, came in without any connection. The same thing happened again in the corresponding passage in the recapitulation. After the performance I tried to convince the conductor of the wrongness of his interpretation, pointing out to him that just as it would be impossible for a rippling brook suddenly to be made to stand still, so it was unnatural to interrupt arbitrarily the flow of the music at this point. To my astonishment I got the answer: "I really don't like it myself, but the people here are so accustomed to it like this from Bülow that I take it in the same way." I thought it useless to make any further effort on behalf of truth and nature, since here it was not a case of misunderstanding, but of a conscious imitation of an admitted fault. This is a sample of the most evil feature of that manner of conducting against which I am contending, since the man's own conviction was here sacrificed and the work knowingly disfigured to comply with the habit of the public, and in fear of incurring displeasure by flying in the face of this habit. In many other cases the trouble mostly came from unconscious defect of artistic feeling, and a certain fumbling after something fine without being quite able to achieve it [—much as the good, childlike Anton Bruckner wrote a "Ninth" Symphony *also* in D minor and would *also* have a chorus for the last movement, in which however the "good God" to whom he had dedicated the work wisely prevented him by opportunely recalling him to the celestial land.

Bülow, by his arbitrarinesses, had drawn more attention than was necessary to his person, and was unfortunately often commended *for that very reason*, and praised as "clever." These arbitrarinesses had now to be not only copied but exaggerated; i.e. the tempo had to be dislocated not only where Bülow had done so but as often and as violently as possible, breath-pauses had to be introduced, extraordinary behaviour had to be indulged in on the platform—in a word, Bülow out-Bülowed in the external features of his conducting, so as to win the same or if possible greater successes than he.] To make their own, however, just that in virtue of which Bülow was really great—the deep seriousness with which (a few exceptions apart, such as the "Carmen" case I have mentioned) he took his calling, the prodigious zeal and the restless devotion with which, even in his last years, when his powers were no longer at their height, he strove to give the most finished performances possible, which were indeed often so perfect that one could forget his personal peculiarities—all this was certainly denied to his imitators. Indeed I have often doubted whether those who wanted to be so "ingenious" really knew properly the works they were playing. When I saw that somebody was incapable of letting one tempo grow out of another, but made every change with a jerk, or that he began what should have been a long and slow *crescendo* with an explosive *fortissimo*, so that nothing was left over for the finish, this in my opinion pointed not only to a want of proper feeling but also to an insufficient study of the work; being surprised and confused by some passage he had not properly thought out the conductor either flew over it, or else, through would-be "temperament," made too sudden a rush at the *crescendo* and spoilt it.

The difficulty of getting a good *ensemble* in the tempo-rubato manner is all the greater when the conductor goes touring. Bülow for some years directed only the Meiningen orchestra, and afterwards only the Philharmonic orchestras in Hamburg and Berlin. He knew these through and through, and the players, who understood him thoroughly, followed him in every detail, so that even his caprices were rendered with faultless technique. But a conductor who comes before a strange orchestra, and wants to take the works not in their natural way—wherein the feeling of the players will always assist him—but to distort them, has not the time, in the few rehearsals that are usually allowed him, to elaborate properly all these *ritenuti, accelerandi*, little *fermate* and breath-pauses by which he hopes to make an effect; and so it may happen that some of the players follow the conductor and the others their natural feelings, and the greatest ambiguity results. It has struck me that eccentricity of this kind has been carried to further extremes in foreign tours than in our own country, apparently because the public abroad is supposed to be more easily imposed on. At least I have found in the orchestral parts abroad some markings which, had I not seen them with my own eyes, I should have thought impossible. Having often been asked by the players, before the rehearsal, whether I would adopt this or that peculiar *nuance* of one of my predecessors, I generally found it necessary to say categorically: "Ignore all markings; follow only the printed instructions as to phrasing." Since in spite of this there were misunderstandings, owing to the parts being in many places so covered with "readings" that the original was obliterated, I often protected myself later on by taking my own copies with me.

The saddest part of the business was that the chief arena chosen for all these varieties and experiments was our glorious classical music, especially the holiest of all, that of Beethoven, since Bülow had acquired the reputation of a master-conductor of Beethoven, and his followers wanted to outbid him even there; though one would have thought that reverence—to say nothing of love—for this unique genius would have put all vain thoughts of this kind to flight.

To take only one example, how the C minor Symphony has been tampered with! Already the gigantic opening has brought into being a whole crowd of readings, notably that according to which the first five bars [(with the two *fermate*)] are to be taken quite slowly. Even the "spirit of Beethoven" was cited* to justify this misguided attempt at emendation, for which, however, not Beethoven's spirit but that of his first biographer, Schindler, is entirely responsible. Schindler, the key to whose character, I think, is sufficiently given by the fact that after the master's death he had visiting cards printed with the title "Ami de Beethoven," has told in his biography so many anecdotes whose untruth has been proved by Thayer, that we may unhesitatingly reckon among them the story that Beethoven wanted the opening of the C minor symphony to be taken *andante,* and the faster tempo to come only after the second *fermata.* Is there even a moderately satisfactory explanation

---

* The fourth edition adds: "by a 'General Music Director' in Munich."

why Beethoven, instead of specifying so extremely important a change of tempo, should have marked the passage *allegro con brio* when what he wanted was *andante*? Liszt's opinion on the point will be of interest. In the previously-mentioned concert of the Meiningen orchestra in Eisenach, where I made Bülow's personal acquaintance—he took the opening of the C minor symphony, that time at least, in a brisk *allegro*—Liszt told me that the "ignorant" and furthermore "mischievous fellow" Schindler turned up one fine day at Mendelssohn's, and tried to stuff him that Beethoven wished the opening to be *andante*—pom, pom, pom, pom. "Mendelssohn, who was usually so amiable," said Liszt laughingly,* "got so enraged that he threw Schindler out—pom, pom, pom, *pom!*"

Near the end of the first movement there is at one place a five-bar group—

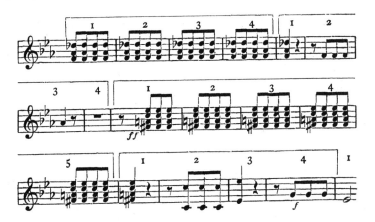

Now whether we look upon the fourth bar of the second group (the pause) as a short *fermata* and the first bar of the succeeding five-bar group as the up-take—according to which there then comes another four-bar sentence—or whether we take it that the opening theme of the *allegro* occurs in the recapitulation the first time thus—

---

* The fourth edition adds: "and with a descriptive gesture."

and the second time with an extra bar, thus—

however we calculate the thing mathematically, in either case the short breathless silence and the ensuing outburst of the chord of the diminished seventh become, just by their prolongation, terrific, gigantic, powerful, menacing, overwhelming, volcanic. It is like a giant's first rising from the earth. Will it be believed that almost everywhere I found the indescribable effect of this passage simply destroyed, either by a bar of the diminished-seventh chord or by the pause itself being *struck out?*

The most tasteless rhythmic distortions, the most absurd breath-pauses, have been calmly indulged in in order to appear interesting; the result has been, however, to turn a supreme stroke of genius into a mere piece of irregularity; *because* the thing must go as a four-bar phrase. *O sancta simplicitas!* The offenders always father their audacities on Bülow. I cannot believe he had so many sins to answer for.*

Towards the end of the same movement, in the passage where the chords come rattling down like devastating masses of rock,

* [Not long ago] I discovered indeed something that made me doubtful as to Bülow's understanding of Beethoven, namely, his cadenzas to the G major concerto. Of all the delicate works of Beethoven's middle period this is perhaps the most delicate. The themes are spun out of perfume and light, the treatment of them is full of chaste, refined charm; it has an atmosphere of immaculate maidenliness that suggests the perfume of lovely flowers. Bülow wrote for it two cadenzas—explosive, full of virtuosity, "leit-motivic," soulless, unmelodious —that have the effect of verses by Josef Lauff dovetailed into a poem by Goethe. [In Paris, where unfortunately I could not prevent the performance of them, since I knew of them for the first time at the final rehearsal, a humorist asked me after the concert whether the pianist had made a mistake and interpolated cadenzas belonging to a piano concerto by Tchaikovski.]†

† Addition here in fourth edition. See Appendix, p. 51.

I found the two *sforzati* corrected to an elegant *piano,* and a delicate *diminuendo* marked before them, making the passage like an elegiac sigh.

I freely admit that I have never been fully satisfied with the rendering of the second movement of this symphony under any conductor but Bülow.* Beethoven marks it *andante con moto.* The older conductors overlooked the "con moto" and played the movement *andante*; the modern ones, on the other hand, appear to see only the "con moto," and drop into an *allegretto,* thus giving the wonderful theme

a dance-like character that is quite alien to its nature. My own conception of it,† in which the *andante* is maintained while the *con moto* is regarded as the spiritual breath that unites and animates the movement, I cannot adequately express in words; I must refer to the performances I am permitted to give of the work.

I may mention a tragi-comic incident I once witnessed in this movement. After the conductor had begun in the usual *allegretto,* he played these bars—

in so slow a tempo that he had to beat each semiquaver of the triplet separately! But enough of these examples.

I‡ need mention no names in order to point out that several

---

* Revised in fourth edition. See Appendix, p. 51.

† Addition in fourth edition: "which coincides with Bülow's."

‡ Revised in fourth edition. See Appendix, p. 51.

ON CONDUCTING**ON CONDUCTING**   **33**

conductors of importance have refused to have anything to do with
these perversions of style. I may also say that my remarks refer for
the most part to an epoch now somewhat removed from ours. When
I published this book in 1895, my object was to try to show how
much the art of conducting had developed up to then, since the time
when Wagner had given it a new basis both by his deeds and his
words. If on the one hand a decided progress could be noted—
greater competence in the orchestra, a more perfect *ensemble*,
more feeling for vital phrasing than hitherto, thanks to Bülow and
some excellent conductors who had become great under Wagner's
direct influence—on the other hand there was imminent danger that*
the vanity, egoism and caprice of younger conductors should make
fashionable a style in which the masterpieces of music should be
merely pegs on which to hang a conductor's own personal caprices.
This is all the more dangerous as an audience with little artistic
education may, in its astonishment, take the arbitrary for the
genuine thing, and, its healthy feeling once perverted, always hanker
after these unsound piquancies, so that finally it thinks the trickiest
performance the best. Wagner's treatise combated the philistinism
that suffocated every modification of tempo and therefore all vitality
of phrasing in a rigid metronomism; my own book on the other
hand combated† the errors that had arisen through exaggeration of
these modifications after the necessity for them had gradually come
to be admitted. It was therefore no plagiarism of Wagner's, as was
of course asserted, but its counterpart, or, if you will, its continuation in the spirit of our own day. If Wagner opened new paths, I
believed it my duty to warn people against mistaking a senseless
trampling of the grass for progress along new paths.‡

[But when I saw that my conduct was looked upon merely as
unprofessional and prompted by the desire for self-exaltation, that
my right to enter into literature was denied, and that in the end,
in spite of the rapid spread of my book, all I had fought for was
wilfully ignored and I myself described as the worst of the tempo-
rubato conductors, I consoled myself with Goethe's fine saying,
that it more becomes the good man to do the right than to be con-

* Added in fourth edition: "the harmful influence exerted by Bülow's
weaker traits and."
† In fourth edition: "combats"; other past tenses also become present
correspondingly.
‡ Addition in fourth edition. See Appendix, p. 51.

cerned whether the right is realised. So in the first place I sought by conscientious self-education to remove from my own conducting everything that, externally and internally, might savour of false attempt to be a "genius," and laboured to become an ever more faithful interpreter of the masters by intimate comprehension of the peculiar style of each of them. I had the joy finally to succeed with what I had recognised as right. My taste must indeed have received thereby a powerful purification, which alienated me from many things I had thought significant, and drew me towards many things that I had misjudged. In the last few years I have heard very little. I sometimes see in the journals one of the younger conductors specially praised for his "simple" and "grand" readings, from which I conclude that the "tempo rubato" is not at such a premium as formerly, and that its unhealthy excrescences represent a fashion that is gradually dying out if not yet quite extinct. We know however that fashions may return, and so when a third edition of this book was called for, I felt that I ought not to shirk the trouble of a careful revision, and then send it out into the world once more.

Some demands that I made at that time on every conductor I still hold to be valid to-day, wherefore I repeat them here:

The conductor must before all things be sincere towards the work he is to produce, towards himself, and towards the public. He must not think, when he takes a score in hand, "What can I make out of this work?" but, "What has the composer wanted to say in it?"

He should know it so thoroughly that during the performance the score is merely a support for his memory, not a fetter on his thought.

If his study of a work has given him a conception of his own of it, he must reproduce this conception in its homogeneity, not cut up into pieces.

He must always bear in mind that the conductor is the most important, most responsible personality in the musical world. By good, stylistic performances he can educate the public and promote a general purification of artistic perception; by bad performances, that merely indulge his own vanity, he can only create an atmosphere unfavourable to genuine art.

To have given a fine performance of a fine work should be his greatest triumph, and the legitimate success of the composer his own.

To this I will add the remarks of two masters who were themselves great conductors. In a letter to the music director Praeger of Leipzïg, Weber, after having expressed himself on the subject of indispensable modifications of tempo, goes on to say: "The beat (the tempo) must not be like a tyrannical hammer, impeding or urging on, but must be to the music what the pulse-beat is to the life of man.

"There is no slow tempo in which passages do not occur that demand a quicker motion, so as to obviate the impression of dragging.

"Conversely there is no *presto* that does not need a quiet delivery in many places, so as not to throw away the chance of expressiveness by hurrying."

He continues immediately, however:

"But from what I have here said, for heaven's sake let no singer★ believe himself justified in adopting that lunatic way of phrasing that consists in the capricious distortion of isolated bars, and gives the hearer the same intolerably painful sensation as the sight of a juggler violently straining all his limbs. Neither the quickening nor the slowing of the tempo should ever give the impression of the spasmodic or the violent. The changes, to have a musical-poetic significance, must come in an orderly way in periods and phrases, conditioned by the varying warmth of the expression."

He concludes:

"We have in music no signs for all this. They exist only *in the sentient human soul;* if they are not there, then there is no help to be had from the metronome—which obviates only the grosser errors—nor from these extremely imperfect precepts of mine, which, considering the extent of the subject, I might be tempted to pursue much further, were I not warned by painful experiences how superfluous and useless they are and how liable to be misconstrued."

Wagner also was afraid of his remarks on this point being misunderstood and thereby giving occasion for exaggerated phrasing. After having devoted to the necessity of *artistic* modifications of tempo almost the whole of his treatise on conducting and many other passages in his writings, he expresses the following opinion, in which, when we survey the post-Bülow period, we must admire his prescience:

"It is certainly a really valid warning against these (to me) necessary modifications in the cases I have named, that nothing could harm the works more than capricious *nuances* in phrasing and tempo, which, by opening the door to the whims of every vain

---

★ Of course the same thing holds good of the conductor. [Author's Note.]

and self-complacent time-beater who aims at "effect," would in time deform our classical music beyond recognition. To this, of course, no reply is possible except that our music must be in a bad way when such fears can be entertained; since it is as good as admitting that we have no belief in a power of true artistic consciousness among us, against which these caprices would at once be broken."*]

There† remain some special points for me to discuss—in the first place, conducting from memory.‡

This makes a great impression on the audience, but I do not place too high a value on it. In my opinion a conductor may really know a work by heart and yet fear that his memory may play him a trick, either through pardonable excitement or some other disturbing influence. In such cases it is always better to use the score; the audience is there to enjoy the work, not to admire the memory of the conductor. I recommend doing without the score only when knowledge of it is combined with such a mastery of oneself that reference to it is more a hindrance than a help, and the conductor, though he may read a page now and then, yet feels that to use the score throughout the whole work would be putting a needless fetter on himself.§ It is all a purely personal matter, however, that has nothing to do with the perfection of the performance. If the conductor is so dependent on the score that he can never take his eyes from it to look at the players, he is of course a mere time-beater, a bungler, with no pretension to the title of artist. Conducting from memory, however, that makes a parade of virtuosity is also inartistic, since it diverts attention from the work to the conductor. Now and then we see a conductor put a score on the stand *although* he conducts from memory, his object being not to attract too much attention—a proceeding that I think commendable. But I hold that it is entirely the conductor's own concern whether he will use the score or not. A good performance from the score has value; a bad one done from memory has none. For instrumental artists also, playing from

* See Mr. Ellis's translation, in Wagner's *Prose Works*, Vol. IV, pp. 336, 337. [Tr.]

† In the fourth edition, Section III begins here.

‡ The opening of this section is different in the fourth edition. See Appendix, p. 51.

§ Addition here in fourth edition. See Appendix, p. 51.

memory is in my opinion a matter of quite secondary importance; it can be done by anyone who has a quick and reliable memory. But if a player has difficulty in learning by heart, it is better for him to devote his time to mastering the intellectual and technical structure of the piece and to play from a copy at the concert, than to be in continual dread of a lapse of memory and of having either to stop or to pad with something of his own, which means disfiguring the work. I have even heard Bülow, who had a remarkable memory, "improvising" in this way in his piano recitals. Here, as in so many other cases, it only needs someone with the courage to begin and the others will follow.

Bülow, in his witty way, divided conductors into those who have their heads in the score and those who have the score in their heads. I might distinguish them, perhaps rather more deeply, by means of the following antithesis—some conductors see only the notes, others see what is *behind* the notes. Then again there are conductors who destroy the unity of a work that is one and indivisible, and others who can shape the *apparently* fragmentary into a unity.

Some conductors are reproached with making too many gestures —not without reason, for the mechanical element in conducting is by no means beautiful in itself, and the black dress-coated figure with the baton-wielding arm can easily become ludicrous if the arm gesticulates wildly instead of leading the men, and the body also twists and curves in uncontrollable emotion. A pose of assumed quiet is however just as repellent. In our music there are, thank God, moments when the conductor must let himself go if he has any blood in his veins. An excess of movement is therefore always better than its opposite, since—at any rate as a rule—it indicates temperament, without which there is no art.* We should not laugh at a talented young conductor whose vehemence prevents him bridling himself, but exhort him in a friendly way to keep his body quiet, and to train himself *not to make any more movements than are necessary*. The expression of each passage will then generate an appropriately great or small motion of the baton. A complete harmony between music and gesture will indeed only come with the years; but as a general thing it may be pointed out that short, quick motions ensure greater precision than very extensive ones, since in the time taken up by the latter the strictness of the rhythm may easily be deranged.

* Addition here in fourth edition. See Appendix, p. 52.

A further question, much discussed at one time and even now and then to-day, is the relative artistic value of touring-conducting. What indeed can there be to object to if the same conductor secures excellent performances to-day in Dresden, for example, and a little while afterwards in Petersburg? A "question" arises only when the performances are less good by *reason of the touring*. If however the public the whole world over has opportunities of hearing the great violinists, pianists and singers, one cannot understand why it should be denied it to listen to the orchestral interpretations of notable conductors. There are two ways of managing this. Either the conductor travels alone, and in many cases performs with an orchestra that he does not regularly conduct, or he travels with an orchestra that is permanently under him, or at least exclusively at his disposition for the tour in question. The latter plan appears to be preferable, on account of the perfect understanding between orchestra and conductor and the absence of the necessity for fatiguing rehearsals when once the tour has begun. It has however this disadvantage, that the greater expense of the transport and maintenance of a whole orchestra necessitates a great number of concerts—generally one every day—with numerous repetitions of the same programme, since, a great part of the day being often spent in travelling, it is impossible to rehearse new works during the tour. The absence of rehearsals indeed obviates some physical fatigue, but on the other hand intellectual lassitude seizes upon both conductor and orchestra when the same piece has to be played too often, in addition to which there is the physical exhaustion of the travelling. As varied programmes as possible, and as short railway journeys as possible, together with proper comfort not only for the conductor but for the players, are factors—not easily to be managed—to which the organisers of such tours must before all things attend, if they are to serve not merely business but art.

The conductor who tours alone must take care that adequate rehearsals are allowed him, the number of which will depend upon the quality of the orchestra, the degree of his familiarity with it, and the difficulty of the programme. A mere "getting-through" with the concert and pocketing of the fee is a sin against art, whether at home or abroad; on the other hand conductors who are above the feeling of offended *amour propre* or foolish rivalry can under this system get into closer touch with and stimulate each other, learning from each other in every way to the ultimate enriching of art.

[Moreover it must be recognised that the two great concert organisations in Berlin, and latterly also the Vienna Philharmonic concerts, are now in the hands of visiting conductors, and that no intelligent person will try to infer from that fact any diminution in the value of those concerts.]*

I† have so far spoken only of conducting in the concert-room, not of that in the *theatre*. That is a chapter in itself, and unfortunately not a pleasant one. The conductor of a small concert-society in a small town has generally at his command a fair if not a strong orchestra and a tolerably well-taught chorus, with which two factors, given much industry and some ability in the conductor, really good performances can often be given. Now and then such performances in the smaller towns—not so-called "music-centres"—are surprisingly good. [I may mention as an instance the chorus and orchestra at Chemnitz in Saxony.] At the theatres in small towns, however, the great obstacle to all artistic effort is the horrible singer-proletariat, which, like so many other afflictions, is a product of this nervous, hurrying epoch of ours, when every one wants to get money and glory as quickly as possible, but scarcely considers whether he is really doing anything good. If nowadays a decent voice appears anywhere, there is not, as formerly, a long course of years devoted to its training and to the general artistic education of its fortunate possessor, but the singer takes lessons, often for not more than half a year, from the first teacher that comes to hand. Then some leading parts suitable to his range of voice are drummed into him by a chorus-master. He learns how to bring off some dazzling *tours de force*, but in every other respect sings as incorrectly and unintelligently as possible, and generally acquires no knowledge at all of what his *rôle* in the opera signifies or what the opera is all about. Afterwards he falls into the agents' hands and is sold to the theatres, of which there are some hundreds in the German-speaking territories. So the poor devil is usually sent first of all to a little theatre, where he draws a miserable salary that is scarcely enough to live on; out of this, however, he has to pay the agent a percentage which, if not much in itself, means quite a handsome sum to the agent because of the number of theatres he provides. The agent grows fat, but art goes to ruin. Scarcely has the novice got an engagement when it is a case of "On to the stage!" At best he gets a piano-rehearsal and

* Addition here in fourth edition. See Appendix, p. 52.
† In the fourth edition, Section IV begins here.

now and then an orchestral rehearsal, so as to have an inkling of how
to find his way about. [No part gets more. Often he really does not
know what he has to do, and stands in despair by the prompter's box,
where he sings his notes, as far as he knows them, with awkwardly
sprawling arms and legs. He meets with malicious colleagues, who
have knocked about for many years on the "world-significant"
boards and have no voice left, but know the ins-and-outs of the
stage and make use of this knowledge to trip up the novice who has a
voice, especially if a trace of talent is suspected in him that later on
may be dangerous to them.] For some years he wanders from one
wretched stage to another, and at last, sung-out, tired out, sick of
the paint, his rosy hopes deceived, he looks round for a business in
which he can get employment. With women, whom passion or need
has driven to the stage, it often goes still more sadly. To comparatively very few of them, who happen to be both talented and lucky, does
a better lot fall. Add to this that in the small theatre orchestras there
are four first violins, one contrabass, and one viola-and-a-half—for
one of the two is usually to be reckoned only as half; that the chorus
numbers perhaps ten men and ten women; that the decorations and
scenery are in tatters; and with material like this "Fidelio,"
"Freischütz," "Zauberflöte," "Tannhäuser" and "Lohengrin"
are given—nowadays even the "Nibelungen." It is quite clear that
under such conditions there can be no question of conducting
as an art.

But even at the larger municipal theatres, where the singers are
of better quality and often highly paid and the orchestra is finer,
art is sometimes difficult to detect, since too often a man is at the
head who has no notion of art, but uses the complicated apparatus
simply to fill his own pockets. The most unscrupulous exploitation
of forces is not unusual in these theatres, and the "Herr Director"
can finally so arrange things for himself that he loses nothing if a
member has worn himself out as the result of the excessive demands
made upon him and no longer stands at the height of his capacity.
[The way in which the earlier theatre-agreements permitted one to
be given up body and soul to incredible caprice can be estimated
only by one who, like myself, has been in the sad condition to have
to subscribe to such agreements. Much has indeed been done by
theatrical unions in conjunction with high-minded and intelligent
theatre-directors; but much remains to be done.]* Is it then sur-

---

* A new passage is substituted for this one in the fourth edition. See
Appendix, p. 52.

prising if singers who have the melancholy certainty of losing, through a comparatively short illness or even through an obstinate indisposition, their bread for perhaps a month, if not altogether, take care of themselves and try to retain their vocal powers as long as possible? Since this cannot be done, however, if they are to do their almost daily work properly, they reserve themselves for especially important representations, e.g. *premières*, "guest"-engagements, evenings when the press attend, and so on. For the rest however, they take things easily, often simply sing at half voice, and do their work very negligently. Indifference, that direst foe of all art-activity, has become master. What can the conductor do with a wearied, ill-humoured lot of assistants? He soon resigns himself to beating through his usual three hours and for the rest to letting the Herr Director look after his own pocket.

The relatively greatest possibility of artistic achievement exists in the richly subsidised court and other theatres, whose chief, employed by the town, is not forced to work for his pocket and in addition to worry about meeting his rent. Yet even here there are some extremely serious defects. In the first place, only in a very few towns, and even there not entirely, is it fully recognised that the supreme direction of opera should be in the hands of an artist— of a musician, in fact, with an administrative committee under him that shall have no power of veto against him in artistic matters. Then again at all theatres, the large as well as the small, *too much* is played.* No theatre is in a position to give daily performances of equal value; it would need at least more than twice as many soloists, chorus and orchestra, and more than twice as many adequate rooms for rehearsal, to allow of a sufficient number of rehearsals taking place without over-fatiguing everyone. An opera that has been put aside and then revived is bound to suffer if it is not carefully and critically rehearsed afresh, especially when long intervals elapse between these unrehearsed repetitions. The *ensemble* that has been produced by such vigilant care is imperilled when, owing to the absence of the players of one or more chief *rôles*, other singers who have studied only their own parts, and who, supposing them to have been present at the preliminary rehearsals, have been merely looking on, are put in with a cursory stage rehearsal. "Guest"-visits of foreign artists are the absolute enemies of finished, artistically rounded performances. [But the so-called "Festival Performances" that are nowadays arranged by our theatres with pompous *réclame*,

* Sentence revised in fourth edition. See Appendix, p. 53.

and to which famous singers from all parts are invited who often do
not attend even the general rehearsal, are the merest absurdity.
"Thrift, thrift, Horatio!"]*

Need there be a performance every day? This question opens up
further questions, the answers to which now-a-days, when money-
making is the war-cry and the box-office statement trumps, look
rather utopian. Nevertheless I will try to give the answers, in spite
of their uselessness. Could not the public be gradually made to see
that it would be better, for the same money that is spent on the
average in going to the theatre, to go less often and pay higher
entrance-prices, but have thus the certainty of seeing only first-
class performances, and so get more real elevation instead of often
very superficial enjoyment? Fewer but better-prepared performances would then yield about the same receipts. Or—and here
indeed I touch upon the province of the apparently impossible—
will courts, states and towns never comprehend that the theatre
must be a place not of luxury and thoughtless amusement, but of
popular education like the school, only in a more spiritualised sense,
and at any rate of higher ethical significance than the church?†
Will people "above" cease to obstruct the perception that noble
dramatic and musical plays—which, if the grievous concept
"deficit" no longer existed, could be made accessible also to the
lower classes—would perform a powerful culture-work, weaken the
lower instincts and strengthen the higher, to the good of the nation
that cultivates them? [Germany has in many things taken a splendid
lead. To emancipate the dramatic art gradually from private
interests, and tend it as an inestimably important part of the life of
the people, would not this in its way just as much assure Germany's
world-position as armies and navies?]‡ Is it not unpardonable that
the worthiest works are rarely given, because the public has lost
touch with them? But why? Simply because it hardly ever gets a
chance of hearing them. [In this vicious circle one evil emanates
from another. Take Gluck, for example. Now and then one of his
sublime operas appears on the German stage as a stop-gap, im-
perfectly rehearsed, badly sung and with worn-out decorations. At

* A new passage is substituted for this one in the fourth edition. See
Appendix, p. 53.
† See Appendix, p. 53, for revision.
‡ A new passage is substituted for this one in the fourth edition. See Appendix,
p. 54.

the Paris Opéra Comique "Orfeo" and "Alceste" are stock pieces. Make the experiment of giving them in Germany in the way they are given in Paris, and the public will go to them. Does not the positively unheard-of success of the "Midsummer-Night's Dream," so finely produced at the "Neues Theater" in Berlin, prove that many "old Schmöker"—as we piously speak of our master-literature—only need to be given properly for an interest to be created in them? It is just the same with the classical music-drama; also with some notable new works, which after a few performances have been taken off in terror, because the press by zealously asserting that they lacked interest kept people away. This would soon have been remedied if the directors had only had the courage to keep the works on in spite of a temporary falling-off in the receipts, and so restored the confidence of the public. Instead of which there was a sigh of "never mind," and the old humdrum *répertoire* of routine went on and goes on for better or for worse. In this way Cornelius's "Barber of Bagdad" slumbered for decades before it was revived. Goetz's "Taming of the Shrew" passed out of remembrance, until it reappeared in our own day in Berlin, this time to be joyfully welcomed; and Verdi's delightful "Falstaff" is still as good as forgotten. The "Trumpeter,"* however, or "Cavalleria" and similar stuff endure and draw full houses.]† *Mundus vult Schundus*, jested Liszt with bitter irony; and our theatres take the greatest pains to avoid bettering this state of affairs.‡

Conviction, conviction—a theatrical director should prove he possesses this. He can only do so, however, if he is independent of daily receipts and press scribblers,§ and can fully and freely fulfil his task of educating the public in the noblest sense of the word— the public, that does indeed too easily incline towards the bad and the superficial, but still has enough freshness and *naïveté* to receive the good willingly if it is only offered to it. To this end the director must in the first place be indeed an artist, who thinks of something more than receipts and criticisms; and in the next place a *character*,

* The reference is to the comic opera "Der Trompeter von Säckingen" by Victor Nessler (1841–1890), founded on the mock-heroic poem of the same name by J. V. von Scheffel. [Tr.]

† A new passage is substituted for this one in the fourth edition. See Appendix, p. 54.

‡ The epigram would have no point in a translation. "Schund" means literally "rubbish," "offal." [Tr.]

§ Instead of "press scribblers" the fourth edition has "all other such things."

who not only knows what he wants, but means to fight for it and
to get it.*

But an end to these dreams.

As for the special function of the conductor in the theatre,
Wagner says very truly that just as the right comprehension of the
melos of a piece of music suggests the right tempo for it, so the right
way of conducting an opera presupposes the true comprehension
of the dramatic situation on the part of the conductor. As a matter
of fact he must before all things have the stage in his eye. This will
give him, consistently with due fidelity to the markings of the
composer, the criterion as to whether he shall take the tempo faster
or slower, how he shall modify it, and where he shall expand or
contract the volume of orchestral tone. He will not allow himself to
draw a melody out at length when the phrasing should be free and
animated; he will not beat out a fast tempo, effective as this may be
from the merely musical point of view, where the dramatic development goes more slowly; nor will he elaborate orchestral *nuances*
that drown the singers or divert people's attention from the events
on the stage.

Of special importance is his relation to the singers. Only a
significant individuality can create a significant performance, and
this only when the individuality can express itself in the performance
fully and without hindrance. Drill counts for nothing; it may be
necessary with the less endowed singers, who for better or for worse
are just put into their proper places in the frame of the whole.
Admirable artists however *must* have, within this frame, room for
the free play of their own conceptions—indeed, they must be held
to the necessity of thinking out their parts for themselves. At the
piano rehearsals the conductor should in the first place impress it
strongly on the singers that they must learn their parts correctly
down to the smallest detail, which is the only way to attain precise
co-operation between orchestra and stage, and so secure the fundamental condition of any good performance—a faultless *ensemble*.
When, after thorough study, individual liberties begin to be taken
by the singers, he should see that these do not contradict the spirit
of the whole work—which he must have completely assimilated—or
the character of the particular passage. The artistic perception of
the conductor and of the singers may be measured by the degree in
which they secure the fine medium between rigid correctness and
living freedom.

* Sentence revised in fourth edition. See Appendix, p. 54.

[Once more] I must cite Weber, with whose almost forgotten writings I strongly advise every artist to make himself acquainted. In them will be found artistic intuitions of such delicacy as to make doubly painful to us the early death of this splendid master and the unhappy circumstances that hindered his full development. He writes in the above-mentioned letter to Praeger:*

"It is the individuality of the singer that actually and unconsciously colours each *rôle*. A man with a nimble, flexible voice and one with a big quality of tone will render the same *rôle* in quite different ways—the first certainly in several degrees more animatedly than the second; and yet the composer can be satisfied with both in so far as they have rightly comprehended and reproduced the gradations of passion he has indicated, each according to his measure. But it is the conductor's business to see that the singer does not go too far and merely do what seems to him at first sight apt." Weber thus convincingly lays it down that the worth of an opera conductor is not, as many think, to be estimated by how far he is able to comply slavishly with the whims of the singers—which is routine but not art.

Further, the conductor should not allow himself to be tempted by convenience to make inartistic cuts, and when he conducts foreign operas must see to the improvement of the translations, which are generally very bad in the matters of phraseology, sense and musical declamation; for nothing corrupts the artistic feeling of the singers more—to say nothing of the harm done to the whole performance—than when they are forced to memorise the conventional doggrel of opera-translations, which is mostly quite unfit for music. It is essential, then, that the conductor should understand at any rate French and Italian at least well enough to be able to make what improvements are necessary.

On the whole the work of the opera conductor is less independent because it relies on and is supported by more factors than that of the concert conductor, who alone is responsible for the whole of his own performance.

Anyone in whom the dramatic sense predominates will be the better opera conductor; the better concert conductor on the other hand will be one whose perceptions are mostly purely musical. Anyone in whom both gifts exist in equal measure will be equally successful in both styles.

* In the fourth edition: "He writes a letter to the Leipzig music director Praeger."

I must mention one more defect which, in the light of pure reason and of all that Wagner has said and done, seems really ludicrous, but which, notwithstanding, is rooted in our theatres so deeply as to be almost beyond the possibility of extirpation, namely the complete separation of the stage management, the machinist's department and the musical direction. If a new opera is given on which the theatre does not mind spending a little, a commission is sent to a scene-painter—often to a foreign firm of repute—along with a text-book, while the stage manager arranges *his* book and the conductor rehearses the singers. When the scenery comes to be set up, the stage-manager generally finds that he will have to alter *his* business, since a good deal that he had planned will not fit in with that particular scenery. Then when the conductor comes in with singers and orchestra it is clear that, e.g. such and such a chorus cannot do its musical work properly if it stands with its back to the audience, that such and such an actor requires a lot of room for his action in a rather long *ritornello*, while he has been allowed only about four square feet; and so on. Then bad temper, a scramble, and the best face possible put on it, which however only leads to further mischief; and at the last rehearsal but one the end of it is that they would all, if they could, gladly begin again from the beginning. But the day of production is fixed, the booking guaranteed, the mere idea of a postponement therefore monstrous; so let it go as best it can. This system of work often results in some good stories; for example, at three large theatres I have known Brynhilde to wake up in quite another stage-setting than the one she went to sleep in. Years had elapsed between the staging of the "Valkyrie" and of "Siegfried." The scenery had been ordered of different painters, who had not come to an understanding as to the identity of the scenes in the two works. The proposal, however, simply to use in "Siegfried" the scenery of the "Valkyrie" was vetoed by the chief machinist, on the grounds that for technical reasons this scenery could not be put in after the fire-transformation. With the careless remark, "The public does not notice," they went on to the order of the day, and the enchanted Brynhilde was spirited away each time to another sleeping-place.*

Since however an operatic performance can be artistic only when all the factors work together, the proper distribution of the labour is this:—When the stage management and the music are not in the

---

* The fourth edition adds: "—no one being upset in the least."

hands of the same man—which is not much to be recommended, since the conductor, when he is in the orchestra, cannot possibly attend to every detail of the stage picture—then stage manager and conductor, *before* the rehearsals begin, must come to a perfect understanding between themselves as to how the work is to be done. *Both* must be clear and of one mind as to the atmosphere of the opera, the action, the scenic pictures, the tempi, and the dynamic effects, so that later on at the rehearsals only trifling changes may be necessary. Only *after* this preliminary work should the scenic artist and the machinist receive from stage manager and conductor their precise orders, compliance with which, however, does not mean the paralysis of their own imagination, which can work more freely and fruitfully within the artistic boundaries prescribed by the work in question than outside them.

For this understanding between stage manager and conductor two things are necessary. In the first place the conductor must have a knowledge of, an eye for, and an interest in the stage, and not merely bury himself in his orchestra to the ignoring of everything else; in the second place the stage manager must be a man of musical perception and musical *education*, who is just as conversant with the scope as the conductor is. In my opinion no conductor should be appointed to a theatre who has not shown that he can stage an opera, and no stage manager who cannot rehearse the musical part of the work. It is perfectly nonsensical that sometimes people should be made operatic stage managers who are not at all musical.*
[The result may be made evident by some experiences of my own. I once asked one of these people to call a piano rehearsal for the eight Valkyries. At the rehearsal there appeared also another lady for whom there was nothing to do. Between the stage manager and myself the following dialogue ensued:
Myself: Why have you summoned Frau N. to this rehearsal?
Stage Manager: You asked me to call the Valkyries.
Myself: Well, which Valkyrie does Frau N. take?
Stage Manager: Why, Fricka!
Some days later the same manager posted up this notice—"Orchestral rehearsal for 'Siegfried,' for principals and *chorus*." Everyone knows that is no chorus in "Siegfried."
During the preparation of Berlioz's "Benvenuto Cellini" I saw unloaded before the theatre a number of specimens of that statuette

* Addition here in fourth edition. See Appendix, p. 54.

of Perseus that is necessary in the third Act (Cellini's studio). I asked the stage manager why he had ordered so many, since only one is required; he replied that they were counting on further performances, and Cellini would have to smash one of these statuettes each time. Then, to my horror, I realised that the good man thought Cellini had to smash the model, instead of the mould out of which the statue itself comes. Only by energetic representations in higher quarters could I prevent what would have been an indelible blot on our reputations. In most cases, however, when I aimed at the removal or at least the diminishing of obvious absurdities, I was politely told that my place was in the orchestra and that I need not worry myself about anything else. Notwithstanding this, however, they never gave me sufficient power as regards the orchestra to prevent the engagement of incompetent but favoured players.

For these and many other reasons I look upon the fourteen years I spent in the theatre as a time of uselessly squandered labour, forcible suppression of my capabilities, and—a few isolated bright spots excepted—vain struggles to get even one step nearer the ideal. I cannot recall it without bitterness.

Finally, one word more on the art of conducting itself. More and more I have come to think that] what decides the worth of conducting is the degree of suggestive power that the conductor can exercise over the performers. At the rehearsals he is mostly nothing more than a workman, who schools the men under him so conscientiously and precisely that each of them knows his place and what he has to do there; he first becomes an artist when the moment comes for the production of the work. Not even the most assiduous rehearsing, so necessary a pre-requisite as this is, can so stimulate the capacities of the players as the force of imagination of the conductor. It is not the transference of his personal will, but the mysterious act of creation that called the work itself into being takes place again in him, and, transcending the narrow limits of reproduction, he becomes a new-creator, a self-creator. The more however his personality disappears so as to get quite behind the personality that created the work—to identify itself, indeed, with this—the greater will his performance be.★

★ Long addition here in fourth edition. See Appendix, p. 55.

Appendix

Preface to the Fourth Edition

When I published this essay in 1895, its reception was not exactly friendly. The delusion of Bülow's infallibility was still in full force, and it was considered unheard of that a young artist should dare to oppose it. My right to engage in literary activity at all was contested. My reply to this was a second polemical essay on the subject of the Bayreuth infallibility delusion. Now the limit had been reached, and it was impossible to heap enough blame upon my doings. Not distracted by the turmoil, I sought my way in creativity and observation, adhering to Goethe's saying about the virtuous man: it is more proper for him to act justly than to worry about whether justice is done. And I found my way.

When in 1905 a third edition of my essay *On Conducting* became necessary, I based it on the experience I had meanwhile acquired; thus, a considerable enlargement was called for. The present fourth edition differs from the third chiefly in a clearer arrangement of the material.

St. Sulpice, Vaud   FELIX WEINGARTNER
August 1913

p. 4, line 14:
   In the fourth German edition, the first part of this paragraph reads:
In the youthful works of Mozart and Haydn, as well, we find few instructions for execution, probably for similar reasons. It was only later that the wider distribution of their compositions compelled

★ See Publisher's Note, p. v.

these masters to add more detailed indications, which especially in Mozart's mature period attain a high degree of sophistication. We know that not only Mozart, but Weber . . . etc.

p. 9, last line:
In the fourth edition:
Those whom it concerned, with the exception of the Royal Opera House in Berlin, where Bülow was shown the door rather than finding his theories accepted, recognized that it would not do . . . etc.

p. 11, line 19:
In the fourth edition:
. . . into a meaningless semiquaver and preventing the extremely important rests from being blurred, whereby indeed, as Wagner says . . . etc.

p. 16, line 19:
In the fourth edition, a new paragraph is inserted at this point:
Bülow's career marked the beginning of sensationalism in music and of that distressing personality craze which goads any nonentity into claiming special rights, as long as his behavior is sufficiently unpleasant, and which also dazzles the talented weakling into undertaking senseless deeds. But if we keep in sight the examples of great men, we see that it is precisely a conscious moderation, even when progress is boldest, that is the noblest sign of a great personality. Bülow had no notion of such moderation and thus laid the groundwork for the direst aberrations, which are all the harder for us to bear today now that those personalities are no longer with us whom we might partially forgive for such aberrations. What Bülow did was at least interesting, because he was a personality, even if he was a personality who had gone astray and was at war with himself. But where is there a Bülow today?

p. 23, line 5:
In the fourth edition:
Even his concert-speeches were imitated, as I learned in New York.

p. 26, line 11:
In the fourth edition this sentence is preceded by the following:
Even a good quality can be wrongly assessed.

p. 31, insertion at end of first footnote:
As of today the extremely difficult problem of writing cadenzas for this concerto has been solved only by Eugen d'Albert, the truly brilliant interpreter of this indescribably beautiful work.

p. 32, line 6:
In the fourth edition this sentence is replaced by the two following:
What bad mistakes are often made with the tempo of the second movement! Here for once conductors should actually imitate Bülow, who took it ideally.

p. 32, last line:
In the fourth edition this paragraph begins as follows:
The object of this essay is to show how the art of conducting has developed since Wagner gave it a new basis . . . etc.

p. 33, line 28:
In the fourth edition this paragraph continues as follows:
If Wagner's essay strove for liberation from mindless formalism, mine is a warning against that formlessness which tries to be hyper-intellectual, and thus is just as mindless. Formalism and formlessness both spell the death of art. However, beautiful form is inseparable from living art; precisely because form is nourished by the spirit of art, it makes this spirit perceptible to the world. This is true of every type of art, and thus also of conducting.

p. 36, line 9:
In the fourth edition this section begins: "There remain some special points for me to discuss. First I must contradict an opinion that has considerable vogue." *Then there follows, with a few insignificant alterations, a passage that in the third edition had occurred earlier in the book: the passage, beginning with* "The interpreter—in our case the conductor" *and ending with* "generally done with that specific end in view," *included with the bracketed section on pp.* 14 *to* 16. *Following this in the fourth edition is a new paragraph, beginning:* "A further point to discuss is conducting from memory." *This paragraph then continues with* "This makes a great impression on the audience . . . etc."

p. 36, line 21:
Added at this point in the fourth edition:
Then the French designate this by the delightful expression "diriger par cœur."

p. 37, line 30:

At this point the fourth edition includes a passage that in the third edition had occurred earlier in the book: the passage, beginning with "Temperament, however, can be given neither by education" *and ending with* "flying in the face of a *plébiscite,*" *included within the bracketed section on p. 8. Following this in the fourth edition is a new paragraph, beginning:* "Temperament as such should never be blamed, only its aberrations." *This paragraph then continues with:* "We should not laugh at a talented young conductor . . . etc."

p. 39, line 5:

Added here in the fourth edition is a passage which incorporates elements from the revised passages on pp. 4, 23 and 24.

In conclusion, I should like to set forth two general rules.

One is concerned with tempo:

No slow tempo must be so slow that the melody of the piece is *not yet* recognizable, and no fast tempo so fast that the melody is *no longer* recognizable.

The other is concerned with dynamics; its author is Bülow, who coined the clever saying:

"*Diminuendo* means *forte, crescendo* means *piano.*"

This is only an apparent contradiction, since to start playing *piano* at the very beginning of a passage marked *diminuendo* and to start playing *forte* immediately at a *crescendo* indication is to destroy both *diminuendo* and *crescendo.* Mozart was overjoyed in Mannheim when he found an orchestra that could perform *crescendo* and *diminuendo* at all. The difficulty of increasing volume over long stretches uniformly and without sudden spurts is still present today, even with the best orchestras; this is why I call attention to it here.

p. 40, last line:

In the fourth edition, this passage reads:

Finally, he can hardly be blamed for this, since he cannot be expected to sacrifice his money for his subordinates or for "ideals." A reform in theatrical contracts, which would no longer give all the rights to the director and load all the responsibilities on the members of the company; a firmer legal supervision of the theatrical union, under whose governance directors are even today allowed the gravest arbitrary procedures; greater material security for directors and company in cases where they are prevented from performing through no fault of their own—these are indispensable necessities, which the government should attend to with energy.

p. 41, line 25:

In place of the sentence "Then again . . . is played" *the fourth edition has:*

But even in these circumstances the most brilliant director will not be able to make full use of his talents as long as too much is played at all theaters, the large as well as the small. With this I touch on the sore spot of our theatrical life; this is where a remedy is in order at once if there is ever to be a healthy recovery.

p. 42, line 3:

In the fourth edition, this passage is substituted for the one in brackets:

But how often we find that even the largest theaters have such a poor distribution of personnel that such guest appearances are essential to prevent the cancellation of performances. Every attempt at bettering this situation is wrecked by the absolutely frightening necessity of opening the portals of the "temple of art" to the public every evening, and often in the afternoon as well. There is never a heartfelt, mature performance! Breathlessness, overexertion, living from hand to mouth, getting through one chore so as to go on to another one—these are the dispiriting signs of that theatrical heavy industry of ours which mercilessly crushes all finer art. Who among older actors and singers does not happily recall the time when the theater was sometimes closed at night so that a rehearsal could be conducted? We were glad to rehearse from five till midnight. Is there any one old enough to have experienced the friendly charm of those evening rehearsals who can forget them? And how fresh and ready for action we were the next day! All gone, a thing of the past! A bad performance that takes in a few marks is preferred to a good rehearsal!

p. 42, line 19:

In the fourth edition, the words "and at any rate of higher ethical significance than the church?" *are replaced by* "and with that lofty ethical, indeed religious significance associated with it by the Greeks?"

p. 42, line 29:

In the fourth edition, this passage is substituted for the one in brackets:

Let the man who altogether lacks feeling for any higher artistic urge amuse himself daily with music halls, bad operettas and the like, as far as I am concerned. Let the theater of noble character open its doors less frequently, but then only onto perfect performances.

"Is it not unpardonable . . . etc." then opens a new paragraph.

p. 43, line 22:

In the fourth edition, this passage is substituted for the one in brackets:

Gluck, Mozart and Weber no longer arouse interest. *Fidelio* can always count on empty houses. Wagner, whose whole life was devoted to ennobling the German stage, is today lost beyond recall to the snob element. Good and bad performances are acclaimed in the same way. New compositions of a fine nature have little chance. *The Barber of Bagdad* slumbered for decades before it was revived from time to time. *The Taming of the Shrew*, Verdi's delightful *Falstaff* and Berlioz' operas are as good as forgotton. Great singers, who could reestablish our master composers on the stage, are fewer every year, and when they appear America snaps them up. We poor Europeans are left with the mediocre, which we must be contented with as we find it, while dramatic art resembles a funeral adorned by song, mime and dance.

p. 44, line 2:

In the fourth edition this reads:

Of course, to this end a man who is an artist and at the same time has a strong character, who not only knows what he wants, but means to fight for it and get it, must be given a firm guarantee for years to come that money will play no role and that no incompetent person will stand in his way. Then, perhaps, an exemplary theater would be possible.

p. 47, line 25:

In the fourth edition, this paragraph ends with the sentence: "But it is precisely what is nonsensical that always has the best chance to be held on to as zealously as possible." *Then, in the fourth edition, Section V begins with* "What decides the worth of conducting . . . etc."

p. 48, last line:

After this point, the fourth edition goes on with the sentence: "These are the demands that I make on the conductor who aspires to be an artist." *Then there follows a passage that in the third edition had occurred earlier in the book: the passage, beginning with* "The conductor must before all things be sincere" *and ending with* " 'against which these caprices would at once be broken,' " *included within the bracketed section on pp.* 33 *to* 36 (*within this passage, the third-edition phrase* "In a letter, to the music director Praeger of Leipzig" *becomes in the fourth edition* "In his above-mentioned letter . . . etc.").

After this transposed passage, the fourth edition concludes with two new paragraphs:

What Wagner feared has come to pass. Today the door is open to fantastic caprices, and not only to those (since "fantastic" after all presupposes the presence of imagination), but also to arbitrariness coupled with complete lack of imagination; and this is true not only in conducting, but in every art. The most irremediable idiocy can count on at least one clique that will howl its praises in every key and outlaw all who do not howl along. Just as anarchy has become a dangerous enemy in the existence of nations, so in the existence of art there is a threat of anarchistic confusion unless the true consciousness of art, the lack of which was already painfully felt by Wagner, comes to life and grows into a force that will destroy the antiartistic breeding of senseless and vain caprices as surely as healthy blood kills the bacilli that endanger life. We have had to absorb too much that is morbid; too much that is repellent, trivial and irrelevant has diverted our art from its true path for recovery to be able to occur quickly and for our defunct consciousness of art to be able to develop again all at once. We are so firmly set on impossible possibilities and possible impossibilities, so hemmed in by luxuriating weeds, that we should be happy to discover a narrow path that would at least offer the hope of leading us out of swamp and jungle onto the road to grandeur and beauty. This road we have abandoned, so that we can no longer enter into the sacred temple of art, can no longer even catch sight of it. Instead we build straw huts and fill them with idols, which we worship with a devotion directly proportional to their hideousness, while from all sides specious hymns numb our senses with the lying assertion that things are not only absolutely splendid just as they are, but a thousand times more splendid than they ever were. And yet again and again they appear before us, the sad countenances with the hesitant question in their sunken eyes and on their pale, whispering lips: "Will things never, never be different? Is a fresh breeze never to blow into this fearsome sultriness which robs us of breath? Is a genuine sunbeam never again to warm us in place of these smoldering torches set up before the idols with which the false priests wish to give us the illusion of daylight?" Then for a moment it becomes light. Some glowing thing passes by overhead whose glittering rays play upon the leaves of the jungle, through which all at once a bit of blue sky becomes visible. But something wondrous resounds within our hearing, a long-absent, delightful, melodious song. The pale countenances listen, alarmed and delighted at the same time. But, as if by pre-arrangement, the hymns and prayers to the idols swell to a furious roar, so that it is no longer possible to hear the music descending from above. The glowing vision passes on toward other, more beautiful countries far away, and things remain just as they were with us.

It is not the modern conductor, not even the modern writer, who will lead us for good out of that labyrinth of the arts into which we have strayed. This will be the lot only of the creative artist, who will be the true and genuine—and probably also the crucified—savior. But both the writer and the conductor can do much to help; the writer if he is manly and fearless, the conductor if he regards it as his sacred task to present the works of our great classical masters to us with purity of style and with emotion that grows out of their own spirit. Of course he will first have to cleanse himself thoroughly of all he has acquired from a false tradition. Only there, in those great creations of the classical age, still so near to us in time but already so far away in spirit, does that pure heavenly fire gleam with which a chosen man can kindle the Promethean torch so that he can set ablaze our straw huts and idols along with all the jungle plants surrounding them. Thus he will drain the noxious swamp and allow fresh air to blow once more over a healthful, fertile soil. Then there will also be room for the development of the true consciousness of art that Wagner longed for, and a period of painful transition like ours today could hardly recur. Or has our era already become so inartistic and industrialized that the Promethean torch can no longer catch fire? "Terrible if you were right," says Max in *Der Freischütz*. Let us hope that this time Kaspar's answer holds true: "Strange that you ask!"

ON THE PERFORMANCE OF BEETHOVEN'S SYMPHONIES

Translated by *Jessie Crosland*

Preface to the First Edition

The secret of the artistic rendering of musical compositions, and hence the secret of the conductor's art, lies in the style. The reproducing artist, in this case the conductor, must have absorbed into himself the peculiarity of each master and each masterpiece, and his rendering must be subordinate to this peculiarity even in the smallest details. As regards the time, the phrasing, the treatment of the sounds in the orchestra and even the technical manipulation, the conductor must assume a different personality according as he is conducting the *Eroica* or the *Pastorale*, *Tristan* or *Die Meistersinger*, according as he is trying to reproduce Haydn or Beethoven, Berlioz or Wagner. I believe I am not going too far when I say that a conductor of genius unites in himself just as many personalities as he reproduces masterpieces.

One of the essential conditions of the style of an execution must be *clearness*, and this is the quality which will occupy us here with regard to Beethoven's symphonies. This is precisely the point in which these greatest of all orchestral compositions offer the greatest difficulty, for even a perfectly correct rendering does not always make the intentions of the master as clear as they become by the reading of the score, or even by the playing of the pianoforte reductions. Indeed, it must be confessed that many passages awaken a feeling of confusion rather than of pleasure. And yet we should be renouncing at once all idea of a true reproduction if we passed these problems by, and took refuge behind the mere correctness of our rendering.

Wagner, in his valuable work *On the Execution of Beethoven's Ninth Symphony* (*Zum Vortrag der neunten Symphonie Beethovens*), to which I shall often have occasion to refer, says: "Just as we should never leave a difficult passage in a philosopher until we clearly understand it—as otherwise, on reading further with increasing

carelessness, we end by misunderstanding the teacher altogether—
so we should never glide over a single bar in a symphony such as
those of Beethoven without having a clear consciousness of what
it means." He also points out that Beethoven's intentions were far
in advance of the instrumental means at his disposal; Wagner
devotes his chief attention to the management of horns and
trumpets, which in Beethoven's day included only the natural
harmonics and one or two more or less questionable stopped notes.

With his penetrating mind and fine understanding, Wagner also
felt and frankly declared "that after the period of his deafness had
begun, Beethoven's mental conception of the orchestra grew fainter
in proportion as the dynamic relationships of the orchestra became
less familiar to him; and these conditions lost their distinctness
just when they were becoming most indispensable, namely, at a
time [that of the late works] when his conceptions needed a
constantly changing manipulation of the orchestra."

We do find, in fact, that the horns and trumpets often come to a
standstill simply because it was impossible to obtain a suitable
sound for a given chord on the instruments of that time, and that
for the same reason they often break off the melodial design entrusted to them and either proceed merely with harmonic notes or
pause altogether. We see that these instruments are often obliged to
make dangerous and apparently aimless leaps because they could
follow the progress of the musical structure in no other way.
Finally, we see that sometimes the most important part becomes
inaudible because it is entrusted to instruments which are drowned
by others with a louder sound playing a much less important part.

It is true that this state of things may be improved by instrumental
changes; but unless those changes are conducted with the utmost
prudence and good taste, there is great danger lest the most important thing of all, Beethoven's own peculiar style, may suffer; for, in
spite of the indisputable imperfections mentioned above, Beethoven's
handling of the orchestra is so entirely peculiar to himself that the
greatest caution is necessary if it is to be in any way interfered with.

The present work has undertaken the task, among other things, of marking as definitely as possible the limit within which such interference is artistically justifiable. Since the later years of Bülow's activity all kinds of distortions as regards time and phrasing have unfortunately become the fashion in the rendering of Beethoven's works. We have also—though not through any fault of Bülow's, for his perceptions were too fine for this—witnessed instrumental encroachments which do violence to Beethoven's spirit. It is well known that I have not only avoided such distortions when conducting myself, but have waged war against them in speech and in writing. And I have no hesitation now in condemning as inexcusable frivolity the addition of instruments which Beethoven never employed, the inclusion of trombones in passages for which no trombones were prescribed and similar foolish experiments. Beethoven's works were written at a time prior to the reform of brass instruments through the introduction of valves, which has been in many respects beneficial. I believe I am not mistaken in feeling in his manner of writing an anticipatory longing for this reform. But on the other hand it must not be forgotten that, at any rate with respect to the horns, even with natural instruments, a far richer and more varied application was possible than that which Beethoven gave to them. We can learn this from a glance at the scores of his contemporary Weber, the greatest master of horn writing. We are justified therefore in sometimes helping to render some of Beethoven's intentions clearer by the application of our more extensive means, but on no account are we justified in a re-instrumentation of his works according to the principles of the modern orchestra.

Since I have been conducting in the concert hall, I have honestly endeavoured to grasp and to reproduce faithfully the style of Beethoven's works. Numerous concerts which I have conducted have given me constantly recurring opportunities of working at this ambitious task, of perfecting myself in it, of quickening my appreciation and of striving with all my might to come nearer to my ideal, viz., to reproduce faithfully in my interpretation the characteristic features of Beethoven's orchestral work, while at the same time combining them with the utmost clearness. The following proposals have the advantage of being based throughout, not on theoretical considerations but on practical and, in many cases, oft-repeated experience.

I tried first of all to animate the execution by means of careful notation, where this appeared necessary, and endeavoured to render obscure passages clearer by this means, without altering the instrumentation. By careful notation I made the more important parts more prominent and put the less important parts more in the background; not with the idea of producing arbitrary shades of expression, but simply to preserve the unbroken melodic progress of the symphony, a clear understanding of which is the only safeguard against obscurity in execution. In many cases where I had originally thought an instrumental alteration to be indispensable, I found to my joy that a carefully executed notation not only amply met my own requirements, but also corresponded much more to Beethoven's intention than the alteration contemplated.

Passages do occur, however, where notation alone would not suffice, and in such cases I was obliged to have recourse to instrumental interference. This book, in which every one of these cases is examined and justified in detail, is sufficient proof of the careful consideration with which I proceeded in the matter.

Such alterations are of different kinds. In some cases I made the second voice of a woodwind instrument, which had just come to a rest, resume in unison with the first voice in order to strengthen it. In several symphonies I not only doubled the number of the woodwind instruments when there was a strong string section—this other conductors had done before me—but also marked with the utmost care every passage in each individual part where this doubling was to come in and where it was to stop. This is treated in detail in the introductory remarks to the *Eroica*, and taken up later in connexion with each particular symphony.

Other alterations are necessary in those passages in which both horns or both trumpets are playing in octaves, but where Beethoven has been obliged through lack of a natural note to allow the second voice to make a disproportionate leap. Wagner, as he tells us himself, used "generally" to recommend his second wind players, in such passages as the following:

always to take the lower octave and play thus:

But this "general" instruction goes too far, for it is just these intervals which are often so characteristic; and just as a great master can often turn to advantage the very imperfection of the means at his disposal, so here this striking use of natural notes often corresponds exactly to the peculiarities of Beethoven's style, and any attempt to improve it would only have the opposite effect. I have therefore examined each of these cases singly, and have only ventured on an alteration, i.e. a transposition into the lower octave, where Beethoven's action is clearly due to the limited compass of the instruments of his time.

Much less numerous than these modest modifications are those passages in which I have made actual additions and have inserted harmonic notes in the pauses of brass instruments or slightly changed the succession of notes in these parts for the benefit of the melodic expression. I have only done this where there can be absolutely no doubt that Beethoven would have written it in the same way, had not the oft-mentioned imperfection of these instruments compelled him to do violence to his conceptions; and he would certainly thank us for these alterations were he in the land of the living.

Real innovations, with the participation, of course, only of the instruments prescribed, I have undertaken partly in accordance with the proposals made by Wagner and partly on my own responsibility; they occur only in the very rare cases in which there was absolutely no other means of obtaining the effect which Beethoven wished to produce. I invite a disinterested examination of the cases which I have attempted to expound thoroughly in the present work and, if necessary, a practical comparison, in which these passages could be tried first as they stand in the original and then in the altered form which I have suggested. I may mention here that whenever I have had the passages executed in their altered form, I have never been reproached with it—indeed no one has perceived the alteration—but that, on the contrary, surprise has sometimes been expressed that, in my rendering, so much became "clear" which had never been so before.

I have thought it necessary to revise very carefully the metronome marks. The metronome is an instrument which, as Berlioz says, is only meant to guard us against gross misapprehensions. Moreover, every composer will admit that one's view as to the time of a composition of one's own often alters considerably as soon as the creation of one's fantasy is handed over to the reality of execution. Maelzel's invention only came into use after Beethoven had already become hard of hearing. He must have been open to error in supplying metronome marks for his works since he was scarcely capable any more of verifying them with his hearing. An attempt to play Beethoven's symphonies according to the metronome marks will prove how unreliable they often are. I would point out emphatically, however, that my directions in this matter can only be of an approximate nature, for an artistic conception of time is not so firmly established that it can be regulated by numbers with absolute certainty.

With regard to my instructions on the advisability of obeying repeat signs, I followed my personal feelings and taste. Proofs of correctness can hardly be supplied in such instances.

In the numbering of pages and bars I have followed the complete edition of Breitkopf & Härtel.*

And now, if anyone wishes to draw profit from my work, I would ask him, not simply to glance through it and single out what perhaps specially appeals to him, but to go carefully through the scores of Beethoven's symphonies with the help of my directions, at least once, and to note these directions down in the scores with the utmost care. By this means only will he obtain an idea of what I wish to say to him and some understanding of my conception of these works. And if anyone finds then that I have gone too much into detail, that I have delayed longer than necessary over points of minor importance and that I have repeatedly referred to things which any intelligent musician could find out for himself, let him remember, first, that in art even the most insignificant things are important, if they serve the perfection of the whole; secondly, that I am writing not only for the elder masters of the conductor's art who have already endeavoured to master Beethoven's style in their own way, but even more for the younger conductors, for the coming generation, who—partly through having been spoilt by the much

---

* PUBLISHER'S NOTE: This is not the case in the present volume, in which, for greater convenience, the references are to bars numbered consecutively throughout each movement.

more easy-going modern scores where everything "tells," and so feeling as uncomfortable in the presence of Beethoven's more reserved orchestra as they would before a sphinx propounding insoluble riddles, and partly through the exaggerated imitation of Bülow's style of conducting which is still more or less in vogue— imagine that they must find salvation in trifles, instead of allowing themselves to be guided by the genius of beauty and truth. I have therefore, in addition to the above-mentioned hints, always explained my own manner of interpretation wherever it seemed to me that it might be of use, and in so far as it was possible for me to do so in words.

The most minute observance of all my directions, however, cannot possibly ensure a perfect execution if the spirit of the artist is wanting, for this alone can give Beethoven's symphonies a living form. My task then is to provide, not an apodeictic book of instructions for rising conductors, but a loving guide by which they may avoid the reefs and dangers which beset the path through these greatest challenges to the conductor's art.

It is with this object in view that I offer this book to the public.

Munich   FELIX WEINGARTNER
July 1906

Preface to the Second Edition

The suggestions I gave in this book have been adopted on many occasions, to my great pleasure. I may therefore assume that they have been accepted. The second edition contains only a few revisions; the text is basically unchanged.

Darmstadt   FELIX WEINGARTNER
March 1916

Preface to the Third Edition

On the Performance of Beethoven's Symphonies, now appearing in a third edition with minor alterations, was followed in 1918 by *On the Performance of the Symphonies of Schubert and Schumann* and in 1923 by a volume concerning three symphonies of Mozart. This yielded the general title *On the Performance of Classical Symphonies*. The great necessity for discovering and clarifying the masters' intentions in many works, either by exact indications or by retouching or sometimes even by reinstrumentation, is shown by the wide distribution enjoyed first by my book on Beethoven's symphonies. The preface and contents of this book expressed these basic principles emphatically as early as 1906. But the necessity is also confirmed by the growing interest in Schumann's symphonies among those conductors who, having used my hints, no longer feel bound by the original instrumentation of those lovely works, which is sometimes deficient. Thus I may look back with satisfaction upon the labor I expended on these fundamental books.

Basel   FELIX WEINGARTNER
March 1928

First Symphony

First Movement

Bars 5 and 6. First flute and first bassoon are important parts for the melody and, whilst the rest of the orchestra remains *p*, must be rendered distinctly audible, thus:

The horns, in spite of the unison with the bassoon which begins in bar 2, must be considered as harmony parts and therefore remain *p*.

Bar 12. The four demisemiquavers in the strings are generally played as grace notes, which is wrong; they must have exactly the value of a quaver. They receive their true melodic importance when the Allegro con brio which immediately follows is played in such a way that the value of a half bar corresponds precisely to that of a quaver in the preceding Adagio molto. It is true that this does not agree with the metronome marking, but it gives more character to the principal theme than if this is played at full speed at the very beginning. The speed should gradually increase until full speed is reached at the *ff*, bar 31. We must emphasize the fact that both here and in all similar observations we are concerned with fluctuations, not with any dislocation of the time of the piece. An intentionally slow beginning of the Allegro would be just as displeasing as the gentle, preparatory holding back in the first bars (which allows the chief part to grow out of the introductions, as it were) is pleasing and effectual.

Bars 25, 27 and 29. Every *sf* to be executed as *sfp*.

Bars 33–41. There is a danger here lest the imitations of the violin passages by the flutes, the clarinets and the first bassoon should be drowned by the horns, the trumpets and the kettledrums, or even by the string section if this is numerous, so that the audience only hears emphatic brass notes and constantly recurring string chords. I therefore propose the following notation:

Flutes
Clarinets
1st Bassoon

Oboes
Horns

Trumpets
Kettledrums

Violins

Violas
Violoncellos
Contrabassos and
2nd Bassoon

The strings still remain *mf* in bar 42 and are joined by the wood-winds in the passage

likewise in *mf*, thus rendering possible the *crescendo* prescribed to last during the next three bars. If, on the other hand, the whole passage reproduced in our last example but one be played *ff* as prescribed, the volume must either be suddenly lessened so as to enable us to produce a *crescendo*, or else the *crescendo* must be sacrificed altogether. The directions given above, however, not only render the bars in question clearer, but they also deliver us from the dilemma just mentioned.

Bars 53–56. To obtain a graceful rendering of this passage the following nuances are recommended, but it must be remembered that the $>$ are to be executed in such a way as to enliven the passage in a pleasing and gentle manner; the slightest forcing of the notes would be detrimental.

What we have just said in regard to the $>$ may be applied also to the *sf* in the four following bars. They are *sf* in *piano*, not in *forte* (a difference which must always be carefully observed), and must therefore be played very delicately. It is advisable to allow them to be followed by a short $>$, so that for the flutes and clarinets the passage will be as follows:

for the strings:

for the first bassoon:

and thereupon for violas, violoncellos and contrabassos:

Bars 61–64. Directions for the parts containing the melody, violins, first flute and first oboe, the same as for bars 53–56.

Bars 67 and 68. I recommend the following notation for all parts:

not however a strong *crescendo* with a startling *p subito*, but a gentle intensifying of the sound, followed by a return to the *p* which reigns in the whole of the preceding passage.

Bar 77. With this bar begins one of the most characteristic episodes of this symphony. The wonderful bass passages, the original modulations and the speaking phrases of oboe and bassoon give us a foretaste of Beethoven's later works. In order to give the expression its full due here, I believe I am justified in placing a *poco meno mosso* at the beginning of the bar in question. Then in bar 85 begins a gradual increase of speed which lasts for three bars and finally reaches the original *allegro* (tempo I) in bar 88.

The marking ⌒ for the violins and violas given in the first two bars only, holds good for the whole passage as far as the *crescendo*, at which point a more vigorous bowing might be introduced.

Bar 93. All parts to be provided with a ⟨ leading up to the coming *ff*.

Bar 97. The modern make of the instrument allows us to write

for the flute in this bar instead of

Beethoven never ventured to write anything for the flute above the high A, and this, as we shall see presently, often led to curiously abnormal treatment of the melody.

Bar 99. The unnatural leap in the parts of the second horn and the second trumpet is simply due to the fact that the lower D was wanting in the instruments of that time. In this and in similar passages, which will be mentioned in their place, we may therefore make the correction

with full justification. The second horn in the following bars also can always take the lower D instead of the higher one until the repetition mark is reached.

I recommend the repetition of the first part in this movement, in which, as the first subject is no longer preceded by an introduction, there is now no reason for holding back the time. The repetition can therefore be begun at full *allegro* tempo, for which ♩ = 112 is a fairly correct metronome mark.

Bar 125. All parts to be provided with a $\prec$ leading up to the following *f*.

Bars 122–125 form a period of four beats, to which the passage of four beats immediately following corresponds. Although this second period is only a transposition of the first, it needs a different mode of execution, as it concludes *p* instead of *f* and leads to major instead of minor. I have therefore introduced the following graduation in all parts for bars 128, 129 and 130. The second horn plays the lower F during these bars, a note which did not exist in the natural instruments.

Bars 131–135. The first flute is the part which carries the melody in this passage. It is quite sufficient in itself during the *crescendo* in bars 131 and 132, but from bar 133 on, it may easily begin to seem weak as the string section has already become fairly strong and in bar 134 has reached *ff*. It is therefore advisable for both flutes to play the passage

in unison. The oboes should not make the *crescendo* on E♮ G too emphatic.

Bar 136. Wagner, with special reference to Beethoven's compositions, has already pointed out the importance of a *p* following immediately upon an *f* without any intermediate *diminuendo*. I would again repeat this here, and would add that the sudden change should take place in tempo, without any separation to break the rhythm before the *p*, i.e. without any so-called "air pause" (or "breath pause"). At the same time I would declare that I consider the introduction of these "air pauses" into classical masterpieces, and hence in Beethoven's symphonies also, as one of the most horrible examples of bad taste in the modern manner of conducting. In spite of the artistic freedom of execution, the great sequence of the time must never be broken. This is one of the very first demands which I make on every conductor, and he will educate himself to it with all his strength unless he wishes to be a mere strainer after effect. I quite admit that this sudden introduction of a *p* belongs to those difficulties of a good execution which can only be conquered by a careful training of the orchestra.

Bar 144. Even the best orchestras tend to get too fast after this bar. This must be carefully avoided. The little rhythms

scattered over the different parts like spots of light, must form a whole with perfect precision like the links of a chain, whilst all players must maintain during fifteen bars a light *piano* undisturbed by any gradation. Then the short *crescendo* in bar 159 should be executed with a so much greater degree of energy.

Bars 160–167. If the different E's in the horns, trumpets and clarinets are played *ff* throughout, the melodic phrases of the flutes, oboes and bassoons cannot possibly obtain their true value. This, however, can be effected by the following phrasing:

Bar 178. Here the principal theme is introduced for the first time in its full splendour. It is therefore advisable, whilst maintaining the energetic expression, to modify the time rather in the broader direction, and to prepare for this modification by an almost imperceptible slackening of the time in the four *crescendo* bars preceding the *ff*. In the following gradual *crescendo* which begins in bar 191, an opportunity presents itself of gently quickening the speed again so that with bar 198 the original time is established once more. But the conductor should see that the strings execute the short semiquaver figures with gradually increasing strength and are not already playing *f* where *crescendo* is indicated.

Bars 184–187. Second horn and second trumpet can play the lower D here. Not so in bars 191 and 192, however, because the lower D of the second horn would hinder the progress of the bass entrusted to the second bassoon. The following low E of the horns, in spite of the analogous progress of the second bassoon, has no influence on the bass leading, as this is executed here by the violoncellos and contrabassos.

Bar 205. In spite of the fact that the flute and clarinet come in gently on the fourth crotchet, I believe a $>$ in the strings is justifiable, leading up to the *p* in the following bar.

Bars 206–222. What was said above for bars 53–68 holds good here with suitable adaptation to the altered instrumentation.

Bar 230. *Poco meno mosso* (as before).

Bars 238–240. Quicken a little (as before).

Bar 241. Tempo I (as before).

Bar 246. $<$ in all parts (as before).

Bars 251 and 252. An attempt to treat this passage for the horns and trumpets in the same way as the corresponding passage beginning in bar 98 would be unsuccessful. The high A and the high F both stood at the writer's disposal. Moreover, a comparison of the different instrumentation of the two passages shows clearly that Beethoven saved the brass for the emphatic introduction of the dominant followed by the tonic. This one example is quite characteristic, and should serve as a warning to those who think that instrumental alterations will be helpful everywhere because in some places, as we shall see, they are indispensable.

Second Movement

Bar 1. I propose ♪ = 104 as metronome mark, instead of ♪ = 120.

The principal theme here easily falls a prey to the following trivial manner of execution:

I therefore recommend, in whatever part the theme occurs, to give as delicate an accent as possible to the upbeat; this can only be represented as follows:

The same holds good for several other passages in this movement, as for example the beginning of the second part:

Bars 11 and 12. For second violins, violas and violoncellos the following notation will serve to animate the execution:

Bar 16. For the sake of clearness I have changed the *crescendo*, which lasts for nine bars and thus has to be very gradually increased, to a *poco cresc.* in this bar, and have placed a *più cresc.* in bar 22.

Bars 27–34. The following notation is to be recommended in a very skilful performance, in order to enliven the execution:

(Violoncellos uniformly *p*)

(this *cresc.* and *dim.* everywhere,
except in the Horns, which remain *p*)

From the upbeat in bar 34 to bar 38 the second violins, first flute and first oboe may play *poco espressivo*, whilst the first violins give their descending semiquaver passage *pp*.

Bar 46. Oboes and bassoons begin to play *forte* at the C and do not wait for the G, which is a correction that I was once surprised to find. The same holds with reference to the F and C for all winds in bar 146.

Bar 57. In this bar a *diminuendo* can be introduced, then the four following bars may be played slightly more *piano* than the three bars which precede the *diminuendo*, thus forming a kind of softly dying echo. At the third quaver of bar 61 we return to the normal *p* prescribed, which closes the first part so gracefully.

The direction to repeat should not be observed.

From about bar 71 a slight quickening of the time will naturally occur until the original tempo of the principal theme is reached by about bar 87 through a series of gradations. For bars 97–100 I have adopted the following manner of execution:

but I always warned the first violins against a sentimental mode of expression in the last two bars. If I supported the execution of the short oboe and bassoon phrases by means of a slight *ritenuto*, I allowed the original time to come in already in the two bars in question and did not wait for the return of the principal theme.

The figurations accompanying the return, which begin in the violoncellos at bar 101, cannot be performed tenderly and gracefully enough. I have therefore inserted a *pp* also in bar 113 for the second bassoon and also for the violas, violoncellos and contrabassos.

Bar 117. Here too only *poco cresc.* at first, and *più cresc.* not before bar 122.

Bars 127–138. See what has been said for bars 27–38.

Bars 157–161. Same as for bars 57–61.

Bars 163 and 164. The little solo for the first oboe to be played with expression and a fairly marked *crescendo*, but with no diminution of the speed.

Bars 176–180. In order to ensure the melodic domination to the woodwinds in this passage, where they play *f* throughout, it is advisable, should the strings be numerous, to adopt for the strings the notation I give here for the first violin:

Bars 186–190. This repetition of the preceding four bars is played *pp* in contrast to the preceding *p*. The *pp* begins in the flute at bar 188, in the oboes at bar 186 on the third quaver, in the clarinets and bassoons at bar 188, in the horns at bar 186, in the first violins at bar 187, in the second violins and violas at bar 186 on the first demisemiquaver, in the violoncellos and basses at bar 186 on the third quaver. In bar 190 the horns resume the customary *p* on the third quaver, whereupon the *pp* prescribed by Beethoven from bar 192 on has a particularly fine effect, especially when accompanied by a slight diminution in the speed. The *f* which immediately follows must, however, bring back the original time.

Such observations as these are intended to serve merely as hints, not as directions. It would be better not to observe them at all than to follow them unintelligently or with exaggerated effects.

Third Movement

Bars 16 and 17. For the sake of the melodic structure, I had the C D-flat (upbeat and first crotchet) in the first and second violins played *p*, or at most *mf*, at all events in distinct contrast to the *f* which is introduced again on the second crotchet of bar 17. It seems to me that this must have been Beethoven's design, as otherwise he would have had no reason for prescribing *f* again in the violins at this second crotchet. The modulation into G-flat major introduced in this bar is one of the numerous striking new features of Beethoven which already distinguish this first symphony. The *ff* at the entrance of this G-flat major (bar 19) must be played by all instruments concerned with special emphasis.

Bar 80, Trio. For the first sixteen bars of this Trio I have adopted the following notation. The first time the woodwinds and horns play as follows:

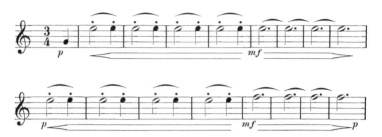

and the violins as written, in a uniform *p*. At the repetition however, these sixteen bars, as well as the following ones until the repetition mark, should be played *pp*, without the <*mf*> which I have added. The violins then, of course, also play *pp*, that is, more softly than the first time. The *sf* in bar 102, which even in the first playing only represents an accent in *p*, should be scarcely noticeable in the repetition.

I would deprecate a too frequent use of these echo effects, which I have introduced here and also once or twice in the Andante of this symphony. They easily give an impression of affectation, especially in compositions of a serious character. They do not seem to me misplaced in this cheerful work, which was evidently written under the influence of Haydn's style. But in the later symphonies we shall scarcely meet them again.

Bar 104. The passage beginning at the double bar should not be begun too quietly, in order to render possible the *diminuendo* which shortly follows.

Bars 120 and 121. I would warn against an exaggeration of the < >, which would have a grotesque effect.

The first part of the main section is so short that I should recommend a repetition of it even after the Trio, in order to avoid the impression of a too hasty flitting past, which seems to me unavoidable if it is only played once. This proceeding forms an exception to be allowed in this symphony only, and which should never be adopted in any other symphony, whether of Beethoven or any other master.

Fourth Movement

Bars 1–6. The first *fermata* on the G is maintained for a considerable length of time and then taken off, so that there is a short pause before the entry of the first violins. The following passage was apparently already executed by Bülow in the character of an improvisatory introduction. I do not know how this was done as I never heard this symphony conducted by Bülow. I have supplemented Beethoven's directions in the following way:

In the Allegro molto e vivace I adopt the metronome mark ♩ = 138 instead of ♩ = 88, by which means unpleasant haste is avoided.

Bars 34–36. The short phrase in the first flute, first clarinet and first bassoon

is not sufficiently in evidence if the trumpets, kettledrums and oboes play *f* as prescribed. It would be contrary to the whole character of the passage, however, to weaken this *f*, and yet it is most important that the merry, almost comic figure of the woodwinds should be distinctly heard. I have therefore allowed the second flute, second clarinet and second bassoon to accompany the first parts in unison and all six instruments to blow *ff*; by this means the effect evidently desired is obtained.

Bars 56–63. The first and second violins play this graceful and spirited theme with the following gradation:

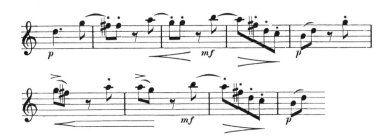

Bar 85. Second horn and second trumpet take the lower D.

Bar 96. The first part of this movement should be repeated.

Bars 106 and 107. Attention should be called to the difference between the *pp* of these bars as a noticeable weakening of the preceding *p*, also to the fact that the violins ought on no account to prepare by means of a $<$ the *ff* which is introduced quite suddenly in bar 108. In order, however, to render these fine and yet strong differentiations absolutely distinct, it is of the utmost importance to avoid a too great hastening of the time, which is a point against which I would warn here expressly, in the interest of the charming gracefulness of this whole movement.

Bars 117–121. For the first violins the following mode of execution may be recommended:

The following passage, with its attractive alternation of *legato* and *staccato* runs, only produces its proper effect when it is faithfully executed *sempre p* without the slightest attempt at a *crescendo*. But then the *crescendo* should come in at bar 138 as prescribed with all the more force.

Bars 160–163. It is of great importance that the *p* in the woodwinds should make its entry here suddenly. If we prepare for it by a *diminuendo* in the first two bars the whole effect is spoilt, although that is easier for careless wind players. In order to avoid any error, I have written *ff* in bar 160 for flutes, clarinets and bassoons, and have added a *subito* to the *p* in bar 162. To my surprise, not only once but several times the compliment has been paid me that I had

really "made" something quite special out of this passage. I have
never understood what there was "special" in faithfully carrying
out an instruction, and still less have I been able to understand how
any other mode of execution than the one described could have been
adopted in this passage. This fine stroke, that the *ff* of the whole
orchestra has a sort of echo for two bars more in the woodwind
instruments and then gives way suddenly to the *p* of the returning
principal theme, is so absolutely characteristic of Beethoven that it
cannot possibly be misunderstood.

Bars 183–188. Although it is a temptation here for the second
trumpet and second horn to take the lower D, I would decidedly
dissuade from it. Especially in conjunction with bar 189, I find the
leaps

too characteristic to justify any weakening process.

Bars 192–199. See bars 56–63. The following four bars will then
of course also be played

and possibly, in accordance with the melodic character, with even
more decided emphasis than the eight preceding ones.

Bars 234–237. The series of chords

represents a closed melodic and harmonic complex; hence the
second *fermata* should be taken off, but not the first, which should
also be held on for a short time in order to avoid an unsuitably
strong interruption.

Bar 246. This entry of the *f* on the last but one note of the theme, which thereby receives a sudden and quite inexplicable jerk, almost makes me believe in a slip of the author's; I think therefore that I may venture on the following alteration in the notation for bars 246 and 247, which I feel to be in keeping with Beethoven's intention.

Bars 275 and 277. It should be specially mentioned that both the *sf*'s in the oboes and horns are here only "accents in *p*" and should therefore be very delicately executed. The wind players concerned must remember that bars 274–277 are a *piano* repetition of the preceding identical *forte* passage. It is just these two *sf*'s which so easily mislead them into playing these four bars loud also.

Second Symphony

The Second Symphony stands in need of fewer hints as to execution than the first, and the alterations here, with the exception of one single passage, are of a less important nature. It is so simple and the orchestral colouring is so bright and vivid that an animated mode of execution seems to come almost of itself. Joyous youth, cheerful fervour and unbroken strength seem to constitute the foundations of its being. To approach it in a spirit of pale reflection is to spoil it at once.

First Movement

Bar 1. The *fermata* must not be removed, nor any pause be inserted after it. We can gather this from a comparison of the first bar with the fifth, in which the same melody proceeds unbrokenly. The first crotchet with the *fermata* must be sustained for a considerable length of time, then the conductor should pass straight on to the second. This is immediately split up into two quaver-beats; the whole orchestra holds on the first quaver, as dotted crotchets are prescribed, and the parts in which a pause occurs do not cease until the conductor gives the second quaver; then the oboes and bassoons continue their theme starting straight away from its first note, the D of the *fermata*.

The metronome mark ♪ = 84 does not agree with the direction Adagio molto, so I have adopted ♪ = 72.

Bar 10. It is not advisable here to change the high F of the second horn into the low one. In the next bar the low G was at Beethoven's disposal and yet he has not used it, so evidently there must have been some reason for it. Perhaps he wished to give a certain sharpness of sound to the F and G, and considered that the unison of the deeper octave, where it could be obtained, would have weakened it. Nor does the interval of the second in the horns in bar 22 seem to justify an alteration of the unison in the preceding bar. Wherever it can be clearly seen that Beethoven would have

83

written the lower notes had they been at his disposal, and that he only obeyed necessity in writing otherwise, the correction may safely be made. But in all other cases this transposition should be avoided, and the thoughtful musician will have no difficulty in recognising such cases if he will only take the trouble to educate his artistic taste for Beethoven's style.

Bar 18. The *sf* in the oboes seems rather weak in relation to the naturally much more powerful *sforzato* which precedes and follows in the horns. I have already heard the proposal to strengthen the oboes here by means of the clarinets. This is unnecessary, however, when we observe that the whole passage bears a *piano* character, in accordance with which the horns must produce their notes very gently; then the naturally rather piercing oboes will obtain their full value.

Bars 24–26. A *poco espressivo* should be added in the melodic passage for the violas and violoncellos. During the second and third crotchets of the last of these three bars these instruments should play slightly *diminuendo*, and should continue their figuration in bar 27 *p*, leaving the sustaining of the melody now entirely to the violins.

Bar 34. Allegro con brio. As metronome mark I recommend ♩ = 92 instead of ♩ = 100.

Bar 73. This is another of those sudden *pianos* so characteristic of Beethoven. They should on no account be either overlooked or prepared for by a *diminuendo*, nor should they be in any way facilitated by means of a so-called "breath pause." I shall in future not call attention to each individual case as it occurs.

Bars 120–125. Here we have evidently not got to do with a *sforzato* in *piano*. The notes marked *sf* must be given shortly and sharply, in contrast to the others, which are to be played *p*.

Bars 152–165. The quaver passages in the woodwinds stand in strong opposition to those of the strings. That is apparent to the eye but not to the ear in the present notation. If this passage is played *ff* throughout as prescribed, the woodwind section is almost inaudible. The short semiquaver passages also, which are played by only one flute, one oboe and one bassoon

are too weak in comparison with those of the first violins. This passage, then, is one of the few where a radical remedy cannot be held to be impious; on the contrary, in my opinion it is urgently demanded by a pious veneration for the great work of the great master. Wagner hits the nail on the head when, in reference to a similar radical remedy in the Ninth Symphony which we shall mention later, he writes: "In deciding such questions, we have to make up our minds whether we prefer listening to a piece of music such as this for some time without obtaining a clear idea of what the composer wished to express, or seeking to do it justice by means of some judicious expedient." In order therefore to render Beethoven's intention as clear for the ear as it is for the eye, I propose the following alterations.

The second flute should play in unison with the first from bar 154 to the end of the passage in question. The low notes of this part in bars 155–158 are of no value as regards sound compared with the very strong string chords and the other woodwind parts, which, as we shall see, are also correspondingly strengthened. The low notes may therefore be sacrificed without hesitation to a more powerful treble.

In bar 158 the second oboe plays

and then blows in unison with the first to the end of the passage.

The following part may be inserted from bar 153 onwards for the clarinets, where a rest is prescribed for them in the original:

The sustained notes of the second bassoon part in bars 155, 157 and 158 are of no importance in so far as the same notes are given by the horns or violoncellos separately or by both together. From bar 152 the part of the bassoon can be played as follows:

Then the second bassoon can play in unison with the first to the end of the passage.

In bars 157 and 158 the second horn blows the lower F. In addition to this, every semibreve in the horns and trumpets throughout the passage should be marked *sfp* instead of *sf*. In bar 158, in which a specially strong accent is needed for these instruments also, the *ff* should be changed into *ff* $>$.

If, with these alterations and additions, the woodwind section does not even yet acquire sufficient strength—this depends on its position, on the number of strings, on the acoustic properties of the hall and so on—the strings also may play *sfp* in bars 155 and 157 and then set in with renewed strength in each next bar respectively.

Bars 186–194. In this passage even the best orchestra tends to hurry and to allow the *crescendo* to make its entry too soon. This should be avoided, as it quite destroys the charm of this sweet passage.

Bars 254–258. Here we should expect

instead of

but as changes in the theme when it is repeated are characteristic of Beethoven we dare not make any alteration in the text.

Bars 292–297. See what has been said for bars 120–125.

Bars 318 and 324. The instruction given for the second violins and violas, as well as for the oboe and first bassoon in the second of the two bars mentioned, should be carefully observed, viz. that the upbeat (the four semiquavers) should still be played *ff* and that the *p* should not make its entry until the first crotchet which follows. These notes, which are so important for the theme, are often inaudible, because the players generally prolong the *p* of the immediately preceding passage over the upbeat notes. If in spite of the *ff* they are still not sufficiently in evidence, a weakening of the other instruments in the second half of the bars in question at the conductor's discretion might be advisable.

Bar 324. The second half of this bar can be provided with a $>$ in the instruments playing in chords, in order to make the semi-quaver figure in the oboe and bassoon clearly audible.

Bar 335. I recommend that the trumpets should make their entry here *mf* and play *crescendo* until the *ff* of the following bar.

Bar 342 and following ones. The use of open trumpet notes often introduces an ugly-sounding, noisy "blare" into the classical symphonies, and this is specially the case with Beethoven. It is therefore necessary not always to allow these instruments to play with their full force even in the *forte* passages, but to reserve this for the points where the climax is reached. Skilful players will feel where such gradations in the *forte* can be made. Those who have not got sufficiently fine feeling will have to be guided by the conductor. It would take me too long if I were to point out each individual passage where such treatment might be required; I will therefore merely indicate one or two cases which will serve as prime examples. Thus, from bar 340 onwards the distinctive feature is the splendid contrast between the violin leaps and the bass figures. I should therefore let the trumpets, and also the kettledrums, though these with slightly diminished strength, play *mf* from the above-mentioned bar onwards. In bar 346 the very natural accent prescribed should be given, and thereupon the instruments in question should resume their *mf*, with a slight *crescendo* in bars 348 and 349 so as to be able to play the final fanfare in all its splendour. A suitable treatment of the loudest instruments, such as I have just described, will often present these longer *forte* passages in an extremely favorable light, whereas a continuous, uniform *ff* in those parts which are so strong already by nature often merely produces a most unartistic noise.

Second Movement

Bar 1. As metronome mark I have adopted ♪ = 84 instead of ♪ = 92.

Bars 17–20. The strings might phrase carefully as follows:

Bars 25–28. The clarinets and bassoons should phrase this passage in the same way the strings did previously, whilst the strings and horns play quite *pp*.

Bars 41 and 42. The second horn plays the lower F from the upbeat onwards.

Bar 45. The conductor should use his own judgment as to whether this *pp* is not better played by the first horn only, in which case the second would make its entry at the *ff* in the following bar.

Bars 48–50. The first violins might phrase this passage in a gently animating way as follows:

whereas during the following demisemiquaver variation a very uniform *p* must be maintained.

Bars 87–89. First clarinet and first bassoon should be somewhat prominent; they might be marked *mf*. In the third bar a *diminuendo* begins, and lasts till the first crotchet of the next bar, which must be played *p*. The same holds for the analogous passage later on, viz. bars 251–253.

Bars 108–112. This beautiful passage will bear a very slight, scarcely noticeable diminution in the speed; then the *crescendo* in the two following bars leads to the resumption of the original time at the *f*. The same holds for the similar passage, bars 118–125. In bar 117, the E minor chord in the flutes, oboes, bassoons, horns, violas, violoncellos and bassos should be furnished with a *staccato* dot and played short, in order to avoid the clashing of the G with the immediately following G-sharp in the second violins.

Bars 128–135. In order to bring the other parts more into prominence, the second violins and violas should play the constantly recurring C with slightly diminished force (*mf*). The full *ff* does not come in again in these parts until bar 136.

Bars 154–157. The preceding *crescendo*, with its melodic and harmonic gradation, which lasts through eleven bars, together with the energetic rendering of the *ff* (six bars before) will naturally have caused a quickening of the time, which in these bars can be brought back gently to the normal time of the theme by means of a *poco ritenuto*.

Bars 174–178 and bars 182–185. See bars 17–20 and bars 25–28.
Bars 212–214. See bars 48–50.

Third Movement

Bar 85. It is advisable to take the Trio a bit more calmly than the main section; this is advantageous to the graceful theme, and also to the characteristic middle part (F-sharp major in the strings). Any hastening of the whole movement should be carefully avoided.

Fourth Movement

Bar 1. I adopt $\bd = 132$ as metronome mark instead of $\bd = 152$.
Bars 12–18. Should the first flute, the first oboe and the first bassoon not be considered penetrating enough here, they may be strengthened by the second instruments playing in unison. In any case I should recommend a slight weakening of the sound in the horns and trumpets after the *f* and the *sf*, unless the players concerned have a true enough perception to do it on their own initiative. The

full *f* enters again at the last crotchet of the last bar. The same holds good for bars 196–202.

Bars 26–29. Violoncellos, second violins and violas should play *espressivo dolce*; clarinets and bassoons should do likewise in bars 32–35, whilst the string section accompanies them *pp*. In bars 30 and 31 I have adopted for the whole string section the phrasing which I give in the following quotation for the first violin:

All this is done with a view to obtaining a dignified animation in the piece, not an unartistic affectation. From bar 32 to the first crotchet of bar 36 the first horn alone will possibly suffice.

Bars 140, 142, 146 and 148. First flute and first oboe may be strengthened by the second parts playing in unison in so far as the acoustic conditions seem to demand it.

Bar 151. In order not to drown the woodwinds it is advisable here, especially when the strings are numerous, to begin only *poco crescendo*, and not to introduce the full *crescendo* until bar 155. Then the flutes and oboes may be doubled by means of the second parts, as follows:

Bars 165–167. As the flute and the oboe cannot be doubled here on account of the characteristic entry of the second parts a little later on, it is of the utmost importance to introduce a diminution of sound in the horns every time after the *ff* and *sf* in the semibreves, and to play *ffp* and *sfp*. The same holds for the horns and trumpets in bars 171 and 172. The full *ff* should not make its entry before bar 177.

Bars 210–219. See bars 26–35.

Bars 252–255. A gloomy minor tone suddenly disturbs the exuberant gaiety of this symphony like the presage of some awful

fate. I have applied the *pp* of the deep horns, trumpets and kettledrums, which give such a wonderful sound, to the whole orchestra,
and then allowed these four bars to be played distinctly more softly
than the preceding major passage. By this means the following
variations in force which occur in the passage up to the joyful *f* in
bar 268, produce a greater effect. The *sf* in bar 267 should barely
be observed. The strings start from *pp* on the following *crescendo*,
which should be most delicately executed. The *p* in the string parts
had thus better be deleted.

Bars 306–312. In order to make a stand against the stormy entry
of the strings, it may be necessary to strengthen the first flute and
the first oboe by the second instruments in unison from the upbeat
notes onward. Then, from the entry of the horns and trumpets
(bar 310) the second bassoon may also possibly play the two bars
starting from B-flat, instead of resting. The system of doubling the
woodwinds in large orchestras for some of Beethoven's symphonies
will soon be discussed in more detail.

Bar 335 and bar 337. Both *fermatas* are taken off and then brought
in again after short rests; the same holds for the *fermata* in bar 415.

Bar 362. We have here a *pp* preceded by a $>$ which lasts for
four bars. As, however, the part which precedes this $>$ is also
marked *pp*, evidently the lightest sound which the orchestra can
possibly obtain is designed for the passage which follows this mark.
It is specially important for the six bars in which the string section is
playing alone (bars 366–371) to produce a feeling of breathless
expectation, which is then happily relieved by the magnificent
entry of the chord of the second in bar 372.

Bar 415. In the eight bars which follow the *fermata*, the time
should be held back in a tender, I might almost say "furtive,"
manner; then at the entry of the *ff* (bar 424 with the upbeat)
normal time can be resumed again and maintained to the end.

Third Symphony

For the Third, Fifth, Seventh and Ninth Symphonies, and also for some parts of the *Pastoral* Symphony, it is advisable for the woodwind section to be doubled (i.e. four flutes, four oboes, four clarinets and four bassoons), if the strings are numerous. It is not so much with the object of strengthening it that this may be done, but rather for the sake of clearness, as I hope I have made plain in the previous cases where I have recommended a doubling of the woodwinds. It is therefore not sufficient simply to tell the additional players to accompany in the *forte* passages—a very primitive proceeding which often does more harm than good—but the places where the double strength will be beneficial must be very carefully and tastefully chosen and accurately noted. Moreover, as we shall see, the woodwinds should not all be strengthened simultaneously; it may easily happen that one or two parts, sometimes even a second part alone, needs the doubling. The most practical method of procedure is the following. At the beginning of the passages where the doubling is to occur a *D* (double) is written, and an *S* (single) is written where it is to stop. The supplementary player can take his place at the reading desk of the chief player (in the first or second part) and must then be given the strictest directions to play only what comes between a *D* and an *S*—not a note more. In a small orchestra there is of course no object in doubling, as the woodwinds would be rendered quite out of proportion to the strings. My recommendations on this head refer only to large orchestras with some sixteen first violins and eight contrabassos.

First Movement

Bar 1. The metronome mark = 60 produces such a quick time that many passages, e.g. the violin figures at bar 186, cannot possibly be clearly brought out. Moreover, if this time were uniformly observed, the whole movement would acquire a hasty, even trivial character which is quite contrary to its nature. I have therefore adopted for the initial tempo the metronome mark ♩. = 54 or thereabouts, by which I do not mean to say that many parts must not be played even more calmly still. I would also observe that this notation by no means involves the instruction to conduct this movement in whole bars (i.e. one beat for each bar) throughout. This manner of conducting would be quite right for many passages, but there are others in which the beating of the three crotchets, or at any rate the marking of the first and third, is necessary. The melodic expression and the spirited rhythm will be the best guides in this case.

Bar 45. Second horn and second trumpet take the lower D.

Bars 45–54. Here, and wherever the melody is similarly broken up into short phrases on different instruments, the dotted notes of each phrase should be carefully held, the quaver should not be played too short, nor the last note too loud—in fact, it should be slightly dying away and therefore weaker than the two preceding ones. This might be shown in writing as follows:

where the — signs must not be confused with the *sf*'s which are prescribed in bars 53 and 54, and which must be executed in these bars only. A very slight slackening of the time, just enough to prevent the melody from seeming hurried, is justifiable here, but this must give the impression of being a result of the feeling, not of being done intentionally. If anyone does not feel capable of doing this, he had better not vary the time at all.

The conductor must decide whether it is better to let the first horn play alone in bars 47–53. In any case the second horn might take the lower D in bars 55 and 56, as well as in bars 59 and 60.

Bars 77–82. Second horn and second trumpet should take the lower D. I should advise also that in bar 79 all the wind instruments begin *p* and play *crescendo* to *ff* during this bar and the following. The natural expression will probably have carried the strings away and they will be playing *ff* before this is prescribed in the score. The above treatment of the wind instruments, however, will obtain the increase of dynamic expression intended by the author, without restraining the strings, which would not be right here.

Bars 83 and following. A skilful conductor will be able to hold back the time at the entry of the secondary theme to just the extent that the execution of the *portamento* characteristic of this theme demands, without interrupting the course of the piece. This slowing down of the time might perhaps slightly increase from bar 95 onwards, so that the *pp* beginning in bar 99 can be played comparatively slowly, by which means the tension is increased. The entry of the quaver movement and the *crescendo* then lead back quite naturally to the principal theme.

Bar 122. The *sf*'s in the preceding bars naturally cause a slight weakening of the three notes which immediately follow them. In this bar therefore a powerful *crescendo* is desirable, to meet the sharp *ff* of the following shocks.

Bars 123–126. It is evident that here it is only due to the imperfection of the instruments at his disposal that Beethoven was hindered from making use of the full power of the horns; I have therefore taken upon myself to complete the horn parts in these bars by the addition of the notes designated by arrows in the following passage:

I did not think it advisable to make a similar addition in the trumpets also, as this would destroy the increased effect (with respect to the present passage) obtained in the analogous passage (beginning with bar 526), where the trumpets participate throughout. I should recommend, however, that in this passage the trumpets and kettledrums play only *mf*, as an *ff* in these instruments, which only come into play for a few chords, would lessen the value of the orchestral shocks, which were evidently intended to be uniformly strong. The following six *sforzato* strokes might then be executed at full *ff*.

Bars 136–139. For the first violins and the first flute I recommend the following mode of execution

with a view to a gently graduated preparation for the coming strong *crescendo* (bars 140–142).

Bars 142 and 143. Second horn and second trumpet take the lower D.

In this movement I think it is desirable to omit the repetition of the first part and consequently the ⌐1⌐. The effect of the wonderful development and of the unusually long coda is thereby enhanced, because the hearer's receptive power remains more unimpaired than if he has to experience the first part over again. It always seems to me, too, that the transition of the ⌐1⌐ is rather conventional compared with the rest of the movement. The continuous *pp* at the ⌐2⌐, which must on no account be disturbed by sentimental variations of the sighing order, must only be increased to a moderate *crescendo* and *sf* in bars 164 and 165. If the conductor finds it necessary to introduce a slight moderation of the time at the beginning of the ⌐2⌐, he must not fail to revert to the normal tempo in bar 166. For the execution of the melody scattered over different instruments in bars 166–177 and bars 220–235, see what has been said for bars 45–54.

Bars 186–193 and bars 198–205. To facilitate a clear rendering of the figuration, which is endangered less by the wind players than by the powerful octaves of the violins, I have adopted the following notation for the violins in these passages:

I need not mention that the bassos and violas should give the principal theme with as much force as possible.

Bar 243 and following. From here to the end of bar 279 the woodwinds can play doubled; this is very advantageous for the imitative interpolations and also for the following powerful *tutti* passage.

Bars 248–259. The enormous weight of this passage leads us to suppose that the resting of the brass instruments in some bars is merely due to the fact that the suitable notes for certain chords were not at Beethoven's disposal. (He evidently very much disliked the dull sound of the stopped notes in the natural horns, as he has obstinately persisted in using them as seldom as possible.) In bars 254–259 I formerly replaced the rests in the horns and the trumpets by new parts and printed these parts in the first edition of this book. Later I changed my mind. Even if these bars sound a little sparser than those preceding, the entry of the brass in bar 260 with the kettledrum joining in forcefully, is so powerful that it should not be weakened by an immediately preceding participation of the same instruments. This must be counted as one of the cases in which Beethoven made a virtue of necessity. So then, play this passage as it is written, without retouching, and bring out as much power as possible in the strings. In bars 248–252 the second trumpet can take the lower D.

Bars 284–297. From the fact that all accents in the E minor passage are marked *sfp*, whereas the same accents in the following analogous A minor passage are marked *sf*, we can conclude that the second passage has to be played with a somewhat more intensified expression than the first, so that it is not simply a transposed repetition, but is destined also to form a transition to the energetic period beginning at bar 300. A more distinct rendering of the *sf* than of the *sfp* will also justify us in placing a short *crescendo* before, and a short *diminuendo* after the marks in question,

both of which must be animated and full of feeling, but not affected or exaggerated. Bar 298 should remain *p*; then the following *crescendo* comes in with all the more effect.

Bars 304–309. I have introduced the following notation for the trumpets:

In accordance with this, the trumpets and kettledrums in bars 316–319 may gradate as follows:

Bars 330–333. When the preceding melodic passage of the woodwinds has been executed with great expressiveness, it seems to me that these four bars ought to be played a gentle *p*, without the ＜ and ＞. Then, with the corresponding change of the *sf* in the whole string section, the following four bars may be graduated throughout, as in the following quotation (for the bassos).

Bars 338–361. Here the woodwind section begins a wonderful imitative passage, which forms a splendid contrast to the ever more boldly rising bassos. The parts are not all of equal importance. At the beginning, for example, I think the second flute has to come into

greater prominence than the first, because it has to imitate the
bassoon and the clarinet with the same notes, that is to say, melodically as well as rhythmically. I therefore recommend that first
bassoon, first clarinet and second flute be doubled. From bar 352
the first flute should play double, and the second single; from bar
355 the second clarinet should be double, and the first single again.
All the other instruments should play single. If no auxiliary woodwinds are to be had, the conductor must let the parts marked double
be rather more in evidence. We then get the following melodic
scheme, which is not only distinct and simple for the eye, but
renders the whole passage particularly luminous:

* The clarinets have been transposed back again here for the sake of greater
clearness.

From bar 358 (the last bar of the above quotation) only the first oboe plays doubled, the rest (starting from the next bar) single. From bar 362 onward during the *ff*, all instruments play doubled; then at the *p* in bar 370 all become single again.

Bars 394 and 395. This extraordinary passage has been much discussed and even corrected. Wagner thought to improve it by changing the A-flat of the second violin into G, but he only made it worse. This strange proceeding has never been imitated as far as I know. I have also heard the view expressed, that a high B-flat horn was meant here and that Beethoven simply forgot to indicate the change of pitch. In the six-bar rest, however, which is all that would have been at the disposal of the second horn, this change of pitch would have been absolutely impossible on the natural horns of that day, where crooks had to be taken off and inserted. We see too in the same passage that Beethoven gives the first horn 41 bars to change from the E-flat to the F pitch, and no less than 89 bars to get back into the E-flat pitch again. There is no doubt that we have to do here with an inspired anticipation of the principal key. I have made no change myself, and I hope that in future no one will feel called upon to explain away this bold inspiration.

Bars 448–457. See bars 45–54.

Bars 482 and 483. See bars 78 and 79. (The kettledrum might give its B-flat *piano*.)

Bars 486 and following. See bars 83 and following.

Bar 516. First flute takes the high B-flat on the second crotchet, instead of the low one, which evidently could not be obtained on the old-fashioned flutes. We shall often have occasion to notice that Beethoven prefers introducing strange changes into the melody to writing this note, which is now at the disposal of every flute player.

Bar 525. See bar 122.

Bars 532–534. I can see no reason why the third horn should not play along here in the *sf* chords as in the analogous passage at bar 124. Probably an oversight of the copyist or of Beethoven himself is at fault here. Thus, the following addition is to be made:

3rd Horn

Bars 539–542. See bars 136–139.

Bars 569–577. I have graduated the very important part of the first oboe as follows:

Bars 589–595. In striking contrast to the very rare use which Beethoven generally makes of the stopped notes, this passage contains no less than seven such notes in the part of the third horn.

Evidently Beethoven had a skilful player at his command. Moreover, there was less danger in this passage of any harm being done by the questionable notes, because the violoncello and the first bassoon were playing at the same time. This passage proves, however, that Beethoven did not abstain from such notes on principle, but on purely technical grounds. No objection can be raised, therefore, to a moderate adjustment of certain passages if care be taken not to interfere with the style of the piece.

Bars 605–614. The woodwinds should gradate as follows:

Bar 619. This second *crescendo*, prescribed so soon after the first one, seems to me to render it advisable to begin this bar with a slight decrease in sound but without a preceding *diminuendo*; this heightens the effect of the short swell which immediately follows.

Bars 640–646. The theme, which seems to be an imitation of the first violins, must be thrown into relief by the horns, but, of course, without interfering with the *piano* nature of the whole passage.

Bars 655–662. Bülow here allowed the theme to be played throughout by the trumpets as follows:

The indistinct character of the theme when played without this correction quite justifies us in adopting it.

Bars 663 and 664. The second trumpet may here take the lower B-flats. The rest in the trumpets in bar 669 is intentional, as Beethoven might have used either the E (g) or the C (e-flat) as natural notes. It is therefore wrong for any addition to be made here.

The woodwinds can begin to play doubled in bar 651 on the second quaver (the oboes naturally in the next bar). From bar 673 they play single again, then doubled from bar 685 (second crotchet) onward.

Second Movement

Bar 1. The stepping-forward character of this movement must be preserved in spite of the Adagio assai. It would therefore be unnatural for the time to be too slow. The metronome mark ♪ = 80 however gives such an alarmingly quick time that it cannot possibly be the right one. I adopt ♪ = 66 as the normal speed, which can be occasionally increased to ♪ = 72.

Bülow has already pointed out that the three first C's in the bassos are introduced by grace notes, and that these, in contrast to the later, written-out, demisemiquavers, must not be played thus

but that the G marks the first point of the bar, followed by the other notes in such quick succession, however, that they only form one rhythmic value. The same holds good, of course, for the similar passage at bar 105. It is striking, however, that here the notes preceding the third C have a different notation from those in our passage, whereas in all other points the similarity is complete. I do not know of any reason for this, but of course the will of the master must be obeyed.

Bars 14 and 15. Here I should recommend letting the first horn play alone.

Bars 56–59. The expression of this passage justifies the following gradation in all parts:

Bars 60 and 61. The weakness of the bass in the second bassoon compared with the strength of the horns united on the C, makes it advisable to play the second bassoon doubled, if auxiliary wood-winds are to be had; possibly even the two free bassoons might also play these two bars in unison with the second bassoon. But the strengthening must cease at the G (bar 62). If auxiliary woodwinds are not to be had, it must be left to the fine perceptions of the conductor as to whether the following part should be given to the second horn, instead of the prescribed part:

By this means, it is true, we get rid of the evil of the weak bass, but the whole passage, to my mind, acquires a character foreign to Beethoven's style.

Bar 69. I have often heard the "maggiore" rendered sentimental by a heavy slowness of the time, or trivialized by a graceful hastening of the speed. There is not the slightest reason for changing the normal time of this melody, so affecting in its simplicity.

Bar 74. In order not to drown the woodwinds, the *crescendo* in this bar should be only moderately given by the strings especially if they are numerous; not before the second half of the next bar, two quavers before the *ff*, should it be energetically executed.

Bar 89. I believe we are justified in this bar in introducing a slight swell of sound in oboe and bassoon, and two bars later a swell followed by a decrease on the G in oboe and horns, which may be noted thus:

if this gradation is skilfully carried out.

Bars 92–97. In order that the playing of the winds may be audible, the strings should pay no attention to the first *crescendo*, and should only begin to play *crescendo* at the indication *sempre più f*, i.e. two bars before the *ff*. Then the *f* for the strings in bar 96 would have to be omitted likewise.

In bars 76–79 and 96–99 the woodwinds should play doubled.

Bar 114 to bar 150. This grandiose fugato should not be in the least hurried; it should advance with brazen footsteps like the chorus in a tragedy of Aeschylus.

The woodwinds should play doubled throughout. In bars 130 and 131 the second horn and second trumpet should take the lower F's; in the rest of the passage they remain, however, as they stand. From bar 135 to 140 the first and second horns should play in unison with the third, as this latter is too weak alone; the following part may therefore be assigned to them instead of their rest:

In conjunction with the possibly doubled clarinets, the theme acquires the true meaning which attaches to it.

Bar 157. The A-flat of the first violins, which is already preceded by a *decrescendo*, must be played in the softest *pianissimo*, then this must be interrupted abruptly by the entry of the bassos, booming on the same note: it is an angel's voice dying away in the air, answered by a chorus of demons from the abyss.

Bar 160 and following. Never has a fearful catastrophe been represented by such simple means as we have here. The immense excitement which is expressed by the triplets of the strings in contrast to the fanfares of the brass (which remind us of the trumpets of the Judgment Day) justifies us here, in my opinion, in introducing a somewhat more animated time. Played in pure *adagio*, these triplets run some risk of producing a noisy, rather than a powerful effect. But here as elsewhere it is only a question of a fluctuation of sensation, not of a complete change of time.

Bars 166 and 167. This colossal chord of the diminished seventh should be played by doubled woodwinds. From the second quaver of bar 168, the flute and afterwards the rest of the woodwinds all play single again. The lower F in second trumpet and second horn would only muffle the incisive effect, instead of increasing it, so it is better to leave the higher note alone.

Bars 173–178. In this passage I let the first oboe and first clarinet play doubled if I had the necessary instruments at my disposal; by this means I obtained a very beautiful penetrating sound of the melody in the midst of the rest of the orchestra which surges around it. At the same time I held fast to the somewhat more animated tempo, as this seemed justified by the mysterious vibrations of the accompaniment, and gave the graduated *crescendo* in bar 182 (which occurs in the melody also) with more passionate expression than in the previous similar passage (bar 18); even here I made no decrease in the speed but maintained the sort of after-quiver which follows intense excitement, until the entry of a more restful expression somewhere about bar 200 gave an opportunity of making the restfulness apparent by gradually bringing back the speed to the normal time. The actual first tempo was reached by bar 209, when the echo of the previous emotion seems completely to have died away.

Bars 177–179 and 195–197. The second horn takes the lower F's.

Bar 199. Only the most unpoetic souls could consider that the pedal on C in the horns, which falls together with the B of the woodwinds and the second violins, could be due to a mistake. The apparent dissonance is one of those peculiarities of Beethoven which neither need nor justify a correction.

Bars 200–203. See bars 56–59.

Bars 204 and 205. A reinforcement of the second bassoon would not be out of place here either (see bars 60 and 61) in spite of the fact that violoncellos and bassos play the F and F-sharp. The sound of the wind chords stands out quite independently of the strings, and if the bass is too weak here, the effect will not be good.

Third Movement

Bar 167. The Trio should be fresh and energetic without any change in the tempo.

Bar 224. For purely practical reasons I believed I was justified here in letting the second horn make its entry thus:

as I had learned by experience that the onset of the horns is rendered more precise by this means, whereas on the other hand the unison of the second horn with the strings is of very little practical importance. However, I do not wish to induce any one to make this change unless he can do it with a good conscience.

First ending after bar 254, second and third bars. Some editions bind these three horn chords also with a ⌒, which is wrong. Each chord must enter afresh.

Bars 356–370. We find here rests prescribed for the third horn, whereas in the exactly similar passage before the Trio (bar 102 and following) this instrument has to be played. Bar 371 differs in the first note from the corresponding bar of the first passage (bar 113). These are probably mistakes, as it is difficult to discover any reason for the change. I think the part of the third horn may be inserted here from the first of the two passages.

Fourth Movement

Bar 1. The extraordinarily quick time ♩ = 76 seems to me very suitable for the introductory bars, which have the character of a stormy, joyful *intrata*. After the *fermata*, however, I absolutely advise a moderation of the time. I adopt ♩ = 116 or thereabouts as metronome mark for the beginning of the theme, bar 12, and this can then be increased until ♩ = 132 is reached.

Bars 31 and 39. The *fermatas* are not taken off. The melodic meaning of this passage is as follows:

and so the A-flat of the strings must follow immediately on the B-flat of the winds.

Bar 55. Some editions place the *fermata* over the E-flat instead of over the D; this is wrong.

Bars 76–79. The first oboe must be more prominent than the first clarinet and the first bassoon, which accompany it with the same rhythmic movement. The horns blow *poco marcato* so that their parts can be felt to be thematic.

Bars 95 and 103. It seems to me advisable to make the first *fermata* short, in consideration of the breath of the first oboe player, then the second one longer and very energetic; neither of course can be taken off.

Bars 107 and following. I would warn here specially against hurrying, which is a great danger here even for the best orchestras. The fine structure of the fugato which follows is rendered obscure if the time is too quick.

Bars 166 and following. The splendid entries of the woodwinds might produce even more effect if the wood be doubled. Then from bar 175 everything should be single again.

Bars 191–198. The flute solo, which must be played with a very slight *staccato* but on no account too quickly, in order to avoid its becoming an étude, should be accompanied by the strings in softest *pianissimo*.

Bar 198. A *crescendo* in the string section is not prescribed, it is true, but it seems to me not only justified but demanded by the expression.

Bars 207–255. Woodwinds may play this whole passage doubled.

Bars 211 and following. I have heard this splendid passage, which calls to mind Hungarian melodies, played both with accelerated tempo and slackened tempo. In either case the effect was spoiled. It is most effectual when played in strict normal time.

Bar 256. It seems to me advisable to introduce a somewhat more restful time at the entry of the C major (bar 258) by means of a slight *ritenuto* in the two preceding bars (the G of the horns). It is also better for the following fugato, which is essentially more complicated than the first one beginning at bar 117, not to be played too fast ($\boldsymbol{\mathsf{J}}$ = 126 at the most).

Bars 266–277. Here the melody passes from the second violins to the violas, and from these to the bassos. I have therefore gradated as follows:

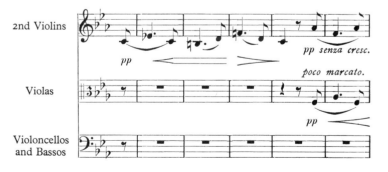

* It is better to omit the ═◁ ▷═ prescribed here by Beethoven, for the sake of the bass part.

Bars 292–296. The flutes may play these five bars *p* and with only a moderate rendering of the *sf*, but they must be played with the utmost clearness and pregnancy in the rhythm. If four flute players are to be had, they might all play this passage in unison. This produces a better effect.

Bars 303–307. In this movement I should recommend that six horns be employed if the string section is strong, or at any rate four, as every orchestra possesses this number. We shall speak later of the employment of six horns in certain cases. In this passage, which has to be distinctly prominent, the first horn can play with the third and the second with the fourth; then the theme becomes quite strong and distinct without the sound being forced. But on no account must all six horns be used as early as this point.

Bar 314. I believe I may take the responsibility of letting the flutes make their entry this soon and play this bar and the two next ones as follows:

Besides this, all the woodwinds should be doubled from here to the entry of the *poco andante*, bar 348. The trumpets in bar 316, in accordance with the theme, play

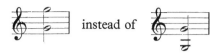

instead of

Bar 348. The *poco andante* should not be taken as an *adagio*, it is true; but the metronome mark ♪ = 108 gives such an impossible *allegretto* tempo here that I have adopted ♪ = 84 or thereabouts.

In order to animate the execution, I have adopted the following gradations to be executed very discreetly:

Bars 358 and 359:

Bars 360 and 361:

Bars 366–369:

Bars 373–376:

In addition, from bar 373 to 376, the first and second violins, the violas and contrabassos play in the softest *pianissimo*, whereas the violoncellos and the second clarinet need not muffle their triplets too much. The horns, however, in bars 373 and 375 should play the semiquavers as lightly and tenderly as possible, otherwise they are too much in evidence. In bar 377 a *poco crescendo* might be added in the strings also, and this is followed by the prescribed *p* in the following bar. Then in bar 379 the first and second violins make a strong *crescendo* from *p* to *ff*. From this point a reinforcement of the melody in the horns is absolutely essential, but it would be barbarous to allow the trombones, for example, to blow in unison. The instrumental colouring of the *Tannhäuser* Overture is not suitable for the *Eroica*. No objection, however, can be raised to increasing the numbers in the first horn part, as this would merely be a change in quantity and not in quality. If six horn players can be had, the first horn part can be strengthened by the three other horns playing in unison with it. If however only four horn players are available, I should advise that three play the melody up to bar 396, and that the fourth play the part of the second horn. The third horn almost always plays in unison with the second trumpet, and in the two bars where this is not the case throughout, it is better to dispense with these few filling-up sounds than to lose the brilliant splendour of the theme, which is rendered clearer and more perceptible by this playing in unison of several horns. From the last quaver of bar 380 to bar 384 (the first quaver), the woodwinds will of course, if possible, play doubled. The whole passage then, if executed in this manner at a somewhat broader tempo, produces an absolutely sublime effect.

Bars 416–420. I formerly felt an obligation to fill out the rests in the horns and trumpets harmonically. Afterwards, however, I gave this up, and now I warn against the proceeding. The entry of these instruments in bar 418 is much too characteristic to justify us in weakening it by allowing them to blow continuously. The woodwinds, however, might play doubled in these bars.

Bar 431. The metronome mark ♪ = 116 for the *presto* is evidently a mistake, as it produces an *allegretto* instead of a *presto*. I have adopted ♩ = 108. The woodwinds, and also the horns, if six are obtainable, can enter doubled here, and the magnificent piece ends in one glorious shout of joy.

Fourth Symphony

In the Fourth Symphony there are even fewer points which call for our attention than in the Second. A fresh and spirited performance of this piece will hardly allow a single doubt to arise.

First Movement

Bar 1. Instead of the very quick metronome mark ♩ = 66, I have adopted about ♩ = 58. The transition to the Allegro (bar 39) produces the most natural effect if the half bars are played just twice as fast as the crotchets in the introduction. The corresponding metronome mark for the Allegro is ♩ = 126. The prescribed mark ○ = 80 gives an absolutely impossible speed.

Bar 50. In this and other similar cases there can be no doubt that the *ff* in the violins begins on the upbeat, and not on the first crotchet which follows it. (See also bars 248 and 256.)

Bar 90. It is tempting here to fill out the rests in horns and trumpets. As however only the keynote

 (sounding A)

would answer this purpose, and this, in relation to the bassos, would give unseemly part-writing,

or the third,    (sounding C-sharp) which creates the same difficulty with reference to the treble,

and moreover, as Beethoven has avoided the fifth in the harmony of this bar throughout, and we therefore are not justified in adding it, it is certainly better not to alter this passage at all. I only mention this in order to point out once again that the most mature consideration and the utmost prudence are necessary where any alteration is undertaken. I mentioned in the Preface that in several passages where I at first thought an alteration to be inevitable, afterwards, on a careful comparison of these passages in their two different forms, I came to the conclusion that the original form was the right one, and that any change was harmful, or at least unnecessary.

Bars 107 and following. The players of bassoon, oboe and flute should be very careful in this passage not to hurry or bungle the quaver figures; this not only spoils the melody but often leads to single notes being missed. A quite imperceptible slackening of the speed is even advisable, if only to remind the players that they are on no account to hasten it.

Bar 183. The F (crotchet) in the violoncellos and bassos is evidently a mistake. (See also the similar passage, bar 453, where the corresponding note is wanting). It should be omitted, as, at most, it causes the impression of an entry at the wrong place.

Bar 185. The | 1 | seems to be important because of its length and because of its logical connection with what precedes. But more recently frequent performances of this symphony have taught me that the whole movement has a fresher effect without the repeat. I thus decided to omit it.

Bar 202. The upbeat in the first violins is of course *piano* already.

Bars 221–240. For the first violins and the violoncellos, I adopted the following phrasing:

and exactly the same for the analogous passage in flute, clarinet and bassoon. In bars 231 and 232 I added a *poco crescendo*, which was followed everywhere by a *p* in bar 232.

The following clarinet solo is then phrased just in the same way as the two preceding similar passages; then the *crescendo* which begins in bar 237 is brought by a strong gradation up to *ff*. The grace notes in bars 223 and 227 are short. The sentimental mode of execution,

which I have often heard, and which is unfortunately also to be found in orchestral parts, is wrong. The grace note would have to be noted as a crotchet for this to be correct.

Bar 253 on. The calming of the musical expression here will probably bring with it an abatement of the time. I should advise, however, that this abatement should not be exaggerated enough to produce a strong *ritenuto*, as this would destroy the peculiarly expectant character of this passage. The climax of the weakened movement seems to me to be reached in bars 302, 303 and 304. At the entry of the 6/4 chord of the main key (bar 305), however, either the principal tempo must begin again immediately, or else the nine bars which follow (306–314) must be used to lead back to it imperceptibly. The almost imperceptible motion of the expressive and, at the same time, natural execution of music, is so fine that in many cases words can only serve as attempts to transmit one's own appreciation to the soul of another, where it must take independent root if something higher than mechanical imitation is to be produced.

A good effect is produced if a certain transitional character is given to the small flute solo (bars 303–305) by means of a quite slight *crescendo* up to the second D-flat; then the D-flat may be

slurred to the following D, just as the G-flat in the bassos is slurred
to the F:

The mark [,] does not designate a breath pause in the sense of a
delay, of course, but simply a slight break for the elucidation of the
phrase. If the second D-flat (third crotchet) can be imagined
written

it will easily be understood what is meant.

Bar 325. The *crescendo* should on no account be introduced
before it is prescribed, and even then it should be very gradually
executed. There is always a tendency for the strings to begin the
crescendo eight bars too soon.

Bar 333. I cannot help feeling that the climax of the preceding
gradation does not occur in this bar, where Beethoven already writes
ff for all instruments, but in bar 337, where the main theme makes
its entry. I have therefore taken the liberty which I am about to
explain. The strings reach the full *ff* in bar 333 as prescribed. The
kettledrum does not play with full force yet but continues the
crescendo begun previously over this bar to bar 337, in which *ff* is
finally reached. All the wind instruments begin *piano* and make a
strong *crescendo* lasting for four bars; then *ff* may be marked for
them also in bar 337. In this way, Beethoven's intention to have an
ff in bar 333 is carried out by the strings, but at the same time a
gradation of sound up to the entry of the principal theme is
obtained.

Bars 361–364. Nothing should be altered here, and it should be noticed how characteristically the second horn progresses here precisely because the natural notes are wanting.

Bars 381 and following. See bars 107 and following.

Bars 391–394. The melodic phrase here differs from the similar passage at bars 117–120 in the changed position of the grace note, and the whole tone step instead of the semitone step in bar 119. It would be wrong to attempt to make these two passages similar, as evidently Beethoven had his reasons for making them differ.

Bar 402. The B is surprising here, as the ear expects a B-flat to correspond to the F of the previous passage (bar 128). A possible explanation, though not an altogether satisfactory one, I admit, of this curious and apparently capricious divergence from the previous passage may lie in the fact that the following B-flat major produces a fresher effect as principal key for the whole piece, if the tonic is avoided as far as possible beforehand. In the first passage we are not concerned with the entry of the principal key, but the dominant key, and the F perhaps gives a firmer sound for the approaching conclusion of the first part than a much weaker F-sharp. However this may be, it was evidently Beethoven's firm intention to write what he has written, as it is quite out of the question to imagine that he wrote a ♮ before the B in all the parts in the second passage accidentally, and perhaps also by accident omitted the ♯ before the F in all the parts in the first passage. An attempt to make the two passages identical is therefore not to be thought of.

Second Movement

Bar 1. I found here the metronome mark ♩ = 84. This is of course a misprint; it must mean ♪ = 84. But this mark also is too quick, so I should recommend ♪ = 72 or thereabouts.

Bar 10. The introduction of *piano* after a demisemiquaver upbeat which has to be played *forte* is very difficult. And yet the upbeat must not be played *piano*, nor must the two bars be separated by breathing pause. The mode of execution intended can only be obtained by repeated practice of the passage.

Bars 36 and 37. In order to obtain a perfect *piano* effect the first horn will suffice here alone; the second may then come in with the low G in bar 38.

Bar 58. In this bar I think a *crescendo* beginning at the second crotchet is needed; this *crescendo* reaches its climax on the D of the next bar for the first violins, on the C-flat for the second violins, and on the F for the violas and violoncellos. Then by means of the $>$ which follows, it is weakened down to the gentlest *pp* and the wonderful entry of the bassoon is seen thereby in its true light.

Bar 90. The Breitkopf & Härtel complete edition has a troublesome misprint here. The second quaver-beat in the violas should be

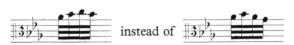

instead of

Third Movement

Bar 91. The extreme limit of speed for the Trio seems to me to be about ♩. = 76; the time prescribed, ♩. = 88, would cause an overhastening of this graceful piece. It should be noticed also that ♩. = 100 for the main section does not denote a very quick time. It is a great mistake, and unfortunately a very common one, to play all Beethoven's Scherzos *quasi presto*.

Bars 121–130. Here too I think it is better for the first horn to play alone. The same holds good, of course, for the repetition of the Trio.

Bar 141 and following. I should recommend here that at first the horns alone give the *crescendo poco a poco*, whilst the strings remain *pp*. The strings can then begin their *crescendo* in bar 151 and increase in strength continually up to the *ff* in bar 56.

Fourth Movement

Bar 1. The finale is marked Allegro ma non troppo. The humour of this delightful piece is quite destroyed if the *ma non troppo* is not observed, and the movement is played like the presto of the last movement of one of Haydn's symphonies. It must not only be begun with a comparatively quiet time, but this time must be maintained throughout, so that the piquant play of the semiquavers does not degenerate into a study, nor the pleasing melody of the secondary theme into a mere commonplace phrase. The great charm of this movement lies just in the contrast between the moderate time and the animated figuration. It gives an impression of speed without really being played quickly. The metronome mark

♩ = 80 does not agree in the least with the tempo indication. I should think ♩ = 126 would be about right.

Bars 44–51. I recommend that this passage be phrased as follows:

Bar 100. Here, too, in performances in recent years I decided to omit the repeat in the interest of the impression to be made by the work as a whole.

Bars 184–187. This is an extremely difficult passage for the first bassoon; indeed, it becomes impossible if either the orchestra, or the conductor, or both, have allowed themselves to become hurried. The four preceding, twice-repeated *sforzato* bars and the short, cutting strokes of the broken minor ninth chords immediately before these offer the best opportunity of keeping to the original moderate time, and even of holding it back if it has become quicker at any previous moment; thus the bassoonist can play his solo at a relatively moderate speed.

Bars 222–225. See bars 44–51.

Bars 294–301. This passage also should on no account be hurried, otherwise both its lucidity and its grace are lost.

Bar 312. I should like to mark this bar *fff*. The *ff* which governs the whole preceding passage would thus be still more increased and would reach its climax, which lasts four bars, in this bar.

Bar 318. The *fermata* must be held on for a considerable time, then taken off. The bassos begin their busy whispering at the comfortable principal time and this is maintained throughout.

Bars 345–350. This passage is formed by the notes of the theme. The *fermatas* must therefore not be taken off, but the following notes must be played immediately. The *fermatas* themselves however seem to me to work backwards to a certain extent, so that I think I am justified in placing a *poco andante* at the beginning of this passage, and in not letting the principal theme make its entry until the semiquaver scale of the bassos, after the last *fermata*, which must also not be taken off.

Fifth Symphony

First Movement

In my work *On Conducting* (*Über das Dirigieren*) I have already
expressed my views clearly as to the folly of beginning this movement slowly and not allowing the quick time to make its entry until
after the second *fermata*. I will therefore waste no words on it here.
But besides occasioning this piece of barbarism, one of the worst
which ignorant conductors have adopted in regard of Beethoven, the
beginning of the Fifth Symphony has given rise in other respects to
various considerations and explanations. It is particularly the
apparently irregular bar interpolated just before the second *fermata*
which has given rise to discussion. The riddle can be solved, however, in a very simple way, if every two bars be taken as one,
whereby the following scheme is obtained:

This explanation, which, as far as I know, no one has ever given
in the same way before, holds good (if this two-bar combination
is imagined throughout) for all the *fermata* passages in this movement where the above-mentioned interpolated bar is to be found.
Wagner has already pointed out that the *fermatas* should be held
long and emphatically, and we can see from the text, and also from
the rhythmic feeling if my interpretation is followed, that the second
must always be held somewhat longer than the first.*
Attempts have also been made to improve on this passage
instrumentally. It has been proposed to let the horns join in. But

* This explanation about taking two bars as one should by no means mislead
anyone into conducting this movement in any way other than by whole measures
(downbeats). [Author's note.]

what possible reason could Beethoven have had for not using these instruments if he had wished to, seeing that out of the four notes of the theme, three stood at his disposal as open natural notes on the E-flat horns, and the fourth (B on the E-flat horn) was at any rate a possible stopped note? At any rate he would have made use of the horns for the first two bars if he had needed them. Moreover, this is the very symphony in which he uses the greatest number of stopped notes (see bars 144 and 205 in this movement, bars 28 and following in the third movement and bars 72 and 115 in the last movement). The explanation that the clarinets are only used here in default of horns therefore does not seem valid to me. I believe, on the contrary, that he purposely reserved the horns for the later and more emphatic entries of the theme. Why this eagerness then to improve? The theme is quite distinct, even with a small string section, if it is played strongly and accurately at the same time. I should recommend ♩ = 100 as metronome mark instead of ♩ = 108, which is really too quick. Two strong beats of the conductor, one for the first bar (quasi first half) and one for the *fermata* (quasi second half), will ensure a good result. Bülow's practice of beating one or more bars in advance is unnecessary. The *fermata* is removed and this gesture of removal occupies the value of one bar, whereupon the downbeat for the third bar follows immediately. This occurs at every *fermata* in this movement. "Inserted" beats have as little to do here as in other places where *fermatas* are removed, a procedure that always demands a pause.

Throughout the whole movement, care should be taken that the thematic repeated quaver, in both *forte* and *piano*, should all be played with precisely the same degree of strength relative to each other. Nothing is more dangerous than the following mode of execution,

which however comes only too readily if the time be taken too quickly, or the players be not kept strictly to an articulate production of each note both in *forte* and *piano*. Only accents are heard then—no melody—and this powerful piece is changed from a Titanic battle to a furious chase. It goes without saying that the strictest rhythmic equality of these quavers is also an absolute necessity.

But it is just in this point that so many people sin. I have only too often heard the passage following the second *fermata* given something in this manner:

until my insistence on rhythmic and dynamic equality of the notes gave the true value to the essential part of the melody, which every true musician will undoubtedly recognise to be the following:

It is just the recognition of the expression of this, I might almost say, latent melody, which is the surest guarantee against the over-hurrying—accompanied by most of the evils which I have just mentioned and deprecated—which is so fearfully detrimental to this magnificent piece.

Bars 63–66. This passage is generally given with the following, absolutely wrong, phrasing:

In the first place let us examine the ligatures. The first three bars are bound together and must therefore be played in the same breath, as it were; the last bar with its short ligature has a final character which would be destroyed by an accent. Then the rhythmical values of the individual bars should be noticed. If, in accordance with our initial concept, two bars are considered as connected and are treated as one bar, we get the following scheme beginning at bar 56:

In this way the first bar of the passage is treated as a kind of upbeat and the chief value is given to the second bar. The suitable phrasing is then the following:

and this is perfectly in keeping with the ligature over the first three bars. This phrasing must always be observed in all the repetitions of this theme. Naturally the object here is not to force each respective second bar of this four-bar phrase into prominence, but simply to produce a gently increasing emphasis which will not endanger the *piano* character of the whole passage. Indeed, a right phrasing of the passage will generally be attained if the players are made conscious of the rhythmic value of the single bars, so that they play the first as upbeat and give the main importance to the second, and carefully avoid the tempting accent which so easily comes in on the fourth bar. If the passage is played in the manner I have described, a phrase complete in itself is obtained, instead of four independent bars, which was surely not the composer's artistic conception. Following my directions one gets, from bar 75 onwards, several further accents which of course are also only intended to be understood in the sense of rhythmic emphasis.

It should be noticed how the position of the ligatures crystallizes the four-bar phrase out of an apparent displacement of the rhythm; this phrase attains its full sway in bar 94.

Such observations as these should not be looked upon as trifling details. Their importance will be seen later to an even greater extent.

Bar 124. The first part should be repeated. It need hardly be pointed out that the re-entry of the theme both at the repetition and after the double bar should be played in strict normal time.

If the repetition passage is carefully examined it will be found that the first two bars of the main theme have a different value when they are repeated and that the original rhythmic conditions are not re-established till the following bars. Thus, if each respective pair of bars be taken together, from the last bar but two before the double bar we get the following scheme:

This shows clearly the variation from the example on page 119, as here we have a 2/4 bar, which causes difficulty in the taking of two bars together. When the theme is written without the bar before the *fermata*, it seems to have a double rhythmic character. This double character is confirmed later beyond a doubt, so that we will confine ourselves here to stating the fact. If we pass from the last bar but two before the double bar on to the second part, we find the rhythmic regularity unbroken, and we can tell from this when we have to take two bars together as one again.

Bars 158 and following. No *crescendo* should be made here, however much one is tempted to make it. It is just the uniform *piano* here which gives the passage an oppressive, uncanny character, which is quite destroyed if the volume of sound is prematurely increased. The *crescendo* must not come in before bar 166, where it is prescribed, and then it should be observed that the gradation at first only reaches a simple *forte* (bar 168). The *più f* is not reached till seven bars later, and the full *fortissimo* makes its entry in bar 179 at the introduction of the theme. All this is clearly prescribed and it may cause surprise that I simply repeat what is already written. But how often have I seen these directions absolutely disregarded; in this passage, for example, the *crescendo* brought in much too soon, and conductor and orchestra bursting into full force where only *f* is written, so that the following gradation becomes quite impossible. I therefore seize this opportunity of pointing out that a strict observance of the given directions is absolutely indispensable for expressive execution, indeed it is often the sufficient cause of such an execution. The experiment ought to be made of playing this passage in the incorrect way I have just indicated, and then in the precise way that Beethoven has prescribed, and then no doubt will remain as to the importance of his directions.

It is unfortunately a very common bad habit to get suddenly much softer at the entry of the *diminuendo* at bar 210, especially in the wind instruments, whereas really the chords should decrease in strength very gradually, and the chord marked *diminuendo* should merely denote an almost imperceptible weakening. A very finely graduated orchestra will succeed in effecting a gradual diminution of sound in such a way that each wind chord sounds the least bit softer than the preceding string chord, and each of these in turn the least bit softer than the preceding wind chord; thus a perfectly uniform, progressive *diminuendo* is obtained until the entry of complete *pianissimo*; this produces a wonderful effect.

Bars 228 and 240. Here our modern system of Leitmotivs has produced a regrettable mistake, which has unfortunately made its way into the printed orchestral parts of the Breitkopf edition. As the theme of the movement begins with a quaver rest, it has been assumed that the *ff* did not begin before the second quaver and the passage has been corrected to this effect. By this means it was hoped that the character of the theme which runs thus

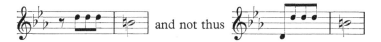 and not thus

would be done justice to in the execution.

Let us see first how the matter stands with regard to a possible mistake or misprint in the score. Supposing that in the first of the quoted bars the *ff* in the strings has been wrongly placed too early, at any rate in the second case the same mistake is out of the question. Here the violins and violas do not have to play the theme at all and yet in each of these parts *f* stands clearly marked. Moreover the crotchet points to an intensification of the tone. In spite of all this the *f* here has actually been corrected to *p*, because it was thought that the Leitmotiv must have its due, even if Beethoven himself had to give way before it. He seems to do so very unwillingly, however, as the *p*, which the strings play in a hesitating, feeble way because they are afraid of not being able to do justice to the *ff* immediately following, sounds so forlorn and meaningless, that this fact alone ought to have been sufficient reason for inquiry as to Beethoven's intention. When we look at the passage from a rhythmical point of view, however, every doubt vanishes as to the horror of this correction. If each two bars be taken together as one throughout the whole movement, from bar 220 we get the following scheme:

We can see from this that the chords degraded to miserable *piano* sighs fall on rhythmically important points, on strong parts of the bar, as it were. We see further that these rhythmically important points are starting points for passages introducing the theme, and these passages in their turn prepare effectually for the entry of the first subject in its original form (bar 248 and following) and the recapitulation of the first part. We see finally that these "castrated chords," as I will call them for want of a better expression, each coming directly after a softly breathing *pianissimo*, represent simply the concentration of energy preliminary to the theme, that they must therefore be played with the utmost energy and not lightly chirped for the sake of the Leitmotiv. Away with the featureless *p* then, and let the two chords be played with the power of the master! The crotchet in bar 240 should be sustained in such a way as to give it a quite special significance, somewhat as though it were written thus

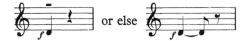

It should be noticed that the first subject on its return possesses exactly the same rhythmical value as at the beginning of the movement, if two bars are taken together in the way illustrated above.

Berlioz in his *Theory of Instrumentation* (see Breitkopf & Härtel edition, page 301) remarks what a curious fault it is that the trumpets so often seem to limp behind when they have to come in after a rest on the first quaver. This is especially likely to be the case here, and if great precautions are not taken, the trumpets, according to an example given by Berlioz, will be heard to be playing

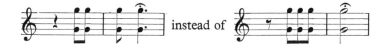

Bar 268. This cadenza in the first oboe only obtains its full significance if not only this bar, but also the whole preceding oboe passage from bar 254, is taken as a solo. This part then, from the bar just mentioned, should be rather more in evidence and the rest of the orchestra should play *piano* throughout. Both conductor and

players should note carefully that the *crescendo* comes in rather later here than in the similar passage in the first part, and this is specially of importance in order to bring into strong relief the following bars:

As the strings should be still playing *p* in bar 266; the *crescendo* for them only refers to the bar before the *ff*. If greater prominence is given to this preceding bar, in which *cresc.* is already indicated, an unmelodious accent is the result. The *crescendo* here is really the task of the oboe and the bassoons. The *p* on the C in trumpets and kettledrums should also be very carefully observed.

The oboe player must neither sustain the first G too long, nor play the beginning of the cadenza too slowly, otherwise he will barely have breath enough to bring the phrase to its conclusion and to sustain the last D for a time at a beautifully restful *p*. I should like the *adagio* in its strict sense to refer to the last three notes only. When the sound of the D has died away the conductor may proceed in the manner of an upbeat, so as to give the oboist an opportunity of taking breath again, and of giving the same sound colour to the F as to the preceding D. The second oboist must of course adapt himself absolutely to the first. I have never been able to bring in a full *allegro* immediately after the *fermata*. The cadenza seems to me to have a kind of aftereffect, and I therefore always began in a somewhat more restful manner, which corresponds in my opinion to the strangely quiet character of this passage, so different from the first part of the movement. I then made use of the following *crescendo* to lead back to the main time of the piece, which I allowed to make its entry at the *f*.

I must repeat again and again that these delicate modifications of the time are really a question of the feeling, and are not mere derangements for the sake of effect. If anyone felt justified by what I have said in proceeding in the latter manner, it would be better if I had not spoken at all. Unless these gentle deviations give the impression of being merely an outflow of natural sensation, to be taken as a matter of course, it would be much better and much more artistic simply to hold fast to the prescribed tempo throughout.

When it becomes evident that the conductor wants to "create" something special, in order that his own mind and inspiration may shine forth, nature, unity and immediacy—and thus Beethoven's own peculiar style—are sacrificed. I therefore recommend a very careful trial of the proposals which I have made. I would much prefer that they should not be followed at all, than that they should be wrongly followed.

Bars 303–306. The transference of the secondary theme played by the horns in the first part of this movement to the bassoons here is merely a way out of a difficulty. Beethoven could not entrust it to the E-flat horns, as he could not use stopped notes for this exposed passage which needs to generate great power. There was no time for a change of crooks and evidently he was unwilling to add a second pair of horns simply for the sake of these few bars. So there was no other way out of the difficulty than to make use of the bassoons. The effect they produce, however, when compared with the idea we obtain from this passage as it appears in the first part, is lamentable, in fact it is simply comic. It sounds as though a buffoon had made his way into the council of the gods. And this bad effect is increased by the fact that both horns suddenly enter with an open natural note *sf* in bar 306, so that this sounds suddenly and unreasonably louder than the three preceding ones. The attempt has been made to let the horns enter *p*; a horn has been added to the bassoons or the bassoons doubled, all of which is of course also only a makeshift. There is only one radical change which can be made, and this is preferable to all these half measures; that is, to replace the bassoons by the horns, and this is certainly what Beethoven would have done had our instruments been at his disposal. The bassoons can rest from the bar in question onwards and need not enter until bar 311, just as they do in the corresponding passage in the first part; then the three-bar rests in the horns can be filled in thus:

This is the only way in which this theme can acquire its true colour and dignity.

Bar 307 and following. See what has been said for the bars 63–66.

Bars 389–394. In reference to this passage, I will quote what I have already said in my book *On Conducting* (*Über das Dirigieren*), third edition:*

Near the end of the first movement there is at one place a five-bar group —

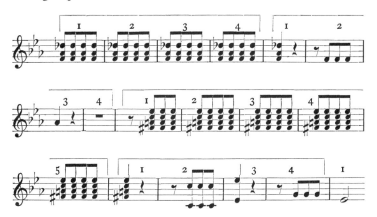

Now whether we look upon the fourth bar of the second group (the pause) as a short *fermata* and the first bar of the succeeding five-bar group as the up-take—according to which there then comes another four-bar sentence—or whether we take it that the opening theme of the *allegro* occurs in the recapitulation the first time thus—

and the second time with an extra bar, thus—

however we calculate the thing mathematically, in either case the short breathless silence and the ensuing outburst of the

---

* PUBLISHER'S NOTE: For this extract from *On Conducting* we have replaced Jessie Crosland's English text by Ernest Newman's, which will also be found in its full context on pages 30 and 31 of the present volume.

chord of the diminished seventh become, just by their prolongation, terrific, gigantic, powerful, menacing, overwhelming, volcanic. It is like a giant's fist rising from the earth.
Will it be believed that almost everywhere I found the
indescribable effect of this passage simply destroyed, either by
a bar of the diminished-seventh chord or by the pause itself
being *struck out?*

The most tasteless rhythmic distortions, the most absurd
breath-pauses, have been calmly indulged in in order to
appear interesting; the result has been, however, to turn a
supreme stroke of genius into a mere piece of irregularity;
because the thing must go as a four-bar phrase. *O sancta
simplicitas!*

Bars 398–468. In the whole of musical literature I know of no
passage which produces a greater instrumental effect. And yet no
more instruments are playing than in one of Haydn's symphonies!
Are they giants whom we hear scraping and blowing? Does the
power of thought speak so forcibly to us that the ear of our soul
hears more than the ear of our body?—Who is so bold as to wish to
fathom the actions of a genius?—

My advice as to the execution is: for Heaven's sake, let there be
no hurry and no false gradation. Strict, not too fast, normal time and
emphatic *fortissimo* everywhere. Every note as if it were made of
iron.

In conducting Beethoven's symphonies one can never be safe
from surprises. With a large orchestra I did not succeed at first in
giving this passage its full value, nor did I immediately discover the
reason. The riddle was not solved until at the next rehearsal I
found that the permanent conductor had prescribed the following
accents:

and that this was followed by some of the players. It is hardly
believable that the idea would occur to anyone to disfigure this
cyclopean structure with a zigzag line of syncopation.

Bar 476. The enormous force of the preceding part seems to me

to justify a slight diminution of speed from perhaps bar 477 onwards; then the main theme, which comes in once again for the last
time with absolutely crushing weight, seems somewhat broadened
here, as it is in no other passage of the movement. The whole
spiritual and physical strength of both conductor and players must
be concentrated once again on this elementary theme, and this is
what I found impossible in full *allegro* time. I then sustained the
fermatas here longer than in the other passages, and began the
incomparably beautiful *piano* passage after the second *fermata*
at a still more restful time, in order to allow the first tempo to
make its entry again at the *ff*—a painful memory, from which one
has to tear oneself energetically away, in pursuance of one's
fate.

If we treat each pair of bars as one, in order to do justice to the
rhythmic value, from bar 469 we get the following construction:

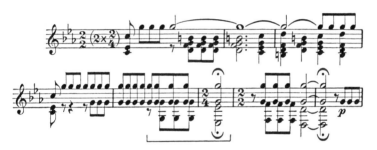

Thus we see that the main theme now has exactly the same
rhythmical character as it had in the repetition of the first part.
Thus first appearance and return correspond on the one hand,
repetition and coda on the other. However, the two bars which
apparently cannot be taken together as one, do actually complete
each other mutually and can thus also be considered as one com-
pound bar. So in this respect, too, the whole movement is wonderfully proportioned, and on this very account the meaning of the
one irregular period (see comments under bars 389–394) is greatly
enhanced.

If the string section is strong, doubled woodwinds are very
beneficial in this symphony. I have introduced doubling in the first
movement for the following passages: bars 1–5; 22–24; 52–58;
94–128; 175–217; 228–232; 240–252; 296–302; 346–386; 390–482;
and 491–502.

Second Movement

Bar 1. The time is Andante con moto, so it is fairly animated. If the *con moto* is overlooked the movement becomes tedious and rambling; if, however, the conductor, in his efforts to do justice to the *con moto*, forgets the *andante*, the whole soul of the movement is taken away and in its place we have an indifferent piece of tinsel with high-sounding phrases. The metronome mark ♪ = 92 changes the *andante* into an *allegretto*. I have therefore adopted about ♪ = 84. In my work *On Conducting* I have already mentioned the difficulty of expressing in words what can only be expressed by a deeply felt and animated execution. To the numerous cases of this kind we must reckon the right appreciation of the time of this movement. I must warn against any sentimental distortion, either of the principal melodies or of the triplets (bars 14, 18, 19 and 20). I would also warn against robbing the magnificent C major passages (at bars 31, 80 and 147) of their freshness by allowing the speed to slacken with the idea of producing a pompous effect.

Bars 88–96. The demisemiquavers and semiquavers in the violoncellos sound finer played with an upstroke only, than with up- and downstrokes alternately. The same holds good in bars 76 and 77 for second violins and violas.

Bar 114 and following. The melodic figure in bassos and violoncellos becomes a little indistinct here, so it is better if these instruments play with their full strength at first. Trumpets, horns and kettledrums are modified to *mf*, and by this means their cessation later, when the harmonic sounds have also ceased, is rendered less noticeable. Wagner had already recommended this modification. I advised the string and woodwind players to play only with sufficient volume so that each one of them could hear the bass figures distinctly. This renders the whole passage clearer. The glory of the passage lies not so much in the brass or the upper chords as in the splendid basses; justice must be done to these at all cost.

Bar 123. The *fermata* should not be sustained too long.

Bar 132. Bülow allowed this *forte* chord to be played *pizzicato* by the strings, though only in his later years, I believe. One can only ask "Why?" in amazement.

Bars 185–190. The partially imitative, but everywhere independently conducted melody of the woodwinds disappears altogether if all the instruments of the orchestra play a uniform *ff*. If auxiliary woodwinds are to be had, this is partially obviated by strengthening the parts of the flutes, clarinets and bassoons (not the oboes) in the bars mentioned. A $\smile$ can be played after the *ff* in the first bar by the oboes, horns and trumpets, who then play the following four bars only *mf*. Then the kettledrums in the third bar also come in at *mf*. In the last bar the instruments in question can play *crescendo* again up to an *ff* in bar 191. (In bar 189 the second trumpet of course takes the lower F's.) The string section, however, phrases in the following manner, which is noted here for the violins only:

The *mf* and *f* in this passage should be understood merely to mean a somewhat modified *ff*. The degree of modification must be decided upon in proportion to the distinctness with which the melody can already be heard in the woodwind section, which is blowing *ff* continuously throughout.

If doubled woodwinds cannot be obtained, then I think there is only one way of doing justice to this counterpart, and that is (in addition to the dynamic gradations already discussed) to hand over the purely harmonic parts of the oboes to the clarinets, and to give the melodic parts of the clarinets to the much more prominent oboes, thus:

An even surer way, though a much more arbitrary one, it is true, is to do away with the filling-in part in the woodwinds altogether and to let all eight instruments play the theme; but in bars 186–190

the part of the oboes might be given to the horns and written as follows:

Every conductor must settle with his own conscience as to whether he can adopt either of these proposals. The acoustic conditions of the hall will have some weight in the decision, but in all such cases the supreme command to be obeyed is "Clearness!"

Third Movement

Bar 1. The third movement cannot be compared with any of the other Scherzi of Beethoven's symphonies. It is heavier and more tragic and must therefore be performed more slowly than the others. The metronome mark ♩. = 96 is excellent and should be retained for the Trio, which for some unknown reason is generally played more slowly than the main part. It is interesting from the point of view of rhythmic value that here too each pair of bars can be taken together as one bar. The beginning, therefore, reads as follows:

and similarly for the whole of the movement (see footnote, page 119).

Bars 44 and 96. I have heard these bars played as though another *sf* were indicated before each *diminuendo*, so that these bars began just as loudly as the two preceding ones (in each case), which were really marked *sf*. I have also heard them played so that the beginning of the bars quoted was already weakened, which naturally occurred because the preceding third crotchet already has a slightly diminished force compared with the *sf*. It thus sounded as though these two bars, in contrast to the two preceding ones marked *sf*, had an *mf dimin.* prescribed for them in the score. And this I believe to be the right mode of execution. This view is upheld, moreover, by the fact that in the second passage *p* is prescribed for the trumpets and kettledrums.

Bar 122. The *crescendo* with which this bar begins must on no account be allowed to cause an increase of speed.

Bar 141. It is important for the whole Trio that the upbeat of the theme should not be indistinctly given, but should be played forcibly and rendered distinct from the following notes, without, how-ever, causing any modification of the time. It is true that the character of the Trio is that of an irresistible storm somewhat regardless of consequences, but it is always dignified and never uncouth.

Bar 231. The *pizzicati* of the contrabassos can bear a slight diminution in the speed, which can reach its climax at the A-flat G. Normal time should be resumed when the *arco* is reached.

Bar 236 and following. There is nothing to be said as to the execution of this incomparable recapitulation except that it would be spoiled if any attempt were made to introduce gradations either into the time or the dynamics. The *arco* grace notes in the violas are a possible source of danger for the breathless *piano* which should dominate all this part, so that I cannot sufficiently recommend the softest possible sound for these instruments.

Fourth Movement

Bar 1. Entry of the last movement. With great force, but not too slowly. The metronome mark is good.

Bars 25–32. At one Berlin performance at which I was present, Bülow introduced the following time gradation:

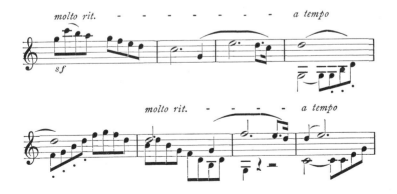

which I merely reproduce as a warning against such senseless dislocations, which merely cause surprise and produce no artistic expression.

It should be observed that the phrasing runs thus:

and not, as it is generally played, thus:

Bars 39 and 40. Experience has taught me that the difference in rhythm and phrasing in these two bars as compared with the two preceding ones can be distinctly rendered by carefully holding the dotted crotchets and placing a significant emphasis on the quavers (D).

Bars 47, 51 and 53, with the upbeat. The phrase of the first and second violins should not be played as a figuration but in a sustained, melodic manner, giving exact value to the triplets and placing no false accent on the first and third crotchets;

is therefore a better notation than

There is a tendency here for the players to hurry. We shall see the
phrase in the violoncellos

acquire such importance presently, that, in my opinion, it is advisable
to bring it rather into prominence already, both here and in similar
passages. This can be done without any change in the notation if
the attention of the players is drawn to the passage.

Bar 85. It is better to omit the repetition of the first part. The
C major coming in after the gloomy anxiety of the third movement
is so supremely powerful that a repetition which is not preceded by
the anxious expectation can only weaken the effect.

Bar 92, with upbeat, to bar 99. First the violas and violoncellos,
then the first and second violins with the violas, may be brought
rather into prominence from a thematic point of view. Compare
what has been said for bars 47, 51 and 53.

Bars 99 and following. In this graceful passage both strings and
woodwinds should play in the softest manner possible. One might
perhaps also recommend the conductor to adopt a rather more
"flowing" time.

Bars 106–112. The thematic leading entrusted to the violoncellos
and contrabassos often sounds strangely weak in spite of the fact
that they are accompanied by the contrabassoon. As the character
of the bassos is here evidently intended to be very weighty and
powerful, I sometimes reinforced them with the third trombone.
The latter, however, should not play with immoderate strength,
otherwise it will destroy the colossal effect of the entrance of the
first and second trombones, which immediately follows. I therefore
gave the following part to the third trombone:

and at once obtained the desired effect. If, however, owing to the
acoustic properties of the hall, the arrangement of the players or the
special excellence of the orchestra, the bassos were sufficiently
audible without the help of the trombone, of course I did not add
the trombone. The first and second trombones, supported by

bassoons and horns, cannot display enough splendour and force in the glorious passage which follows (beginning at bar 112). They must play with true enthusiasm.

Bars 119 and 120. The powerful antithesis in the violins and brass

cannot be strongly enough accented.

Bars 132–136. The woodwind section is too weak here even when it plays doubled. I therefore had no hesitation in letting the horns, which are simply employed here in unison with the short trumpet notes, play as follows:

by which means the passage becomes a regular blaze of glory.

Bar 153. In the 3/4 time I interpreted the tempo in such wise that two bars corresponded exactly in value to one *alla breve* bar; I thus really kept to the same tempo and held it fast until the re-entry of the *alla breve* bar. The reminiscence of the Scherzo has lost all its anxious expectancy here. It is as though years of a rich and full life lay in between; a short lingering over scenes of the past which no longer cause any pain, then immediately a fresh, joyous seizing of the smiling present. Overpowered by the feeling which I have just tried to describe, I have never been able to help giving the return of the main theme (bar 207) in a somewhat more animated manner than the first time.

Bars 244 and 245. For the bassos see what was said for the violins in bars 39 and 40.

Bars 256, 260 and 262, with upbeats. See bars 47, 51 and 53.

Bars 294–302. First the violoncellos, then the first violins must develop as much force as possible in their theme. When the full wind then attack the same theme, they must be exhorted to play the upbeat (bar 302 at the *più f*) with great emphasis and determination and not wait for the first following crotchet, which often happens out of sheer carelessness.

I will here give the result of long experience with orchestras of the most varied kinds. Both trumpets and trombones, especially the latter, when they have to come in *fortissimo*, generally only begin to think about it at the moment when they have to come in; the consequence is that the first chord sounds feeble and the *fortissimo* proper only begins at the second chord. Many splendid brass effects, and not least the beginning of this last movement of which we have been speaking, have been spoiled by this apparently hereditary laziness. The conductor should therefore exhort the winds concerned to have breath, instruments and attention in readiness so that they have all their force at their disposal at the important moment, and do not come into possession of it only when the decisive point is passed.

Bars 312–317. If hitherto the speed has possibly been somewhat increased, these beats give the welcome opportunity of bringing it back to the normal again. In any case I should recommend that the whole passage which follows, from the entry of the bassoon (bar 317) to the *sempre più allegro* (bar 353), should be taken at a speed not greater than that of the beginning. The sublime joyfulness of this passage is then effectually reproduced.

Bars 350–352. No increase of speed is allowable here. On the contrary, the string players must be carefully warned to restrain the tendency to hurry—which, curiously enough, is always observable in this passage—otherwise the quaver figures in the woodwinds and horns sound indistinct and blurred. The increase of speed comes in at the *sempre più allegro*, as prescribed. This direction is more important than appears at first sight. The uncertain hurrying which one generally hears at the first rehearsals is simply horrible.

Bar 362. I think I am justified in looking upon the *presto* as a continuation of the *sempre più allegro*. Thus when I began here to conduct in whole bars, these were at first not really quicker than the immediately preceding bars which were conducted with two beats; in fact, the whole passage, from the *sempre più allegro* to about the *fortissimo* at bar 390, where the full *presto* comes in, seemed like one great *accelerando*.

I need hardly say that if doubled woodwinds can be obtained it can be freely used in the last movement. I should recommend in any case, even in smaller orchestras, the doubling of the horns in this movement; the third can be paired with the first, the second with the fourth, and the parts marked *D* and *S* as in the woodwinds. Two piccolos would also be an advantage; the contrabassoon of course suffices undoubled.

The doubling is generally introduced in the two last bars of the third movement; then, whilst the other instruments are already playing fairly strongly, the strengthening instruments come in at *piano* and make a strong *crescendo* which gives greater intensity to the general *crescendo*. From the beginning of the last movement everything is played doubled until bar 51. Then the doubling comes in again at the following places: bars 58 to 64; 72 to 91; 106 (fourth crotchet) to 153, first bar of the 3/4 time; 207 to 259.

Bar 264. The first flute can begin here; the other reinforcements begin in bar 267 at the *ff* and continue till bar 273.

Bars 281–317 (the bassoon solo single, however). From bar 321 to bar 353 the semiquaver runs of the piccolo may be doubled, but nothing else.

The last doubling begins in bar 390 at the *ff* and continues to the end.

Sixth Symphony

First Movement

Bar 1. The metronome mark $\mathrm{d} = 66$ is too quick and gives rise to the erroneous idea that this movement ought to be conducted in whole bars. I should propose $\mathrm{J} = 108$ or thereabout.

Bar 4. No pause to be made after the *fermata*.

Bar 12. Although *f* is prescribed as recently as the preceding bar, the *f* in the bar which follows and the melodic character of the whole passage seemed to me to justify a slight diminution of force in this bar between the two *f*'s. I have therefore marked it *mf*.

Bar 83. In order to bring the melodic parts—flute and clarinet—into relief, I made the string section, after executing a moderate *crescendo*, begin this bar *piano* again; the four following bars should still be *piano*, then in bar 87 *crescendo* begins which leads up to the *f* in full gradation.

Bars 106, 110, 113 and 114. The second horn plays the lower D throughout.

Bar 138. The first part not to be repeated.

Bar 163. The incomparably beautiful entry of this D major acquires more significance if the orchestra, after the preceding *crescendo*, begins *pp* again and lets the *crescendo* start afresh gradually. By this means, in addition to the poetical effect which is gained by the modulation, the almost inevitable error in a *crescendo* of such length (24 bars) of allowing the full *forte* to begin too soon is avoided. Exactly the same holds good for the similar entry of the E major in bar 209.

Bars 189–190, and 235–236. A conductor with a very fine feeling for modulations of time might introduce a gentle *ritenuto* in these two groups of two bars, and then return to the original time in the succeeding bar in each case. If done without exaggeration this produces a very good effect and is quite in keeping with the spirit of the symphony.

Bars 217–227. Certainly Beethoven would have made use of the horns in this bar if the needed notes had been at his disposal. This is clear from the similar passage in bar 171. I have therefore added the following parts for the horn starting from the bar in question:

This is not absolutely necessary, but it seems rather strange to hear this passage, which is raised a tone (E major in contradistinction to the preceding D major), without the ring of the horns, and to be forced to say that doubtless it was only a technical hindrance which caused this omission. The artistic conscience of the conductor must be the guide as to whether my suggestion should be adopted or not.

Bars 249–254. I propose the following notation for violas and violoncellos (to be performed discreetly):

Bars 261–262. The second horn plays the lower D.

Bars 282–284. The trill should be extended without following grace notes (*Nachschlag*) to the second crotchet of the last bar; it stops there, so that this crotchet is played simply

without trill.

Bars 297–299. Second violins and violas appear here as a repeating continuation of the clarinets and bassoons. The following notation is therefore a suitable one:

Bar 362, see bar 83.
Bars 428 and following. The whole passage would be robbed of its character if the triplets were hurried. The first time, taken in an easy manner, should be the standard to the end of the movement.

Second Movement

Bar 1. This splendid movement is generally taken too slowly. Beethoven marked it Andante molto moto, and ♩. = 50 indicates the tempo perfectly. The image of the flowing brook must be maintained throughout.

The second violins, the violas and the two muted violoncellos are apt to sound too loud in the passages where they have figurations. The conductor should see that these instruments only form a background which brings into relief the tender pictures of the melodic parts.

Bar 15. In order to allow the gently blowing clarinet to present the melody clearly, first violins and bassoon might begin quite *pp* on the F, and play *crescendo* in the next bar with the rest of the orchestra.

Bar 19. In order to obtain a graceful execution I think the following gradation for the first violins is justifiable:

Bars 32–35. I allowed the violins and the first bassoon to play slightly *diminuendo* on the fourth crotchet of the first of these bars; then all players began the following bar (A major) in lightest *pp*. In the next bar the violas and violoncellos joined the bassoon, also as softly as possible, but together with the bassoon animated the expression just the least bit towards the middle of the bar. Then the sound was again diminished in order that the beginning of the last

bar might be quite *pp* again, and this *pianissimo* was sustained until the *crescendo* prescribed by Beethoven on the fourth crotchet:

Bars 40 and 41. The trill on the G in the first violins goes on to the A of the next bar without any following grace notes. Then the flute and first violins enliven the expression towards the middle of the bar in the manner already described for the violas, violoncellos and bassoons (see the last quotation).

Bars 48 and 49. For the sake of clearness the following notation may be recommended:

Bars 58–65. First violins and violas should play the three-note figures in strictest *pp*, as the slightest excess of prominence in these parts thickens the sound unduly. I should prescribe *mp* for the flute from the last crotchet of bar 61, and for the oboe from the bar 63 onwards. In the bar 64 the *crescendo* in the strings and the horns should be only quite moderately executed in order not to obscure the free play of the woodwinds. For bar 65 I have adopted the following notation:

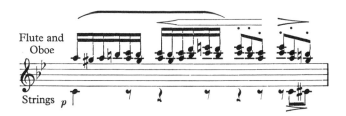

Bars 67 and 68. In the first of these two bars I let the violas and violoncellos play *crescendo* in the first half, then moderate again in the second half. In the second bar I have ventured to change the first *f* into *mf* in all the parts; then I added a $\diagdown\!\diagup$ which leads up to the second *f*, prescribed on the third crotchet of this bar. In reference to the last remark, see the similarly notated passage at bars 77 and 78.

Bars 69–75. For the same reason as in the above-mentioned similar passage, the bassoon and first violins must perform their three-note figures quite *pp*. So too the *crescendo* in bar 75 must be taken in a very moderate sense. Only the solo-playing clarinet may allow itself more freedom. The horns can take the lower F's in bars 69 and 70. Not so, however, in bars 73 and 74. Here the second clarinet sustains a low F (actual sound E-flat), the special sound of which is disturbed if the second horn blows in unison. In bar 75 the second horn may take the lower F again, and in bar 76 the lower D.

Bars 79–82. In the first two bars the flute should be marked *pp* from the second crotchet onwards. In the last two, first clarinet and first bassoon should be marked *pp* just as the rest of the orchestra is; the flutes, however, *ppp*. (See the wonderful combination of the flute notes with the appoggiaturas of the clarinet in the third bar of the passage quoted).

Bars 91–94. From here onwards the whole orchestra should play in lightest *pp* in order to bring the flute, which is of course also playing equally softly, into melodic relief. In the last two bars the second horn (F, D, G) plays an octave lower. See the similar bassoon passage, bars 69–72.

Bars 104–107. See bars 32–35.

Bars 113 and 114. See bars 41 and 42.

Bars 120 and 121. See bars 48 and 49.

Bars 129–136. This splendid passage, distinguished by its ingenuousness and its artistic relation to the whole work, not only produces its best effect but also bears the truest resemblance to nature when it is played in strict time, without the slightest attempt at any special gradation.

Bar 138. In the first half of this bar a gentle, moderate *ritenuto* may be introduced which from the *sf* onwards gradually gives way to the first time again.

Third Movement

Bar 1. As regards the time of this Scherzo also, we gain nothing by comparing it with the other Scherzi of Beethoven. It has an easy-going character and must therefore be taken rather more slowly than, for instance, the Scherzo of the *Eroica* or of the Seventh Symphony. It should be noticed that Beethoven has prescribed *allegro* here, whereas generally his Scherzi are marked either *presto*, *molto vivace*, or some similar expression denoting a very quick time. The metronome mark ♩. = 108 also helps us to get a true appreciation of the time. A really quick time would not only destroy the basic character of this piece but would also be detrimental to a true and adequate execution of the delightful solo passages (bars 91–164), in which we seem to witness the rustic dances of merry youths and maidens. At last, at the end of the movement, when the joyful mood has risen to the pitch of enthusiasm, we see that Beethoven himself has prescribed a rapid time (*presto*). And yet I have often heard the whole Scherzo taken so quickly that at this point an increase of speed became impossible and the movement simply hurried on at the same express speed throughout.

Bars 40, 47, 48, 55, 60, 63, 189, 192, 193, 196, 237, 242 and 245. In these bars the second horn takes the lower C's and D's throughout, as the awkward leaps in this part can only be explained by the fact that the

was wanting on the natural instruments.

Bar 165. The 2/4 bar emphatic and uncompromising, not too quick, perhaps ♩ = 116 instead of ♩ = 132.

Bars 173–188. The important and characteristic part of the first flute becomes inaudible here if the rest of the orchestra plays *ff* as prescribed. This can be avoided, however, by means of a reinforcement, without any other instrumental change. As a piccolo is necessary for the storm movement, the player of this instrument can strengthen the first flute in this passage (with the regular flute, of course, which he will bring with him for this purpose) and the second flute may here also play the part of the first. It matters less that the second flute part be sacrificed than that the part of the first flute be inaudible. If double woodwinds can be had for the storm movement and the last movement, we have a total of at least five flute players (including the piccolo), so that four can play the first, and one the second part. This gives a perfect result.

Fourth Movement

Bar 1. No breath pause should be made after the Scherzo. The *pp tremolo* of the bassos, which represents the distant thunder, comes in suddenly and unexpectedly. This movement is unconditionally *alla breve*, and must therefore be conducted in two beats, not in four as is sometimes done. The mingling of quintuplets in the violoncellos with the ordinary semiquavers of the contrabassos (bars 21–32) shows clearly that Beethoven intended to produce an entirely naturalistic effect here, so that the time should on no account be retarded for the sake of a "correct execution of the bass figures," which is a view that I have sometimes heard maintained. The metronome mark $\bd = 80$ gives the right time.

Doubled woodwinds and doubled horns (third playing with first and second with fourth) are very useful both in this and the last movement. The doubling can come in from bar 21 to bar 56, and from bar 78 to bar 119.

Bar 146 to the end. This wonderful transition will bear a gradual slackening of the time until the entry of the pastoral song, for which $\bd. = 60$ is a very good metronome mark. I cannot warn strongly enough against playing the last two notes of the flute solo an octave higher and thus bringing it up to the high C. It is precisely the interval of the seventh between the high A and the lower B that generates so much warmth and charm.

Fifth Movement

Bars 25–31. Here Beethoven begins to strengthen the part of the violoncellos, violas and clarinets by means of the horns. From the fourth bar this reinforcement ceases in the second horn, as the notes are wanting, and at last, in the last bar of the passage, the first horn also comes to a stop because the A and B are wanting. This breaks into the melody in a most disturbing manner and it not only may, but must be altered. A complete melodic progression of the horns would necessitate the omission of harmonically important notes, first of the second horn, and, in the last bar, of the first horn also. As every orchestra which attempts Beethoven's symphonies at all has four horns at its disposal, I should advise at first the doubling of the horns at the entry of the melody, and then the continuation of the first and second horn from bar 28, thus:

allowing the third and fourth meanwhile to play the original melody. If double woodwinds can be had, the clarinets may also be doubled in these bars.

Bar 66. The trill in the first violins to be played as a short double upper mordent without ending grace note, thus:

Bar 80. The beautiful melody in the clarinets and bassoons needs a particularly expressive execution. I have therefore added a *cantabile* to the *dolce* and marked the parts as follows:

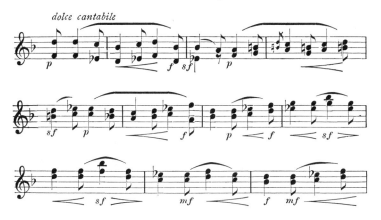

In the last bar of this quotation I let all the woodwinds begin to play *mf* on the third quaver, the violins and violas on the second semiquaver, and extended the *crescendo* (in the original *più f*) over the two next bars to the *ff* bar 93. It may in certain cases be useful to double the clarinets and bassoons until bar 94.

Bars 100–108. Here the woodwinds (exclusive of the horns) may be doubled. It may be advisable in this and similar passages in order to achieve a uniform *diminuendo*, not to let the doubling cease all at once or in all the instruments at the same time. From bar 109 the strengthening instruments might also play the following:

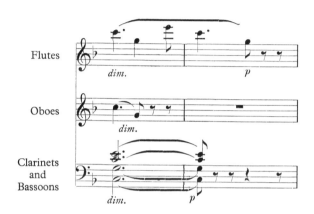

A thoughtful conductor will be able to decide all details of style and expression in such cases.

Bars 117–124. The *pizzicati* of the second violins must be brought into thematic relief, but this does not mean that they should be played *f*.

Bars 125–131. The thematic alternation between first violins and violas must be rendered quite distinct.

Bars 133–140. The variation of the main theme is here entrusted exclusively to the horns. Here too the absence of certain notes in Beethoven's time inexorably demanded a harmonic deviation from the melodic leading. From bar 137, however, this deviation is so in accord with the character of the horn that the absence of a deeper melodic part is not felt at all. But in bar 136 Beethoven was driven to a meaningless and clumsy leading in the second horn, and I believe that every reader endowed with a fine perception will feel that he wrote this part unwillingly, and only because he was forced to do so by the imperfection of the instruments of his day. I have therefore introduced this change into the second horn:

In addition to this the horns should be doubled for the whole passage.

Bars 211–219. If auxiliary woodwinds are available, the first flute may be doubled here, then the first bassoon and first oboe (bar 213) and then the first clarinet (bar 216). After this both oboes, the second bassoon and the second clarinet may be doubled (bar 218), and in the last bar mentioned (bar 219) the horns also. This doubling can last till bar 233, where the strengthening instruments, which must have already made a stronger *diminuendo* than the main instruments, cease playing.

Bars 226 and 227. In order to do justice to the splendour of this magnificent modulation, I introduced a $<$ in the first, and an *fff* in the second bar. This latter was sustained in its full force until the *diminuendo* began (bar 231). It ought to sound as though the whole fulness of heavenly blessing was being poured forth over fields and meadows.

Legend tells of a conductor who added kettledrums in this movement. If this be true, no words can express the barbarism of such a proceeding. Surely no supreme genius, only common sense, is needed to perceive that in this symphony Beethoven has reserved the kettledrums exclusively to produce the noise of thunder and with inimitable fine-feeling has abstained from using them on any other occasion.

Bars 237 and following. The execution of the end of the movement must be extremely simple, warm and sincere, without any trace of sentimentality or any deviation from normal time. In the two last beats, and from bar 254 to bar 256, the woodwinds and horns may be doubled in such wise that the extra instruments begin *piano* (not *forte*) in bar 254, play *crescendo* till the next bar, and thereupon *diminuendo* again, thus:

This in conjunction with the entry of the trombones produces a very beautiful swell, like that of an organ.

In reference to the substitution of lower notes for higher ones in the second parts of the brass instruments, the following hints might be of use.

The second horn takes the lower D everywhere from bar 40 to bar 56. Then it takes the lower F everywhere from bar 86 to bar 93, the lower D from the bar 146 to bar 148, and then again the lower D in bar 163. In the pastoral song the second trumpet always takes the lower D instead of the higher one. This substitution of lower for higher notes is not necessary for either instrument in the storm movement.

Seventh Symphony

First Movement

Bar 1. The introduction is generally played too slowly. It is marked Poco sostenuto, not Adagio, or even Andante. The time is never really slow throughout the whole symphony, and therefore not here, where the vital energy which permeates the whole work seems to be already stirring its wings. What can one say when one hears the violin passages (bars 10–14), which seem to fly up like airy sprites, played in such time that it sounds like a child practising scales; or when the light ring of a graceful round (bar 23 and following; bar 42 and following) is played so slowly that one can imagine one hears the funeral procession of some dead general passing in the distance? One would like to call to a conductor who allows such a proceeding: "For heaven's sake, read the time directions, before you dare to conduct such a masterpiece!"

Bars 39–41. If the trumpets blow *ff* here continuously, they sound extraordinarily shrill and hide both the character-filled leaps of the first violins and the equally uncommon progression of the woodwinds. I tried at first taking the trumpets in unison with the first violins so as to bring out this part clearly. As I grew to understand Beethoven's style better, however, I saw the worthlessness of this remedy. I should therefore warn against it now. But I do think it is good to let the second trumpet occasionally take the lower notes (see the following example) and make a specially strong accent only on the first crotchet of every other bar, where the harmony changes and where the kettledrum can also be more in evidence than on the other beats. These two voices would then be notated as follows:

It is also good to double the woodwinds in these bars if possible.

Bars 57–62. This passage seems meaningless when it is executed in a spiritless manner. In any case those who see nothing in it but a constant repetition of the same note will not be able to make anything out of it, and in their bewilderment will overlook the main point of the whole thing. As a matter of fact, the two last bars before the Vivace, together with the upbeat, prepare the way for the rhythm which characterizes this movement, whereas in the two first bars of the passage quoted the vibrating movement of the introduction dies away. The two middle bars, which represent the moment of the greatest restfulness, give at the same time the feeling of intense expectation which is naturally felt at a moment when the old is dying, and the new is momentarily awaited but has not yet actually made its appearance. Thus, after the first two bars have been played in strictest time and the motion has died away of itself through the transition from semiquavers to quavers, in the next two bars the expectation can be still more increased by means of a very moderate retardation of the speed. From the end of the fourth bar of this passage, where the entry of the new is also indicated by a change of key, whilst, in contrast to the previous passage, the winds lead and the strings follow, the tempo may be very gradually quickened. At the entry of the 6/8 time, a ♩. may be taken as equivalent to the previous ♩, and the increase of speed may continue until full *vivace* tempo is reached in the fifth bar of the 6/8 time, at the entry of the main theme. No gradation in strength should be thought of, except the *crescendo* prescribed in the fourth bar of the Vivace. The *vivace* tempo itself, which has the excellent metronome mark ♩. = 104, should not be too quick, otherwise the movement loses in strength and clearness. It should be remembered that ♩♪♩ in itself gives a very animated musical metre.

Bars 77 and 80. The *sf*'s should not be too emphatic. It should be noticed that they are marked *sfp*.

Bar 88. The *fermata* should not be held on too long, and should be immediately followed by the run. Then the *ff* breaks out in jubilant energy.

From here onwards the second trumpet always plays the lower D throughout the movement, except in bars 324, 326 and 347. The same for the second horn with the exception of bars 437 and 439.

Bars 124 and 126. The imperfection of the brass instruments in Beethoven's time gives rise here to a regrettable disproportion of sound. Each of the bars preceding the two bars quoted has the benefit of the glorious trumpet sound, although it is only giving a chord of the seventh; but the chords containing the resolution are deprived of this splendour, and consequently produce a smaller volume of sound than the preceding chords of the seventh, which is quite contrary to the musical conception. We are therefore perfectly justified here in filling in the rests of each bar in the trumpets with

In the corresponding passage, bars 336–339, the trumpets participate throughout, because here the natural notes fit in with the harmonies of the chords.

Bar 176. It is better not to repeat the first section.

Bar 181. There is too much tendency for orchestras to hurry from this point. The conductor must guard against this.

Bars 205–206 and 211–212. The woodwinds as well as the horns should be doubled here. The second horn plays the lower B-flats throughout the passage, beginning, in fact, at the double bar (bar 177). If auxiliary woodwinds are available, I also recommend their use in the passage which follows shortly:

Bars 236–249. I have succeeded in obtaining a very good effect in this powerful gradation by distributing the *crescendo*, sustained in the winds, in such a way amongst the strings that the volume of sound in the prolonged notes increased in a quite special degree,

whereas the figurations began each time with a somewhat diminished sound and started the *crescendo* anew. Of course these special *crescendos* on the long notes must be graduated among themselves in such a way that they are weakest the first time and strongest the third time. An attempt at a precise notation would be somewhat as follows:

Bars 250–253. Here too the second horn plays the lower B-flat. Then in the last bar both woodwinds and horns, or at any rate the latter, come in doubled and remain so until bar 300. Beginning with the *piano*, of course, everything becomes single again. I need not mention that at bar 254 the entry of D minor, which can be preceded by a *crescendo* of two bars, must be of gigantic force. The trumpets and kettledrums in particular must play with absolutely elemental strength.

Bar 274. After the enormous display of power in the preceding passage we still have a *più f* here, which leads on to the *ff* of the returning original theme. It seems therefore absolutely necessary to obtain a diminution of the sound beforehand. The place most adapted to this seems to me to be the second half of bar 267. The short preceding phrases of the woodwinds and strings (from bar 264) must still be played with great energy, but the passage

should come in *poco meno f*, which of course does not mean a sudden transition to *p*. The following rising figure is played with a gradual *crescendo*. The woodwind section (whether doubled or not) joins in at about *mf* and also plays *crescendo* until the *ff* prescribed in bar 278.

Bar 285. The meeting of the D major and A major in this bar— the woodwinds anticipate the modulation to a certain extent—is a true piece of Beethoven daring, and must not be interfered with or explained away.

Bars 299 and 300. After these *fermatas* no pause must be made any more than in bar 88. I should also advise that the second *fermata* be sustained for a somewhat shorter time than the first.

Bars 304–314. I have allowed myself some freedom in the execution of this wonderful passage. First of all I added a *poco diminuendo* in the first of the bars mentioned, and let the D minor make its entry *pp* in all instruments. Four bars later, whilst the winds were still playing *pp*, I graduated the strings as follows:

In this notation only a very moderate increase and decrease of strength is intended. The solos which follow in oboe, flute and clarinet, I had executed thus:

(*poco*)

whilst the string chords were quite lightly sustained. I also prescribed a *tranquillo* for the whole passage starting from the second *fermata*, and employed the eight bars from the entry of the kettledrum (bars 315–322) onwards for a gradual acceleration of speed until the original time was reached at the *ff*.

Bar 326. The sudden change to *p* is very difficult here. It must however on no account be prepared or facilitated by a *diminuendo*.

Bars 401 and following. In this passage, one of the most sublime in all the nine symphonies, there must be no acceleration of speed, or it acquires the character of an ordinary *stretta*. The first time must be maintained throughout to the end of the movement. The effect is wonderfully increased if the contrabassos, or at any rate those of them which have a C-string available, play the lower octave from here till bar 423, at which point they take the original part thus:

If auxiliary woodwinds are available, they might be introduced *p* in bar 417, support the *crescendo* powerfully until the *ff* is reached, and then continue to blow till the end.

Second Movement

Bar 1. The time signature tells us that this movement is not to be taken like the customary *adagio* or *andante*. The metronome mark ♩ = 76, however, nearly gives us a quick march, which cannot have been the composer's intention here. I have therefore adopted ♩ = 66 or thereabout.

My first music master, Dr. Wilhelm Mayer of Graz, had found a beautiful, poetic comparison for this piece. The first A minor chord is, according to him, a look into a magic mirror. At first nothing can be seen; then forms appear, approach us and look at us with eyes which have seen another world, then pass on and disappear again—and only the dark surface of the mirror (the last A minor chord) remains. Poetic interpretations of pieces of music, which in general I am not disposed to favour, are absolutely individual and cannot be forced upon any one. But it is often of value to learn what impressions are produced by great music on men endowed with imagination; it is for this reason, and not to provide a program, that I have repeated what my teacher told me.

Bar 4. This bar and all others which are marked ♩ ♩, should be played on one bow and not with up- and downstroke or vice versa. It is best, in fact, to take each pair of bars as follows:

Bars 75–98. In a performance of this symphony at Mannheim which he conducted, Richard Wagner, in order to bring the theme of the woodwinds and horns into stronger relief, strengthened it by means of the trumpets. I think this was a mistake. The trumpets, advancing with their fearfully grave and solemn steps from the dominant to the tonic, supported all the way by the stately kettle-drums, are so characteristic that I cannot think they ought to be sacrificed. But even if Wagner, as I imagine, had four trumpeters at his disposal, even then the effect of Beethoven's wonderful trumpets is interfered with if the same instruments are fulfilling two tasks at the same time. The two similar sounds mutually destroy each other. As a matter of fact there is no danger of the melody not being distinct enough if the horns are doubled and the second players play the lower octave where, according to the notation, they ought to play in unison with the first. Every one will agree that Beethoven would certainly have written the lower notes had they been available on his instruments. If the woodwinds can also be doubled, the effect is considerably enhanced. In bars 83 and 84 the first flute naturally plays the higher octave. The second trumpet takes the lower D's throughout the passage. The second horn also might take the lower F in bar 74.

Bars 101 and following. Care should be taken not to render this melody sentimental. It should be played in strict original time. If the string section is strong, it is advisable to let it retard the execution of the *crescendos* a little more than the solo winds. The strings might even play quite *pp* in bars 117–122, and similarly the bassoons and the horns as long as they are sustaining the C.

Bars 140 and 142. The unison of the trumpets on the two high F's easily sounds shrill in spite of the *pp*; it is therefore better for the second to take the lower F. In bar 149 and bars 213–219, on the other hand, the position of the trumpets with regard to the horns will prove to any observer gifted with insight that it would not be advisable here to substitute lower notes for the high ones. In bar 220 only, I should recommend that the second trumpet play

in order to avoid the unnecessary leap to the low G.

Bars 210–213. If doubled woodwinds are not available here, it is better to let the second flute play in unison with the first, as this part easily becomes too weak. In the last bar of the passage from

to bar 221, all the woodwinds can be doubled, but I should not recommend the doubling of the horns in this passage.

As to the shortened repetition of the secondary theme in A major, one can only repeat what has already been said on the occasion of its first appearance.

Bars 243–246. The strangely solemn character and sound of these four *pianissimo* bars seem to me to justify a very slight retardation of the time here; the original time can be resumed at the *ff*.

Third Movement

Bar 17 and following. A substitution of the lower for the higher D's in the second trumpet might possibly destroy the freshness of

the sound here, as both horns are already playing the lower octave;
it is therefore better not to make any change in spite of the leaps in
the second trumpet. On the other hand, there is nothing against
letting only the first trumpet blow the threefold D, and not bringing
in the second till the low G. I should certainly recommend this for
the *piano* repetition in bars 277–284.

Bars 33–36 and 49–52. It is very important for flute and clarinets
to play these four bars *pianissimo*, i.e. in appreciable dynamic
contrast to the immediately preceding bars. This Scherzo is
generally hurried along to such an extent that the poor wind players
are out of breath by this passage, and are thankful if they can blurt
out the notes at all, in which, as often as not, they do not succeed.
In the meantime the *pp*, like many other things, is simply ignored.
Therefore, in spite of the Presto which is prescribed, the time must
not be taken so quickly as to render a clear and faithful rendering
impossible. The metronome mark ($\text{♩.} = 132$) is a little too fast,
perhaps. $\text{♩.} = 116\text{–}120$ would give about the right speed.

Bar 145. The $\boxed{1.}$ must be taken in strict time and the A
sustained in uniform *ff*, but the $>$ during the $\boxed{2.}$ justifies a
transitional *ritardando*.

The Assai meno presto is marked $\text{♩.} = 84$, but the speed which
this represents would greatly endanger an intelligent execution of
the carefully notated first bar, and the Trio would resemble a galop
rather than the joyous and yet deeply moving song which is here
intended. The right time, to my mind, is just about twice as slow
as that of the main section, and might have the metronome mark
$\text{♩.} = 60$. I need not say that it should be conducted in whole bars
and not, for example, in three crotchet-beats, as is occasionally
done.

Bars 207–221. Woodwinds and horns can be doubled.

Bar 221. There is a real difficulty for the trumpeters here which
should not be underrated. They have to give this exposed bar in the
beauty of its strength after having been obliged to sustain the high
G at a magnificent *ff* during the six preceding bars. They should
therefore be exhorted to devote special care to this passage, and at
the same time the conductor should guard against any indulgent
relaxation or *diminuendo* in this bar. The following *fp* in the horns
is a slight accent on the first note, but should not be interpreted as
though this note had to be sharply enunciated and only the following

one played *piano*, in which case the notation would be

A slight relaxation of the time after the double bar suits the nature of the passage, but on no account should a pause be made before the entry of the Presto.

Bar 260. It is of great importance here, though not very easy to accomplish, that the *piano* should be uniformly adhered to without any increase in volume from the third crotchet of this bar to the *cresc. poco a poco* in bar 334. There is also a tendency, owing to the continuance of this same *piano*, for orchestras to hurry in a very detrimental manner. For bars 293–296, also for the corresponding passages at bars 309, 529 and 545, see what has been said for bars 33–36 and 49–52. It seems unnecessary to point out each of these passages individually, but experience has taught me how often it happens that if conductor and players do not make every effort every time to give a good rendering of these passages, all too often they may succeed the first time and perhaps even the second time, but after that they completely fail. In order to render clearer the *diminuendo*, which should be quite perceptible in the bars marked *pp* in spite of the *piano* character of the whole passage, a *p* might be added for the flute and oboes on the third crotchet of bar 334, since it is evident that these bars must be played somewhat more emphatically than the preceding ones in order to render the *diminuendo* possible.

Bars 647 and 648. A very slight retardation of the speed, a weaker rendering of the $<\,>$ than in the two preceding bars and a *diminuendo* in the strings seem to me justified by the melodic character of this passage; a doubly energetic rendering of the concluding bars which follow is also facilitated by this means. The second trumpet should take the lower D in bar 652.

I recommend that all repetitions in this movement should be played, with the exception of that of the second Trio at bar 441, as this has already been repeated. The omission of this repetition seems to me to be justified on structural grounds, as will be seen by the following scheme:

Main section.
First part repeated.
Second part repeated.
First Trio.
First part, with small written-out variant (for the flutes), repeated.
Second part repeated.
Main section.
First part, with small written-out variant (*pp*), repeated.
Second part not repeated.
Second Trio.
First part repeated as before.
Second part not repeated.
Main section.
First part not repeated.
Second part not repeated.

In this way the whole movement in its structure strives towards greater conciseness, and I think this process would be arrested by another repetition in the second Trio, apart from the fact that a fourfold unchanged repetition even of this wonderful theme decidedly weakens its effect and gives a feeling of great length.

On the other hand, I think it is regrettable not to repeat the second part of the first main section (usually the case), if only for the sake of the extremely surprising and affecting return of the passage

after the A of the ⌐1.⌐, which has been sustained *ff* in strict original time.

Fourth Movement

Bar 1. Strangely enough, although I take this last movement more slowly than all the conductors I know, I have always had the quickness of my time in this piece remarked on, either with blame or praise. I can only explain this by the fact that my more even time allows the players to develop a greater intensity of sound, and that this naturally brings with it greater clearness in the execution. It is the impression of strength which I give to this movement that has been mistaken for the impression of speed. As a matter of fact, this movement is marked Allegro con brio, and not Vivace, or even Presto—a fact which is generally overlooked. The time must therefore on no account be too quick. The metronome mark ♩ = 72 is good enough in itself, but I should prefer to change it to ♩ = 138, as the piece must generally be conducted with two crotchets, and not a whole bar, to the beat.

This is one of the strangest pieces that Beethoven has written. The themes in themselves are anything but beautiful; indeed, they are almost insignificant. Small variety in the rhythm, no trace of polyphony, modulations such as any composer can produce, and yet this extraordinary effect which cannot be compared with that of any other piece. It is an unexampled bacchanalian orgy!—To reproduce it impressively is, in my opinion, one of the greatest tasks of the conductor—not indeed in its technical, but in its spiritual bearing. To arouse the superabundance of energy, of strength and of unrestrained jubilation in all the players, to sustain it and increase it irresistibly right to the end, demands a degree of devotion and intuitive communication of the will which is both physically and mentally extremely exacting. And yet without this the piece would be simply a succession of figures and chords. No one can conduct this movement correctly without sacrificing a part of himself. I grant that this may be said more of all true music, but I am convinced that it is quite specially true of this unique movement. And the task must on no account be lightened by omitting any of the repetitions. Even the small repetitions (beginning at bars 5 and 13) must each be played twice when the whole first part is repeated, and not only once as in the case of Minuets and Scherzi. Any curtailing of the dimensions of this gigantic hymn of wildest enthusiasm is bad.

Although the spirit of this piece can only be grasped as a whole, I give a few hints as to individual passages.

Bar 16. The first violins should play this bar with special emphasis and particularly strong bow-strokes, as if it were notated thus:

The same holds good for bar 157.

Bars 26, 27, 34, 35, 37, 38, 39, 41 and 42. The second trumpet takes the lower D's here and also in the corresponding passages

beginning at bars 224 and 237. A glance at the register of the horns
and at the preceding G in the trumpets will explain why in these bars,

in both passages, the second trumpet must keep to the higher D's.

Bars 74–77. The dotted semiquaver in the strings, although *p*,
must be audible every time with the utmost rhythmic clearness, as
otherwise the effect would be

If the time is too quick, however, it is impossible to render it audible,
and the *tenuto* which characterizes all the second crotchets in these
bars loses all meaning. In any case it is better, and especially so in
strongly resonant halls, that the time should be somewhat retarded
rather than hastened. Very short, subtle movements of the conductor's baton are here much to be recommended. The same may
be said with regard to the corresponding passages at bars 84, 285
and 295. I think I may take the responsibility of placing a B in the
second and fourth bars of the passage quoted (at bar 74) on each
second crotchet in the horns, as the contrast in sound to that of
each respective preceding bar becomes too pronounced through the
sudden cessation of all brass. The horns can play

in the passage in question, and

in the corresponding passage at bar 84.

No attempt at an alteration must be made here on account of the fact that Beethoven, without an evident reason, has made the horns play in octaves the first time and in unison the second time, although the instrumentation was otherwise the same in both cases. Nor does it seem to me advisable to make any additions in the trumpet parts, as a corresponding note in the kettledrum would have then to be introduced to restore the artistic equilibrium, and this would weaken the strangely harsh rôle which the high E occupies in this very passage. In the corresponding passages at bars 285 and 295, where trumpets and kettledrums play in every bar, we have a simple interchange of tonic and dominant in the main key, and so the tonic relation is different. The second trumpet there, however, may take the lower D throughout.

Bar 92 and following. Here the conductor, by means of special marking if necessary, should see that the *crescendo* is not made independently in each group of the string section, but that one group takes it from the other, so that this figuration right up to the *ff* (bar 104) is given in one single, uniformly growing *crescendo*. Frequent and careful rehearsals are necessary here and also in the similar passage at bar 307.

Bar 113. The sudden cessation of the brass and kettledrums here on account of the limited number of natural notes is very disturbing. All the chords are marked *sf*, and it is evident from the appearance of the whole passage that they were all intended to be played with the same degree of strength. Some remedy is urgently needed here and I have ventured to fill in the bar in question as follows:

The fact that the A of the kettledrum produced, to a certain extent, a chord of the ninth which Beethoven had not contemplated, did not disturb me in the least, as no hearer, however musical he may be, can possibly distinguish it. If I have been too bold, I think it is a lesser evil than either to allow the kettledrum suddenly to cease, which would strike every sensitive ear disagreeably, or to introduce a third kettledrum (one that would play a G-sharp, let us say) for the sake of this one note, which would be contrary to the style of the piece.

Bars 129–132, 136–137, 138–143. The minims, together with the tied crotchets which precede them, must be sustained with the utmost strength so that there is no trace of a weakening *diminuendo*, such as

which would be utterly wrong. A slight pause might even be made on these notes, but then it is absolutely necessary for the dotted quavers with the semiquaver to be played throughout at full speed, so that the passage is really executed in time and no general *ritenuto* is introduced. The following notation might be adopted:

From bar 144, however, the original time, which is no longer held back by any considerable pauses, should already be energetically resumed. Both in this and the following bar, however, the notes marked *sf* must of course be sustained in full *ff*, and any inappropriate *diminuendo* must be carefully avoided.

Bars 165–169. These bars sound very feeble in the winds in comparison with the strings even when the woodwind section is doubled. I have given them their full value as far as possible by filling in the rests in the clarinets with the following part:

Bars 198–215. The expectancy which seems to be expressed by this *pianissimo*, before the entry of the powerful *crescendo* which prepares for the return of the main theme, must not be weakened by too great haste. The first flute should especially be warned against this.

Bar 389. After the *ff* prescribed from bar 319 right on to the bar quoted, with the exception of a few *f*'s and *sf*'s we find no further directions as to strength. Then here we have *sempre più f*, which is followed by another *ff* in bar 405. It is clear then that there must be a *diminuendo* somewhere if this *sempre più f* is to bear any meaning to us. Wagner strongly objected to a sudden *p* which his Dresden colleague Reissiger introduced for the above reason. And, in fact, a sudden change to *p* in the middle of the passage does seem a rather childish makeshift. The occasional *f*'s in the trumpets and kettle-drums which we mentioned above also seem to prove that Beethoven intended no lessening of sound to take place. And yet when I played all this long section at a uniform *ff*, I could not avoid a certain feeling of emptiness, and moreover I could not succeed in bringing out the *sempre più f*. I determined, therefore, to follow my musical instinct and to make an actual innovation, for which, I must confess, I have no other grounds than the effect which it produces and the immediate willingness with which every orchestra to which I explained my proceeding followed it. I had everything played with the greatest energy until bar 367; I then introduced a slow, very gradual *diminuendo*, which became a *piano* in bar 384 and remained so for a space of five bars. This gave a particularly beautiful expression to the following thirds of the woodwinds. Then instead of the *sempre più f* I introduced a *crescendo poco a poco*, which increased continually with ever growing strength until the *ff* in bar 405. Of course the individual *f*'s prescribed in the trumpets and kettledrums must be correspondingly modified, i.e. either changed to *dim.*, *p* or *cresc.* as the case may be, or simply omitted altogether.

Then in bars 374 and 376 I let the second trumpet take the lower B-flats, and in the later bars of the passage in question the lower D throughout. Not till bar 402 is it better to take the higher D again on account of the intense sound effect.

I am quite conscious of the danger of recommending an innovation which can no longer be viewed as interpretation of the composer's mind, but is an independent conception of the interpreter; dangerous because, according to the saying that what one may do another may do likewise, others may easily feel called upon to undertake similar changes in other passages on the strength of a recognised example. I would therefore call attention to the extreme caution with which I proceeded whenever I ventured on a new marking or alteration of the original, and to the care with which I avoided in any way interfering with Beethoven's characteristic style. I would also point out that, in all the nine symphonies, this is the only passage in which I could possibly be accused of acting arbitrarily; but it is to be noted that precisely here the original notation is unfortunately not only practically useless, but actually confusing. To write *ff*, *sempre più f* and then *ff* again is senseless. If the *più f* is to mean anything, it must be either preceded or followed by a diminution in strength. As the whole structure of the passage excludes the possibility of a *diminuendo* after the *più f*, I have tried, in the way that seemed to me best, to supply the want before it, and my manner of procedure has met with unanimous approval. Repeated performances have convinced me that this whole part produces a much more direct effect when played in the manner I have indicated than when it is simply flogged through at *ff*, because the gradation—evidently intended by Beethoven, necessary and expressly prescribed by the *sempre più f*—cannot be obtained under these conditions.

The doubling of the horns in this movement, and also of the woodwinds, if possible, is of the greatest importance. It starts right at the beginning and ceases at bar 63. The effect of the long *crescendo* at bar 92 is particularly powerful if the woodwind reinforcements enter *p* in bar 98 and the other players, who are already playing fairly loud, are thus supported by means of a renewed *crescendo*. The doubling comes to an end in bar 199, then begins again in bar 218, where the reinforcing instruments come in *p* and during the two bars which precede the *ff* strengthen the already existing *crescendo*. It stops again in bar 274. Then, as in the analogous passage earlier, the extra woodwinds and horns again come in *p* in bar 316, and support the *crescendo* of the other instruments with renewed energy. From this point the doubling proceeds unbroken to the end, even during the *dim.*, *p* and *cresc.* which I have prescribed for bars 367–404.

Eighth Symphony

As this symphony is one of Beethoven's most mature master-pieces, the instrumentation has reached a wonderful degree of perfection. As far as the sound is concerned, the score leaves hardly anything to be desired. However difficult it may be for the conductor to reproduce the incomparable humour of this piece in all its free-dom and subtlety, yet he will find no necessity to attempt to render the execution clearer by means of elaborate notation; or—with the exception of the familiar octave transpositions in the second horn and second trumpet advisable in several passages—to undertake any alterations in the text. I have therefore a very limited number of suggestions to make in regard to this symphony.

First Movement

Bar 1. The metronome mark ♩. = 69 is too quick. I have adopted ♩. = about 56, or better still ♩ = 160, as a motion in three crotchets, not in whole bars, forms the groundwork of the movement although one beat will often suffice for one bar.

Bars 1–3. I have noticed in many concert halls that the theme in the violins is not distinct enough here. In such cases I adopted the following notation for all the wind and the kettledrums:

It is advisable to adopt this if the string section is not very strong.

Bars 5–8. The detestable habit of playing these bars suddenly much more slowly and bringing in the first tempo again in bar 9 must be rejected, although it was favoured by Bülow in weak moments.

Bars 36–37. The execution is aided if the bassoon gently emphasizes the two notes

the G perhaps a little more than the A.

Bars 43 and 51. The *ritard.* should be made only in this bar, not before. The flow of the melody also demands a very fine and gentle retardation of the speed, but not a sentimental *ritenuto.*

Bars 62, 65, 66, 67 and 69. The second horn, and in the last bar the second trumpet also, takes the lower D's.

It is very important that the *sf* should be executed only very moderately at first and then gradually increased to the *ff*, so that the *crescendo* starting from bar 60 may be preserved. See also bars 257 and following.

Bars 73–79. These bars must remain *p* throughout. The sudden entry of the *ff* which follows must not be prepared by any *crescendo.* See also bars 270–276.

Bars 93 and 95. Second horn and second trumpet take the lower D's.

Bars 96–99. These and the four similar bars later on must be played straight off at strong *ff* without an attempt at rhythmic marking. I only mention this because I once found the following meaningless notation:

Bars 132–135. In order to render the woodwinds distinctly audible, it is advisable to perform the *crescendo* in the strings very moderately. In view of the fact that the woodwinds remain *dolce* throughout, there is no harm at all in giving the following *fortissimo*

entry in A major a certain character of suddenness which corresponds to the previous *fortissimo* entries.

Bars 190–198. The theme in the basses and bassoons cannot always be heard distinctly here. An alteration which I have heard made and once tried myself is to support the first and second bars by means of four kettledrums, thus:

but I realized that it is a very rough and ready proceeding. As a true understanding of the theme is what we have to aim at in this passage, there is really no other choice but to let only the violoncellos, basses and bassoons play with their full strength and to adopt the following notation for all the other instruments:

I cannot resist adding the exhortation here to impress continually on the players in the orchestra the great difference between *f* and *ff* and the error of producing a maximum of sound where only *f* is prescribed, and thus rendering impossible any further gradation to *ff* or, as the case may be, to *fff*. It seems hardly necessary to say that the same holds good with regard to *p* and *pp*, and yet how often is this point disregarded!

Bars 201 and 202. Both the *f* of the woodwinds in the first bar and the *p* of the strings in the second have to come in suddenly without any preparatory *crescendo* or *diminuendo*. It is more difficult to give this passage quite correctly than appears at first sight.

Bars 233 and 234. Here too clarinet and bassoon should emphasize the two notes

in the manner I have indicated for the G and A of the bassoon at bars 36–37.

Bars 240 and 248. See bars 43 and 51.

Bars 257–260. The second horn plays the lower octave here, and also the lower E.

Bar 301. No increase of speed should be allowed either during the following *piano* passage with the wonderful clarinet solo or during the *crescendo* which precedes the *ff*.

Bar 332. The three chords marked ⌒ should be given in free and somewhat broader time; the last *fermata* should not be held on too long and should be sharply taken off. Then the music resumes again after a short pause. To prolong the B-flat in the first violins with a languishing *diminuendo* is altogether wrong when playing Beethoven.

Bar 366. The *diminuendo* which begins here will justify a very slight holding back of the time. But the two last bars of this movement must without fail be played in original tempo again.

Second Movement

The metronome mark ♪ = 88 gives a good tempo. The final note of the theme (bar 3) and every quaver that has no *staccato* dot (e.g. bar 4 in the basses, and bar 81) must retain its full value as a quaver and must not be played *staccato*. At bars 26 and 59 the *diminuendo* can be supported by a very slight *ritenuto*. Aside from these hints, this delightful movement should be performed delicately and gracefully without any artificiality.

Third Movement

Bar 1. Wagner's justifiable condemnation of undue hurrying in this movement is so well known, that I need hardly refer to it here. I must give an earnest warning, however, against allowing the time to get too slow, and playing this lively Minuet like the music at the entry of the giants in *Das Rheingold*. The metronome mark ♩ = 126 seems to me too fast. I prefer ♩ = 108.

Although the notation

is clear enough, yet conductors often overlook the fact that the upbeat is to be played powerfully, it is true, but without the characteristic *sf* of the later crotchet-beats. The hearer must realise clearly that this is an upbeat and not the first crotchet of a bar. If the first F is played *sf* like the following ones, the feeling of a first crotchet-beat is produced too soon and an error of rhythmic feeling is allowed.

Bar 38. The obstinate clashing of the tonic in the woodwind (third crotchet) with the dominant in horns and trumpets cannot be given with too great distinctness. Strangely enough, I have heard the view expressed that this is an error in the music.

Bars 55 and 56. These bars can be played somewhat more quietly than the two preceding.

Fourth Movement

Bar 1. The metronome mark ○ = 84 gives an impossibly quick time. I have adopted ♩ = about 132. In bars 4 and 5 after the up-beat, and everywhere else that the third crotchets are not expressly marked with *staccato* dots, they must not be played *staccato*. It would be best to mark them – in the individual orchestral parts.

Bar 17. In order to give this fantastic, half-humorous and half-gloomy C-sharp with the force required, a very slight retardation starting from the *ppp* will be found necessary. Violins and violas must have time after the C in the second beat to raise their bow and to come down with all their weight upon the C-sharp. This C-sharp is then sustained a little beyond its time (*quasi tenuto*), and the original time is resumed in the second half of the following bar. Here, as in all such cases, there is no question of a real change in the time; it is merely a slight modification, which indeed only produces the desired effect if it is slight.

Bars 22–23. The passage

if played an octave higher, as is sometimes done, sounds too ordinary, so it is better to leave it unchanged. The same may be said of the corresponding passage, bar 183.

Bar 38 and following. If we allow the brass instruments to take the lower D's here, we get false basses in the second horn from bar 42 to bar 47. The comparison with the same chord succession in the strings shows us that the lower part of the harmony is entrusted to the bassoons. The higher D's must therefore be retained. In bar 47 only, I should advise that the second horn and second trumpet play thus:

in order to avoid the unnecessary leap to the low G.

Bar 48 and following. The habit of playing the second subject much more slowly and turning this charming melody into a piece of languishing sentimentality is a most objectionable mannerism. Unless the whole movement has been senselessly hurried, the original time is valid for both first and second subject, and it is quite unnecessary for the latter to be cut off from the whole by a change in the time.

Bars 91–94. The *p* in the violas and violins should not be too softly rendered, otherwise the *pp* which shortly follows becomes impossible. See also bars 267–270.

Bars 178 and 179. See what has been already said for the execution of the C-sharp and the bars which immediately precede it.

Bars 255 and 259. Horns and trumpets take the lower D throughout.

Bar 282 and following. A passing note of gravity can be distinguished here through the gay music of this symphony. Therefore I could not bring myself to maintain the original time completely, so I started from the A of the second violins a little more moderately, then gradually returned in the first bars around bar 331 to the quicker original time, which came into possession of its full rights in the second half of bar 345 (D major).

From bar 314 to bar 340 the second horn and second trumpet should always take the lower D and F; the second horn should also take the lower E-flat in bar 322. The B-flat, I think, should not be transposed. In bar 364 the second horn takes the lower D.

Bars 370–379. Although in the first three bars the slight retardation recommended for the similar preceding passages has a beneficial effect, it would be a mistake to prolong it over the short fragments of the original theme which precede the two following C-sharps. These should rather be played in full time, in such a way however as to give the string players time to raise their bows sufficiently to produce the C-sharps with all their force. To this end we are justified in placing a short pause before each of the C-sharps, but these pauses must not last longer than is absolutely necessary for the manipulation of the bows. Just as the passage which I discussed in the Seventh Symphony was the only one in which I ventured upon an arbitrary gradation, so too this passage in the last movement of the Eighth is the only place where I have thought it permissible, in fact necessary, to introduce anything in the nature of a breathing space. Constant practice, however, must reduce this interruption to a minimum. A notation of the passage in which I have taken this liberty would present an appearance something like the following:

Bar 391. This entry in horns, trumpets and kettledrums, which brings in the incomparably ingenious return of the principal key, must be executed with triumphant strength. To modulate from F-sharp minor to F major by magically transforming E-sharp, the leading tone of the former key, into the tonic of the latter key through an enharmonic change is an inspiration so monumental in its simplicity that only Beethoven could have hit upon it. Where are all poetical interpretations when compared with the primitive force of music which is displayed here?

Bars 420–427. A joyful light seems to break forth in one's soul when the rough bassos take up the graceful second subject here. Where is such a trait of irresistible humour to be found in later music? The violoncellos and contrabassos must play this delightful solo with delicate but long bowing.

I might also mention that the first flute can take the higher B-flat instead of the

which Beethoven evidently wrote for safety's sake, in the following places: Bars 26 and 34. (Strange to say, in the similar passage at bar 187, Beethoven has made an exception and has himself written the high B-flat, so that it is difficult to understand why he so anxiously avoided it later in much more important passages of the Ninth Symphony.) Further in bars 195, 209, 219–222, 387, 389, 391 and 393–398. It is not advisable, however, in similar passages to change the

to the higher C. Doubling of the woodwinds should be unconditionally avoided throughout this symphony.

Ninth Symphony

Beethoven's Ninth Symphony is not only the greatest, but also the most difficult of orchestral compositions. A clear and correct, but at the same time sympathetic and powerful execution of this symphony belongs to the most overwhelming tasks of the conductor's art. Here more than in any of his other works Beethoven found himself constantly handicapped by the limited resources of the orchestra, and here more than elsewhere we can see how his deafness made it difficult for him to judge correctly of the different sound effects. That in spite of these hindrances he has created in the Adagio a true miracle of instrumentation only makes us gaze afresh in wondering admiration at this unique genius.

Wagner was the first to recognize the necessity of an occasional interference with the text, either by means of marking or by the introduction of moderate changes, in those places where literal rendering of the piece would only produce a confused image and would fail to fulfil the intention of the composer as clearly evidenced by a reading of the score. In his treatise *On the Execution of Beethoven's Ninth Symphony* (*Zum Vortrag der neunten Symphonie Beethovens*) he makes various suggestions, which with unusual modesty he lays before "seriously minded musicians" in order to stimulate careful thought, but "not to incite to imitation." I will repeat these suggestions of Wagner's here so far as I feel able to adopt them, referring to the work mentioned above for all that concerns their justification in detail.

I would preface my remarks on this symphony by the statement that, not to mention the requisite quantity and quality of the vocal forces, I consider performances of the Ninth Symphony with a small string section to be utterly inadequate; further, in my opinion, doubling of the woodwinds is indispensable when the string section is at its full strength. All my following remarks on this symphony are made on that twofold understanding. With exceptionally numerous forces, for instance at music festivals in very large halls, a corresponding doubling of horns and trumpets (eight horns, four trumpets) is to be recommended. Concert institutions, however, which only have the use of small orchestras, should either not attempt this symphony at all, or should shun neither trouble nor expense to obtain the requisite number of good players, and at the same time of course should not limit the number of their rehearsals. Far better to hear the Ninth Symphony well performed once every ten years, than badly performed several times every year.

I cannot forbear mentioning here the strange and unartistic proceeding of Bülow in executing this work twice successively at one and the same concert. Are we concerned here with a theoretical dissertation, which can be demonstrated to the audience over and over again for the sake of a clearer comprehension, or are we seeking to feel and understand the deep, intense heart-outpouring of one of the greatest men and masters who have ever lived, which penetrates all the fibres of our being and shakes us to our very depths ? Is it possible for a being gifted with a soul that vibrates in sympathy to experience twice in a row with full participation this titanic struggle from darkness to light and from pain to joy, then to cover the sunlight which is just breaking through with stormy clouds again, in order to enjoy the victory *da capo* immediately after ? If Bülow was capable of this, that is, if he so coolly and deliberately undertook the task of changing Beethoven's gigantic effort into a simple problem for the conductor's art, at all events he might have had more consideration for the receptive capacity of his audience and also for the productive capacity of the performers. Numerous witnesses of this double performance have told me with regret that they were unable to follow intelligently the second time and that the second performance did not attain the same level as the first. As a matter of fact just this falling off is the only thing which speaks well for Bülow on this occasion. It simply proves that he himself could not survive the ordeal of the Ninth Symphony twice through, one time after another.

When I became conductor of the Berlin Symphony Concerts, for which the public rehearsals and the performances take place on the same day, after one attempt I absolutely refused to conduct this work twice in one day, even though six and a half hours were to elapse between the end of the first and the beginning of the second performance. The arrangement was therefore made that when the

Ninth Symphony was to be performed, the public rehearsal should take place two days before the concert itself.

First Movement

Bar 1. The metronome mark ♩ = 88 seems to me a trifle too quick. The *un poco maestoso* character would be in danger of being obliterated, owing to the semiquaver motion of this movement. The time of this extremely delicately proportioned piece of music will bear many modifications and many gradations, and may possibly even reach ♩ = 88. But I should not recommend anything more animated than ♩ = 76 for the original time.

The very first bar presents a difficulty, inasmuch as the D-horns are very liable to come in too loudly with their fifths and thus destroy the uncanny twilight effect of the beginning. The horn players should be specially drilled to play these two notes in lightest possible *pp*.

Bar 16. A moderate retardation of the time is advisable in this bar to enable the strings to give a precise and distinct break-off at the demisemiquaver rest and then begin an energetic attack on the magnificent main theme. With the same object in view I let the winds, who are naturally out of breath after the *crescendo*, make a rest of a demisemiquaver before the entry of the theme,

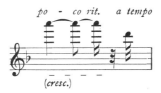

during which they can take a fresh breath. I conducted the second crotchet-beat of this bar as two quaver-beats to render my object clearer. The woodwind section is doubled for the entry of the main theme and the doubling continues until bar 28.

Bars 19 and 20. The second horn takes the lower octave from the E-flat onwards.

Bars 21–23. The imposing effect of these chords is produced by sustaining decisively the dotted quavers, not by retarding the speed.

Bars 24–27. Second horn and second trumpet take the lower F's.

Bars 34 and 35. The strange run in the first violins and violas together with the *diminuendo* seems to me like the sudden vanishing back into the earth of a gigantic, ghostly apparition. It is very important that the same breathless *pp* as at the beginning should be resumed immediately after.

Bar 50. Here exactly the same may be said as for bar 16. Here too the woodwinds come in doubled with the theme and the doubling lasts until bar 73.

Bars 50, 51 and 54. The second horn plays the lower E-flats, and in bar 51 of course the lower C.

Bars 53 and 54. The fourth horn plays the six notes starting from the E an octave lower.

Bar 57. Second trumpet takes the lower D.

Bars 61 and 62. Second horn plays the lower F's and the lower E-flat. But I cannot make the same recommendation for bars 64 and 65. Beethoven could have written

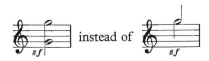

without hesitation and could have let the higher notes come in from the F onwards. He seems to have preferred the sharper sound of the unison. I make this observation in order to point out once again how carefully and cautiously one should proceed in these matters.

Bar 69. The lower C-sharp on the old bassoons was either extremely imperfect or altogether wanting. (See Berlioz, *Theory of Instrumentation*, Breitkopf & Härtel edition, page 100.) This explains the strange upward leap. The lower C-sharp should unquestionably be played here.

Bar 72. The fourth (but not the second) horn plays the lower D's.

Bars 77 and 78. The entry of the flute is no simple doubling here. In view of the preceding phrase on this instrument, which is to a certain extent completed by these five notes, and also in the interest of the melodic leading, which I interpret thus:

(see also bars 339 and 340) I let the flute play with the following expression here:

Bars 80–83. Heinrich Porges, in his report on Wagner's performance of the Ninth Symphony at Bayreuth, emphasizes the fact "that any forced accent was avoided." To achieve this end it is very important that both flute and oboe should be reminded to adapt their method of execution and tone production exactly to that of the clarinet and bassoon, so that the change of instruments may be noticed as little as possible and these four bars may present a melody complete in itself to the ear of the hearer. The >'s should be just hinted at. It is perhaps better for only the first horn to play from bar 82 to bar 88, but if the first and second play they should be reminded to play the E-flats in lightest *pp* and to increase only to *p* in the <. In the syncopated entry of the strings in bar 79 a slight accent may be placed upon the A. I have ventured for this passage upon the notation

a nuance which, as a matter of fact, Beethoven has himself prescribed in a similar passage, bar 278. The strings and the second pair of horns might also play quite *pp* and then make a slight *crescendo*, perhaps to *p*.

Bars 88–91. In this passage I had the small violin figures executed very *pp* and adopted the following expression for the woodwinds,

at the same time bringing the first oboe and the second clarinet somewhat to the forefront.

Bars 98 and 99. In order to bring out the *crescendo* of the clarinets and first flute, which carry the melody here, Wagner recommends the omission of the *crescendo* in the strings and the introduction of a general *crescendo* for the strings in bar 100, where *più crescendo* is prescribed.

Bars 102, 103, 106 and 107. These four bars are played by the doubled woodwinds. Formerly I let the trumpets play in B-flat here, instead of D, and allowed them also to play in bars 103 and 107. I have since abandoned this mode of execution, however, and mention this here so that if anyone should hear the passage executed in this manner, they should know that it does not happen with my consent.

Bars 108 and 109. Strings and flutes should not begin too softly here (*mp*), and should pass over to *pp* in the second bar by means of a $>$. Wagner has already pointed out emphatically the necessity of a thoroughly restful and uniformly quiet execution of the following fourteen bars. The *crescendo* which begins in bar 124 should be supported by means of a gentle $<>$ repeated each time on the G-flat and G (crotchets) in the parts containing the melody:

Bar 119. The fourth horn takes the lower F.

Bars 132–138. From the B-flat (fourth quaver) onwards both flutes can be doubled.

Bars 138–145. Wagner has made particularly valuable suggestions for the execution of this difficult passage. It would be puritanical to deny that his alterations, both here and in the similar passage which occurs later on, without doing detriment to the style in any way, conduce to a clearness which cannot be obtained by means of a merely literal rendering. The alterations themselves in this first passage are still extremely moderate. The extent of their scope is that in the second bar of the passage in question the oboe instead of playing

and in the sixth bar the first flute instead of playing

The dynamic gradations suggested by Wagner are of just as great importance. He introduced the following notation:

This is merely a continuation and an intelligent interpretation of the *espressivo* prescribed by Beethoven. I would merely add that the third and fourth horn players should mark the passage

which occurs three times before the *ff*, each time with *pp*, and that from bar 137 to bar 149 the second horn should take the lower F's and E-flats.

In order to obtain an expressive precision in the very necessary moderate retardation of the time, which Wagner had also suggested, I gave quaver-beats from bar 138 onwards, and only resumed the two crotchet-beats in bars 148 and 149.

Bar 150. The woodwinds should come in doubled here, and the doubling should continue until the *decresc.* at bar 158 is reached.

Bars 160, 166, 170, 174 and 178. These solemn notes in the trumpets should be firmly sustained in spite of the *pp* (*quasi tenuto*). The kettledrum strokes should be soft, but somewhat heavy.

Bars 179–185. In order to bring out clearly the melodic, polyphonic structure of this passage, I have adopted the following notation for the first woodwind parts:

Bars 196 and 214. Strange to say, the *a tempo* in these bars is often overlooked and the short *ritard.* that precedes is carried in each case over the two bars following it. It should therefore be observed that the whole beauty of the execution depends on the *a tempo* coming in just where Beethoven has prescribed it, and on the careful avoidance of any sentimentality of expression. If the quavers are held on dotted, as they should be in spite of the return of the original time, we get a kind of *portamento*, which might be given by the notation,

which is really only a continuation of the notation already prescribed for the three *ritardando* notes.

Bars 198–206. Second horn takes the lower F's and E-flats. The first oboe should sound the third bar of the passage very expressively, thus:

For the first clarinet and first bassoon the following notation might be adopted:

Bar 217 and following bars. Starting from the high G (fourth quaver-beat) the first flute comes in doubled. From the C onwards the bassoons follow suit and then all the remaining woodwind instruments as they make their entry. The doubling remains until bar 252. The whole magnificent fugato up to that bar should be played with the utmost precision and energy, but not too slowly. For a metronome mark ♩ = 80–84 might perhaps be about the right one.

To render the polyphonic structure more distinct, the following observations also are important.

Bars 232–235. After a great many performances, I became convinced that the second violins, even when numerous, could not give the theme here with the incisiveness which it requires. I therefore resolved to bring in the oboes doubled, and prescribed the following parts to fill the rests in these instruments,

and this immediately produced the effect which seems to me indispensable here.

Bars 228–231. Horns play with the following gradations:

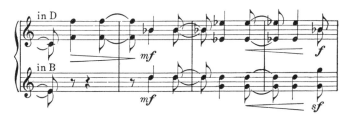

The substitution of the lower F's and E-flats for the higher ones is already shown in the quotation.

Bar 236 and following. Horns, trumpets and kettledrums play only *mf* here, and the *sf*'s may then be played correspondingly somewhat less sharply. In the third and fourth horns the *mezzoforte* already begins on the preceding upbeat (octave G). The second horn takes the lower E-flats during four bars. In bar 244, when the violins make their powerful leap from the low D to the high E, the first and second horns first come in *f* on the fourth quaver-beat (octave G) and then trumpets, kettledrums and the second pair of horns follow suit, also with a powerful *f*. In bars 249–252, whilst violas and basses are playing at full *f*, the following gradations are important:

The *sf*'s and ⊲'s cannot be played strongly enough; it is only by this means that the despairing beauty of this passage can be properly brought out.

The *più p* which follows in bar 254 has, in view of the later *pp*, probably the meaning of a gradual *diminuendo*, not of a sudden lowering of volume. The *p* of the second bassoon and the second flute can then be drawn into the general *dim.*, as there is no melodic ground for allowing these parts to be more prominent than the first ones.

Bars 259–269. The following gradation helps to render the *cantabile* more distinct:

The *cresc.* is then continually increased until, at the fifth semiquaver of bar 270, it becomes an almost hard *f*, which, with uncanny swiftness, vanishes again in the three following notes leading up to the *pp* of the next bar. The climbing of the basses up to the high A must produce an effect of distinct uneasiness.

Bars 275–282. A *poco espressivo* should be introduced in the first four bars for clarinet, oboe and flute, in the following four bars for violoncellos and contrabassos. The phrase in the first and second horns has a melodic value; it must therefore come slightly into evidence, like this:

The transposing of the D and E-flat in the second horn is justified, as it obviates the leap from the low G to the high D, which is incompatible with soft tone production. The final quavers sound better played in unison.

Then the little phrase in flute and oboe (in bars 282 and 283) comes like an answer to these quavers. With a slight change of accent it should be played thus:

The semiquaver figures which follow in the woodwinds begin *p*, just as the strings in the same bar, then make the *crescendo* with the strings and decrease again at the same time. At bar 287 the whole orchestra begins with a *pp*, which is introduced by the short *dim.* which precedes it. The second violins must come gently into relief in bars 287 and 288, the first violins in bars 289 and 290, flute and bassoon in bars 291 and 292 and oboe and clarinet in bars 293 and 294. The first three of these groups return immediately to the prevailing *pp* after they have finished their melodic phrase; first and second horn then come in also quite *pp*. The second trumpet takes the lower B-flat and D throughout.

With bar 295 begins a short but powerful *crescendo* which should on no account be allowed to acquire a character of false pathos through a *ritenuto*. In bar 298 the auxiliary woodwinds come in on the fifth semiquaver. The volume of sound must still be able to increase considerably in bar 300 in order to discharge itself in bar 301 in a crushing *ff*.

Bars 301–336. This gigantic passage presents a difficult problem for execution. It is evident from the notation that Beethoven intended a continuous *fortissimo* of the utmost strength. But if the passage is played thus, the only thing that can be distinctly heard is the roll of the kettledrums, if indeed a player of such excellence can be obtained that he can play for thirty-six bars without the slightest diminution of strength. If his strength gives way, however, the enormous effect (at least in dynamics) thus achieved in this passage is endangered, all the more so because some of the other players instinctively fall off with the kettledrums, while others, remembering the directions of the composer and the admonitions of the conductor, force the notes in a disagreeable manner, so that the last ten to fifteen bars are performed at a weak *mezzoforte*

interspersed with various shrieking sounds. Certainly that is not
what Beethoven intended. After various attempts to bring out the
overpowering meaning of this passage, I at last resolved upon a
radical change in the notation, acting upon my principle that clearness is the most important consideration. The new notation had the
effect of rendering all the details of the passage comprehensible
without affecting the general character of the piece, and the changes
were effected without any instrumental alterations other than
a few octave transpositions. And owing to the great increase in
clearness, I believe that the hearers scarcely ever realize that whole
groups of players are often playing *mf*, or even *p*. Indeed I think
that if both modes of execution, the literally correct and my own,
were heard immediately one after the other, in the latter case an
impression of even greater strength would be given than in the
former. At all events I invite all conductors to try the passage once
in the manner indicated here, and then to pass judgment not only
from the impression obtained at the podium, which is often deceptive on account of the nearness to the orchestra, but from the
impression produced on unprejudiced musicians among the
audience.

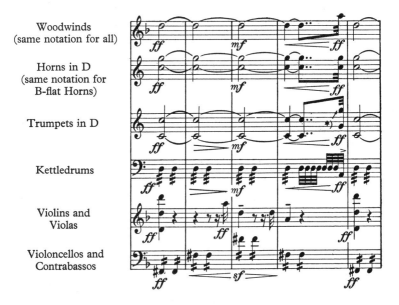

* *The notes marked by an ↗ are altered from the original.*

Violoncellos and Contrabassos as in the original.

One other question I would like to submit for examination; it concerns bar 310. Is there not a mistake of Beethoven's here, and should not the last demisemiquaver here be G, as it is in the preceding similar passages, and not C? The thematic progression AD is certainly just as important here as before. It is in fact actually executed by the flutes and the kettledrum, but it is almost inaudible if the trumpets, contrary to their previous mode of procedure, remain on the C (actual sound D). I have therefore no hesitation in correcting this demisemiquaver to

In the next two bars (beginning at bar 337) there comes at last the relief of a general *diminuendo*, and at the same time a moderate retardation of the original time, which is already somewhat heavy. We have a passing impression of peace during bars 338–344. I should like to insert a *tranquillo* here, and in my opinion the bars ought to be played with a very restful, I might almost say smiling expression, without becoming sentimental by any *crescendo* or other such gradation.

Bars 345–376. At the beginning of this section the conductor has an opportunity of gradually animating the time so that by about bar 359 the original time is reached again. The execution of the woodwinds is easier here (bars 345–348) than in the analogous passage (at bars 80–83) on account of the simultaneous transfer of the melody to oboe and bassoon. For the notes to be properly combined the flute must play its little phrase somewhat more emphatically than the oboe, which is rather prominent owing to the character of its sound. In the oboe part I think it is better for the two A's to be gently connected thus:

The notation for the strings is the same as in the first passage:

I understand the *crescendo* in bars 349 and 350 in a fairly lively sense, and have taken the liberty of somewhat increasing the

in the bassos, and playing the corresponding chord in the second violins (F-sharp A) *mf*. (Trumpets and kettledrums remain *p*.) At the marvellously painful entry of the D minor, however, bar 351, I placed *pp* everywhere and increased the *crescendo* which follows only to *p*, bringing it back to *pp* in the strings in bar 355. Important to my mind, too, was a perceptible weakening of the trumpets and kettledrums for which *pp* should be prescribed in this bar, also an alteration of the *espress.* prescribed for the small phrases of the woodwinds into

For bars 355–358 the same gradations (with corresponding modifications) hold good as for bars 88–91.

Bars 363 and 364. Wagner recommends here the omission of the *crescendo* (in the strings, first pair of horns, trumpets and kettle-drums), by which means the continuation of the theme in the clarinets (bar 364) is brought into relief. During the next two bars the clarinets with the remaining wind instruments, supported by the strings where the *crescendo* comes in at the upward figures, lead energetically up to the *forte*. In bars 365 and 367 the second and fourth horns take the lower F's.

Bars 369, 370, 373 and 374. Woodwinds should be doubled in these bars, just as in the similar passage at bars 102 and following.

Bars 375 and 376. Just as the strings in the corresponding passage (bars 108 and 109), so here the wind instruments should not begin too softly, and should pass over to the *pianissimo* which follows by means of a *diminuendo* in the second bar. The C in the trumpets should be marked *pp*.

Bar 398. In the similar passage at bar 129 the minor changes to major. Here, however, the minor remains. In order to bring out more clearly this striking modification I placed an *sf* over the first B-flat in the violins and clarinets (C), which is such a characteristic note for this passage, and another over the F in the violas and the E-flat (F) in the first horn.

Bars 401–406. Just as the flutes were doubled at bar 132, so here the oboes can be doubled for their characteristic leaps from the fourth quaver of the first bar onwards; the doubling is of course immediately removed at the entry of the *piano*, bar 407.

Bars 407–414. For these bars exactly the same may be said as for the similar passage, bars 138–145. I give in the following quotation the instrumental changes made by Wagner, which are absolutely essential for the clearness of the passage. The notes either changed or introduced by Wagner are in large type, as are also the signs in the notation which do not occur in the original.

Clarinets and bassoons as well as flutes and oboes are furnished with < > and <. The *pp* in the third and fourth horns is introduced just as in the similar preceding passage. The second horn plays the lower notes throughout, thus:

Bar 415. The woodwinds come in here already doubled, as the expression is more intense than in the previous corresponding passage. It is well known that Beethoven never wrote above the

high A for the orchestral violins. The meaning of the violin passage in the next bar which comes in so characteristically with painful sharpness is, however, evidently as follows:

I had no hesitation therefore in letting the violins play in the manner indicated, and first placing the second violins an octave higher and then changing the

into

in bar 418.

Bar 427 and following. The doubling of the woodwinds comes to an end here. The execution of the following magnificent passage, in which there is some danger of the most important woodwind parts being overpowered by the strings, needs a very careful notation, which I will give in the quotation on pages 198–201. A D is entered at the most suitable place for the doubling to commence in the parts to which the melody is entrusted.

From bar 448 the whole orchestra swells to *ff* in a powerful gradation, and when the *ff* is reached the remaining woodwinds are reinforced just as the second clarinet has been already for the last three notes. In bar 451 the first flute (doubled) takes the B-flat and the A in the higher octave.

In bar 457 the doubling of the woodwinds ceases. Continuing his remarks on this symphony, Wagner says in regard to this passage: "Here too, on account of the dynamic disproportion of the instrumental organization, at the new return of the similar passage in bar 457 the first two bars must be played entirely *piano*, the two following with a strong *crescendo* by the winds, and with a weaker

1st Flute

1st Clarinet

1st Bassoon

1st Violins

2nd Violins*

* *Notation for the violas the same.*

* From the beginning of the general crescendo *here, prescribed* < >'s *are executed with constantly increasing energy.*

one by the strings, which should only receive a decisive increase of strength in the last two bars before the *forte*."

Bars 463 and 464. The second horn plays the lower F's.

Bars 469–476. An ideal execution of this horn solo demands a somewhat more moderate speed than that of the preceding bars, and this must be maintained if the strings, henceforth in a minor key, take over the theme (bar 477); the *crescendo* which follows this entry must be given with strong dynamic gradation but without increasing the speed. I do not think any bad effect is produced here if the woodwind figures at the *ff* are swallowed up by the strings and only become audible again at the *diminuendo*; in fact, I have generally found that just this reappearance on the scene produces quite a magic effect on me. If a conductor wishes to avoid this disappearance of the woodwinds, they can play doubled when the strings become loudest.

Bar 468. The second trumpet takes the lower D's.

Bars 485 and 486. The second horn takes the lower F's and D's.

Bars 506 and 510. It need hardly be mentioned that the *ritardandi* refer only to the half bars as before. At the second *a tempo* the moderate original time of the beginning ($\quad$ = 76 or thereabouts) comes in again and remains till the end of the movement without further change. The auxiliary woodwinds come in with the best result at the *più f* at bar 527. In bars 533 and 534 the second horn plays the lower octave. A *quasi ritenuto pomposo* in the final bars seems to me ill advised. Shortly, resolutely and energetically the great man speaks his last word: Rather break than bend.

Second Movement

Bar 1. The metronome mark ♩. = 116 is extremely quick, but does not render the execution impossible. It is quite out of the question, however, to play the Trio (bar 412) at the rate ○ = 116, as a simple experiment with the metronome will soon prove. There must be either a mistake or a misprint here. ♩ = 116 would be more comprehensible, but viewing this both independently and with regard to the beginning, I doubt if this either is the right mark. Beethoven denotes an increase of speed by his indications *molto vivace—stringendo il tempo—presto*, and I therefore consider that former customary mode of performing the Trio at a comfortable speed is utterly wrong. It is true that it was not played quite so comfortably everywhere as in the opera house at Berlin, where, when I took over the concerts, I found the *presto* crossed out, and *adagio* inserted in its place; but even Bülow used to take it pretty slowly, and Porges tells us that Wagner took the *presto* to refer strictly only to the first two bars, the octave leaps, and recommended an "easy and comfortable" (*behäbig-behaglich*) time for what followed. But there is no reason for this. In Beethoven's manuscript we find the original notation

altered in such a way that each pair of bars is bracketed together in his own hand and the direction is given to make them "whole bars." Besides this we find the word "*prestissimo*" distinctly written in pencil in addition to the *presto*. Evidently, therefore, a very quick time is intended—not such as would be given by ○ = 116, however, as this passes the limits of possibility altogether.

If I try again here to put down in words and numbers that instinctive musical feeling which has always been my principal guide as to the tempo conditions of this Trio, I come to the following result, which will serve to supplement and correct a former attempt of mine made in the *Allgemeine Musikzeitung* for the year 1901.

I began the Scherzo at about $\downarrow$. = 108–112. After the *stringendo*, I took the Presto in such a way that a half bar of this Presto corresponded to a whole bar of the 3/4 time, which was already somewhat quickened by the *stringendo*. I conducted the first two bars of the Presto in two beats for the sake of greater precision, so that each beat was equal in value to the immediately preceding 3/4 bar (about $\downarrow$ = 138). Then I began marking each bar by one beat only; this would answer to the metronome mark $\circ$ = 80. But by this time a crotchet-beat of this Presto was about equal in value to a crotchet-beat of the 3/4 time as it was taken at the beginning of the movement.

I have taken up this question, which seems to me so important for the understanding of the movement, before going on to the elucidation of various smaller points.

Bar 6. The woodwinds play this bar doubled but of course immediately after become single again.

Bar 57. The doubling comes in again here and ceases at bar 77.

Bars 93–109. For this passage I give the alterations suggested by Wagner; we learn from what both he and Porges have written, that these alterations were never actually tried. They are designed to render the theme with its peculiar characteristics audible in the winds without having to mute the strings, a procedure which Wagner had already recognised to be a very inadequate makeshift.

If Wagner himself heard this improvement, he would surely have noticed that the horns in D, as he has notated them, produce a false upper voice to a certain extent in bars 1–4 and 9–12. I suggest correcting the horns in D as follows:

Bars 1–4:

Bars 9–12:

In this way the leading melody stands out with fullest clarity.

The woodwinds are of course doubled here. The doubling stops at bar 117. Two bars before this the second horn takes the lower F's.

Bars 127–138. The woodwinds play doubled here. The second and fourth horns play the lower D, F and G throughout.

Bar 150. I recommend the repetition of the small first part, but not of the long second part, so that the ⌐1⌐ at bar 388 can be omitted. If the first part too is played only once, the themes announced here seem to me to flit past too quickly, and this gives a feeling of unrest to the whole movement.

Bars 172–176. The woodwinds should be doubled.

Bars 272–296. The woodwinds play doubled. In bars 276 and 280 the violins and violas play

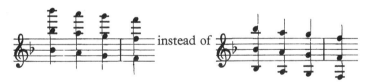

instead of

and the first flute takes the high B-flats both in these bars and in bar 285.

Bars 330–346. Still following Wagner's suggestions, I have altered this passage in the same way as the previous one in C major. In the original the trumpets are brought in here in such a way that, as Wagner rightly remarks, "unfortunately here too they only hide the theme of the wind instruments." He found that, at a performance of this symphony, he was obliged to recommend "a meaningless moderation" (*charakterlose Mäßigung*) to these instruments. In accordance with the view already stated, that if any remedy of an evil be attempted, a thorough cure should be aimed at, I resolved to follow Wagner's instigation and let the trumpets strengthen the theme. The players need now no longer play with meaningless moderation, but with characteristic strength. The woodwinds are of course doubled from the entry of the theme to the *p* in bar 354. In bar 335 the flutes play

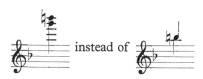

and in bar 343

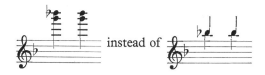

In bar 348 the first flute takes the high B-flat. Other alterations in this passage are as follows:

Bar 356. The second horn takes the lower F. In the passages immediately following, the interval of the seventh in this instrument is characteristic and should be retained.

Bars 364–375. The woodwinds play these bars doubled.

Bar 395. According to Porges, Wagner did not sustain the *fermata* here but broke the note off quite shortly. We have no reason to doubt the trustworthiness of this assertion, but I fail to see any reason for this arbitrary proceeding. My own method of procedure has been to hold on the *fermata* and to go straight on without introducing any pause whatsoever.

Bars 412 and 413. The first two bars of the Presto are played by the doubled woodwinds.

Bars 454–474. The execution of the oboe solo is by no means easy. Freedom of expression must be combined with rhythmical precision. If the time is too quick the passage is not likely to be well rendered and yet, on the other hand, if the time is too slow this tenderly woven, beautiful succession of notes becomes a mere study. I have always waited to see first whether the oboe player himself had not sufficient good taste and skill to hit upon the right expression, in which case I accompanied rather than conducted the passage. My work of training only began when the performer proved himself to be clumsy and helpless. It is very important that the player should manage the breathing properly and have time to take breath. While the slurs last over eight notes a breath can be taken after each. Starting from the *crescendo* (bar 466), which should be begun by all the wind instruments on the second half of the bar, the oboist should not breathe again until immediately before the *p*, bar 471, and he should then take the rest of the phrase until the *fp* in bar 475 in one breath. It is very important that he should arrange his tone production and breathing in such a way that he can execute the *crescendo* with a uniform gradation up to the very last note, and need not be obliged to hurry or make an inopportune *diminuendo* on account of lack of breath. A moment's interruption may easily ruin the whole passage.

Bülow corrected the C of the second bassoon in bar 470, together with the half note to which it is tied, into B, but this correction should be abandoned without hesitation. "Chromatic pettiness instead of diatonic grandeur," is what he would probably have said had anyone else dared to make this insipid correction. See his edition of Beethoven's Sonata Op. 106, first movement, the return of the first subject.

Bar 491. From the $\boxed{2}$ onwards, even in the *p*, the woodwinds can play doubled, and remain so until the *sempre più p* in bar 523.

Bar 523. I should recommend that the execution become gradually more restful starting from the *sempre più p*. At this point I always began to conduct in two beats again. I sustained the *fermata* for a considerable length of time in strictest *pp*, did not then wave it off, however, but allowed it to be terminated very suddenly, and with savage force, by the return of the main theme. I have never performed this passage without observing a movement in the audience which sometimes even culminated in a spontaneous burst of applause, fortunately of short duration. If the *fermata* is waved off the effect of this return is far less "demoniac."

Wagner, as Porges tells us, took the repetition of the main section at a somewhat quicker speed than at its first appearance, and I have adopted this method of execution with full conviction. For the rest, the repetition corresponds in all points to the main section itself.

I consider that a quite small *fermata* on the general rest in bar 556 is indispensable. The last three bars are played with the greatest energy (the woodwinds doubled) and as quickly as a clear and, at the same time, powerful execution will allow.

Third Movement

Bar 1. This finest and deepest of all slow symphonic movements is marked Adagio molto e cantabile. The metronome mark ♩ = 60 is too quick; ♩ = 63 also seems too quick for the Andante moderato which follows. But one thing seems to me clear from this notation, namely that Beethoven intended only a gentle increase of speed in the 3/4 time. Wagner says somewhere that he was perhaps the first conductor to take the beginning of this movement really *adagio*, and thus succeed in emphasizing the difference between *adagio* and *andante*. This announcement was enough to make conductors of the younger school introduce the modern Bayreuth dragging *Parsifal* time into this Adagio, taking the beginning so slowly that the melody became quite unintelligible, but playing the Andante moderato *quasi allegretto* in order to preserve the "difference." I have elsewhere put a distinct veto on all such exaggerations and need only mention here that I consider ♩ = 48–50 to be about the right metronome mark for the beginning, to which ♩ = 54–56 corresponds as a gentle increase for the Andante.

The treatment of the orchestra is so wonderful in this movement, and the use of the horns, which is not generally Beethoven's strongest point, so magnificent, that I almost shrink from adding anything whatsoever to the notation. I only do it with the express request that any alteration which I have introduced may be executed with the utmost care and caution.

Bars 33–42. The part in the first violins, which hovers over the principal melody in a divinely restful manner, must be executed even more tenderly than the melody itself. The *crescendi* which occur in this part must therefore be correspondingly less distinct than in the melody. Porges tells us that Wagner did not sustain the *fermata* on the E-flat at the end of the whole passage. This seems to me to be going too far, although I think a slight retardation of the time before the *fermata*, perhaps in the last two bars, is quite justifiable.

Bar 43. The variation of the main theme which begins here should be conducted in quaver-beats, at least at the beginning and partially later on also. I should therefore propose ♪ = 84–88 as metronome mark. I now give some suggestions as to notation for the first violins which I have recommended to my own players, but destined, as I have said before, only for very discreet execution.

Bar 45:

Bars 49 and 50:

Bar 53:

Bar 58:

Bars 63–64. Here too a slight holding back of the time during these two bars, and especially just before the wonderful modulation into G major (last crotchet-beat), may be recommended. If the first clarinet be a player of outstanding musical talent and artistic feeling he will gradate the last bar before the 3/4 time thus:

and he will thus be able to introduce the new theme.

Bars 65–79. I should recommend a *pp* for the violins and violas throughout this passage and the omission of the *crescendo* everywhere. These pure phrases are so full of expression that they are quite sufficient in themselves without extraneous aid, whereas the *crescendi* tend to destroy the effect of the principal melody in the wind instruments, especially if they are executed with even a little too much energy. In the third and fourth bars the flute, which is written unmelodically with good reason, might both become less prominent and at the same time bring out with greater expression its part, which passes so beautifully into the melodic leading, by means of the following gradation:

The same method of procedure holds good for bars 75 and 76, where the four quavers on C and the B in the flute should also be played *pp*, so as not to take the attention away from the melody, which is here suddenly entrusted to the first oboe alone.

Bar 83 and following. I think we may take the time just a very little quicker here than at the beginning of the movement. The justification for this change lies in the absence of the "molto" after the word "Adagio" and in the transparent character of this whole passage, which is rendered particularly lucid by the employment of the *pizzicati*, especially where these pass over into the triplets. At the same time there must be a slackening of the tempo compared with the previous 3/4 time. The fluctuations of sensation are so delicate here that they can scarcely be expressed in words.

In this whole symphony Beethoven has made use of the stopped note

for the horns more frequently than in any of his earlier orchestral works. But here the free and constantly repeated use of several stopped notes is especially striking. I think we see here an influence of the wonderfully skilful treatment of the natural horns in Weber's *Freischütz*, which Beethoven knew and esteemed very highly. But in any case it is strange that he should have entrusted this extremely difficult and exposed solo precisely to the fourth horn. I admit that in the Kaim orchestra at Munich I once had a fourth horn player— Herr Stange—who gave this passage excellently, but he was certainly an exception. As a general rule it will be safer to assign the passage which follows, from the entry of the 𝄢 onwards, to the third or first horn player, according to their respective merit.

I should recommend a very delicate execution of the following gradation with a view to obtaining a more animated rendering:

* *This slur to the previous G is evidently wanting.*
** *This < > is made also by both clarinets*, not *however by the flute, together with the horn.*

The cadenza in bar 96 should be executed as restfully as possible, *quasi portamento*. If the player's breath will not hold out for the whole passage, he may take a breath, as imperceptibly as possible, after the first high A-flat.

In the bar before the entry of the 12/8 time a very moderate *ritenuto* may be introduced in order to supplement the *crescendo*. I have marked the last crotchet (B-flat major) *f*, but the *p dolce* prescribed on the first crotchet of the next bar must follow immediately without any preparatory *diminuendo*.

In view of the *lo stesso tempo* and the stirring element in the violin figurations, I decided not to return altogether to the very slow original time, but to take this whole long variation at a somewhat more flowing speed, as compared with the principal time, not losing sight, however, of its *adagio* character. It should be specially noted also that the melody lies almost continuously in the wind instruments and that consequently the violin figurations, however finely they must be executed, really only form the accompaniment, or shall we say the arabesque, with relation to the wind instruments, which carry the melody. I would not mention that the conducting should be done in four and not in twelve beats here had I not been told of occasions on which this uncalled-for piece of dilettantism had really occurred.

A few shades of expression which I have introduced for a careful execution will be found in the following quotations.

Bars 104–106:

1st Fl. 1st Ob. 1st Bassoon

1st Viol.

Bars 108 and 109:

1st Viol.

Bar 111. The *crescendo* in the solo horn, the small *diminuendo* on the G and the following *crescendo* must be given very expressively and with true artistic freedom. The deep notes need not be forced in spite of the *crescendo*. The high E which follows the low C of the next bar must be begun *p* again.

Bar 112. The first violins begin *p* again at the low G and make a uniform gradual *crescendo* up to the beginning of the next bar, where the $>$ comes in.

Bars 114–116:

Winds and
Kettledrums

1st Violins
and Strings

Bars 121 and 122. The second horn takes the lower F's just as it does in bars 131 and 132.

Bar 124. The transitional character of the *pizzicato* in the violon-cellos and contrabasses justifies a somewhat stronger entry of the higher E-flat, followed by a gradual weakening until the F is reached.

Bars 125–130:

Bars 133–136. The rhythm in the second violins is to a certain extent an echo of that in the trumpets; it should therefore be played distinctly in spite of the *pp*.

Bar 138. The melodic curve demands a short *ritenuto* on the second half of this bar; this is followed by the *a tempo* at the beginning of the next bar.

Bars 140–144:

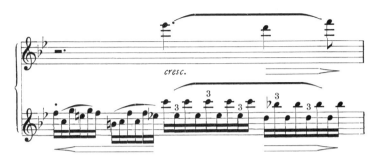

In the first bar the B-flat horns join with the first violins in the
$<\ >$; in the second they play *piano* just like the rest of the strings
during the first two bars. The *crescendo* beginning in bar 142 must
be very gently and gradually executed by all the instruments
except those which have a special marking.

Bar 151. This descending violin figuration absolutely demands a
restful execution in the most uniform *diminuendo*. It seems to me to
indicate a return to the very slow first time which dominates the
ethereally beautiful close. Therefore, from the last crotchet of the
preceding bar I marked the quaver-beats—without really altering
the time, of course—and continued to do so till the end, with the
exception of a few passages which every conductor of fine feeling
will find out for himself.

Fourth Movement

Bar 1. This beginning of the last movement is not merely an
introduction. It is a wild disturbance of the peaceful, unworldly
atmosphere which pervades the Adagio. The eminently dramatic
character of this beginning never seemed to me to produce its
genuine crushing effect when a long pause immediately followed the
Adagio, this pause interrupted by applause and possibly by the
appearance of the soloists, or even of the chorus, on the stage. After I
had often conducted the Ninth Symphony and always suffered
under this unfavourable impression, I resolved to let the last
movement follow immediately upon the Adagio. I only made a quite
short pause after the last chord and guarded against any movement
of applause by keeping my baton raised; I then let the "frightening
fanfare" (*Schreckensfanfare*) of the last moment, as Wagner rightly
calls it, break forth with fearful power.

In order to accomplish this it was necessary of course for all the vocal forces concerned to be ready in their places. In general, I cannot point out too emphatically what a horrible effect is produced when the chorus does not come on till after the Adagio. The long pause, the sudden unrest, the stamping to and fro, the search for chairs and scores, the chattering in the audience, the signs of the ladies when they recognize a friend on the podium or in the hall, the soloists bowing and smiling in answer to the applause, the two lady soloists trying to make room for their trains; all this together is such an unworthy interruption of this holy work that I cannot understand the matter-of-fact way in which it has come to be looked on as part of the performance of the Ninth Symphony and the surprise with which any attempt to improve matters is greeted.

I demand unconditionally that the chorus should all be in their places at the beginning of the performance and should wait quietly until they rise to sing. I request the soloists to do the same but admit the possibility of an exception here. The solo passages in the Ninth Symphony, however short they may be, are very dangerous and not only make high demands on the skill of the singers but also require a perfectly unhampered control of the voice. I have come across singers who willingly acceded to my request that they take their places in front of the orchestra before the beginning of the symphony. Some have even offered to do so in order to hear the performance. Others, however, assured me that although they recognized the justness of my request, they could not fall in with it because their throats became absolutely dry after sitting for almost an hour in a hot room without singing. As this was quite a reasonable objection, I was obliged to give way in such cases, especially if I noticed that the singers in question were in an only too natural anxiety as to the success of their performance, or were perhaps slightly indisposed. Certainly the later arrival of a singer is a lesser evil than the failure of a solo passage. But then I always insisted that the solists should come in after the Scherzo, and not after the Adagio, which was followed immediately by the last movement. The four artists should be urged to come in as quietly and unnoticeably as possible, and the ladies should be specially requested to leave behind in the dressing room the large bouquets which they generally receive, however beautiful these may be. If it is possible, however— and with good will it is generally possible—it is much better for the soloists to be already in their places at the beginning of the whole symphony.

As to the arrangement of the chorus, it should be remembered that the Ninth Symphony is essentially an orchestral composition. The effect of the instrumental part, which is far larger, is sacrificed if the chorus is brought forward in an overwhelming majority and the orchestra placed behind, as in an oratorio. The orchestra must as far as possible take its accustomed place and be surrounded by the chorus in a broad semicircle. The podium must rise in the form of a terrace. If it is very wide it can be arranged thus:

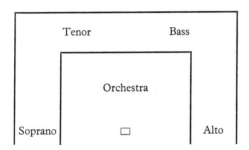

If, however, it is long and narrow, so that with the above arrangement the greater part of the orchestra would be pushed too far back, it is advisable to fill all the front with the violins, and, if possible, with some of the viola and violoncello desks, and then to let the chorus take its place behind on a distinctly raised platform.

Wagner was conscious that the effect of the two *Schreckensfanfaren* did not correspond to the impression obtained on reading the score. He tried to obviate this by letting the trumpets play partly in unison with the woodwind figuration.* Much is gained by this, it is true, but it still leaves something to be desired. In the first fanfare Wagner leaves the original untouched from the fifth bar onwards. The trumpets and the four horns thus unite on the D with full force, but they completely drown the woodwinds, to which the melodically and harmonically important notes are entrusted, so that these, even if doubled, only give a little chirping sound as against the crashing brass notes. In the second fanfare (bars 17–24) Wagner lets the trumpets play in unison melodically to the end, it is true. As, however, in the last bars the horns are silent except for a few isolated notes, only the upper part strengthened by the trumpets

---

* In Wagner's *Literary Works*, vol. IX, p. 242, both passages are incorrectly quoted, with the omission of a bar in each.

is heard, and no harmony. Acting again on my oft-repeated principle that an alteration is only of use when it is thorough and goes to the root of the matter, I extended Wagner's changes in the trumpet parts by letting these instruments accompany the melodic upper part to the end in the first fanfare. Then I brought the horns to the support of the harmony, and this gave the true meaning to the strengthening of the treble by the trumpets.

I also tried to prevent the infinitely important, despairing B-flat of the first chord from being too much hidden by the A of the united horns and trumpets. Reasons of style would not allow me to correct the G of the trumpets into A-flat, as I consider this entry on the dominant to be a necessary counterpart to the later entry on the tonic in the second fanfare; I therefore solved the difficulty by letting the clarinets play the beginning an octave higher. In the same way I succeeded in giving a sharper prominence to the E-flat at the beginning of the second fanfare too; in the lower octave it is already given with sufficient strength by the third horn. Lastly, by analogy to the second passage, I also corrected the unimportant harmonic notes of the first flute into melodic notes in the fifth and sixth bars of the first passage.

In what follows I combine Wagner's alterations and my own, and I ask all those who consider it sacrilege to interfere with Beethoven's instrumentation whether it is not allowable, or indeed whether it is not a duty, to assist in rendering truly effectual such a powerful intention of the Master, when it is clear that the means of thus producing the complete effect were not at his disposal. I think it is unnecessary to add trombones, for instance, as Beethoven was quite free to do so himself; but he wished to reserve the effect of these instruments for a later passage. Any one who has felt deeply the magnificence of the entry of these instruments at the passage "Seid umschlungen, Millionen," will not wish for their entry at an earlier point in the piece.

The object here, then, has been to apply those instruments which Beethoven chose to use to the working out of his intention, with all the advantages which a more advanced technique has given us, but in a way that Beethoven could not do it simply because of these technical difficulties. And I ask, is it better to hide the spirit of the composer behind the dead letter, or to unveil it freely for the comprehension of the hearer?

First fanfare:
Bars 5 and 6:

1st Flute

Bar 1:

1st and 2nd Clarinet

Bars 3–7:

3rd and 4th
Horn in B-flat

Bars 2–7:

Trumpets
in D

Wagner

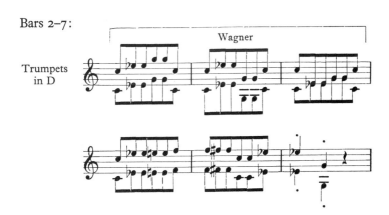

Second fanfare:
Bar 17:

2nd Oboe

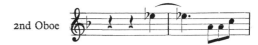

Bar 17:

2nd Clarinet

Bars 21–24:

1st and 2nd
Horn in D

Bars 21–24:

3rd and 4th
Horn in B-flat

Bars 18–24:

Trumpets in D
(Wagner)

The woodwind section is of course doubled in both passages. One contrabassoon is enough. The doubling comes to an end at the *allegro ma non troppo* in bar 30.

The metronome mark ♩. = 96 is too fast for the bass recitative, although not for the fanfares. Whereas the best time for these latter will be the quickest which is compatible with a continuous *fortissimo*, the first two recitatives must be played above all with great energy, with no false pathos and in quick time, but must come in rather more moderately than the fanfares. I therefore adopt the metronome mark ♩ = 168.

The expression of this recitative must be felt; it cannot be explained. I have given up any attempt at a notation and procured the mode of execution I desired partly by singing it aloud, partly by transmitting my will directly to the players. I will therefore confine myself here to a few hints for the execution.

The first two recitatives (bars 8–29) should be in somewhat moderated, but still quick time without any retardation.

At the entry of the *allegro ma non troppo*, the time of the beginning of the first movement, perhaps ♩ = 76. Softest *pianissimo*.

In the third recitative (bar 38) I think a conflict begins between the fearful impetuosity of the beginning and more irresolute, hesitating emotions. I will try to give my impressions.

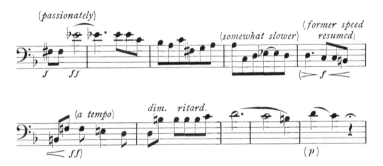

The notes of the Scherzo (*vivace*, bar 48) are merely touched in passing. The time must be correspondingly quick, and a general *p* must be observed.

Wagner has indicated very beautifully the meaning of the F C which follows in the basses, by writing underneath the two words "Nicht doch!" ("No!")—No more looking back, no more deceitful memories!—Forward, with a heart for any fate!—The pause before the *tempo I.* should be quite short. The noble, manly resolution of this recitative justifies a somewhat more restful, although still animated time. I should say about ♩ = 144. The conductor must decide whether the *diminuendo* at the end should be combined with a slight *ritardando*. Some notes of the Adagio are softly sounded. As it is only a short reminder which brings the charm once again before our souls, I should recommend that the time be slightly quicker here than at the beginning of the third movement.

For the following *allegro* I think ♩ = 126 gives the right time. We turn aside, seeking a fresh path, as it were. Is there to be another battle? An increase of speed at the *crescendo* and a quickened, very energetic execution of the notes marked *ff* produces a splendid effect. The winds come in more peacefully. With a view to the melodic and not merely modulatory meaning of the second oboe part, I have ventured on the following mode of execution

It is better to let the first horn come in alone on the D and not bring in the second until the next bar.

Guided by the improvising character of this whole part, I did not give the first appearance of the "joy" melody in full tempo. Without pausing after the preceding *ritenuto*, I began the *allegro assai* at bar 77 somewhat more slowly and made no increase in speed until the third and fourth bars; then I led up to the *f* which follows by means of a spirited *crescendo*.

The *allegro* of the *tempo I.* should be joyously animated (perhaps ♩ = 132). The fifth bar, the rise to the F-sharp, should be executed with a very broad bowing, and should sound like a sigh of relief. If a moderate, but decided *ritenuto* from the G (bar 88) onwards is justifiable, the two chords (bar 91) should not be played solemnly, as though they came after a church recitative, but joyfully and in smart *allegro* time.

After a very short pause the orchestra proceeds again.

I substituted ♩ = 72 or so for the ♩ = 80 as metronome mark for the "joy" melody. I know there are time-beating school-

masters who conduct in comfortable crotchet-beats here, but I
only mention it as a proof that there is not a piece of stupidity in the
practice of any art which is not committed somewhere. All the
crescendi (bars 103 and 111 and the following) should be only very
moderately given. The whole passage bears a character of great
tenderness, especially the coming in of the violins at bar 139.
At bar 156 begins a very warm *crescendo* which lasts for eight bars,
and at the *ff* all instruments (the woodwinds doubled) come in with
exuberant force. The B-flat horns, which rest in the original, can
strengthen the D horns up to the fourth crotchet-beat of bar
187.

Bar 116. In the manuscript at this point there is a pencil indication
in Beethoven's hand: "2 do Fag col Basso." This means that from
this bar onwards the second bassoon is to take over the bass voice of
the cellos, which ends here, and apparently is to double the contrabassos in the higher octave up to bar 164. This later correction
produces a very beautiful effect.

Bars 193–198. This passage cannot be clearly rendered without
doubled woodwinds. In the whole preceding *tutti* the melody
moves exclusively in natural notes, and therefore horns and
trumpets play with the woodwinds. But that must cease here on
account of the modulation. Horns and trumpets now play only a
few harmonic notes, whereas the melody is entrusted entirely to
the first woodwind instruments and disappears as completely for
the hearer as if the earth had swallowed it up. An attempt to let the
brass instruments also play the melody seemed to me too crude a
makeshift, and the same objection prevented me from reinforcing
the horns to any further extent. So I had each first part of the woodwinds played by three players, the second parts, on the other hand,
by one only. This caused a sudden ray of light to fall into this
passage of such apparent confusion. I must confess, however, that if
no extra woodwinds are available, I know no way of rendering
this passage clearly and at the same time preserving its true
character. I hope that some other will discover the means, or that,
still better, a time may come when the Ninth Symphony will no
longer be performed by small orchestras at all. From bar 199 the
ordinary doubling in all parts is resumed.

Bar 200. The second trumpet takes the lower D's.

Bar 203. From here to the entry of the *presto*, the woodwind doubling ceases. It is advisable to beat crotchets at the *poco ritenente* and to continue to do so at the *tempo I* also, in order to be sure of absolute precision in the *tremolo* entry of the kettledrum (bar 207).

Bar 208. In the B-flat horns and trumpets the same changes are made as in the first fanfare at the beginning of the last movement. First oboe and first clarinet begin an octave higher for the reasons mentioned above.

1st Oboe and
1st Clarinet

The time should be as quick as possible here. Woodwinds are of course doubled.

At this *presto* the baritone and the whole chorus rise; the chorus remains standing till the end. Individual members should not take their seats again on account of the disturbance which this creates. As to the soloists, the tenor, alto and soprano stand up after the last words of the recitative ("freudenvollere"). Soprano, alto and bass take their seats at the beginning of the *allegro assai vivace*, bar 331, the tenor at the end of his solo, bar 431. All four soloists stand up at the *allegro ma non tanto*, bar 763, and remain standing to the end. This attention to details should not be considered either trivial or small-minded. Everything is of importance in the execution of a great work of art, and it will be found in the end that time has not been wasted which has been spent on removing everything which would tend in any way to destroy the artistic impression of the whole. And it is just these details, apparently so trivial and superficial, which have this disastrous effect.

Bar 216. The baritone should sing his recitative as an energetic and enthusiastic summons with dramatic expression, as if he wished to control a raging multitude. Wagner demanded a tone of "noble indignation" (*edle Entrüstung*). The singer should begin almost immediately after the orchestra chords, i.e. not later than is shown by the rests. Excellent singers have sometimes found it possible by means of diligent study to sing the last six bars of this solo, "und freudenvollere," in one breath. If this is absolutely impossible I should recommend the following division.

und   freu - - - - - - - - -

- - den; freu - den -vol - le - re.

★ *In this case it is better to bind the two C's together.*

I cannot go further without mentioning the great singer Franz
Betz. He had often sung this solo in Berlin when I was conducting,
and had always bemoaned the fact that he could not manage this
passage in one breath. For this reason he asked me not to count on
him any more for the Ninth Symphony. One day when he was nearly
sixty years old, he came to me beaming with joy and said: "I have
practised it and studied it, and I can do it in one breath now. Let
me sing it just once more." At the next performance he sang it once
again—for the last time—in a simply wonderful manner, and did
actually perform this phrase in one breath.

It would be well for all young artists to take example from the
zeal which fired this excellent man.

Bar 237. From the entry of the *allegro assai* the reinforcement of
the woodwinds comes to an end.

There is no known reason why Wagner suggested singing

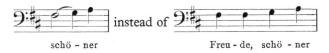

schö - ner   Freu - de, schö - ner

in the baritone solo. He does not give any reason for the change
himself. Alterations are only justified if they spring from a pressing
need, and not if they are based on a difference of opinion.

Bars 312–330. The woodwind section is doubled. The last bar,
the terrific modulation into F major on the word "Gott," should be
sustained for a considerable time and with the greatest force. The
kettledrum rolls *ff* for a short time and then, as though in death

shudders at the approach of the Almighty, makes a *diminuendo* to *p*, so that the *ff* of all the other instruments remains as a simple chord without the thundering of the drums. This direction of Beethoven's is often overlooked.

Bar 331. ♩. = 84 seems rather slow for an *allegro assai vivace* in 6/8 time. I have therefore adopted ♩. = 96. The woodwind section plays single again here. The beginning must be played with the softest sound possible and the *crescendo* which follows should be made very gradually. The auxiliary woodwinds come in *p* at first on the third quaver in bar 415, then help to increase the volume of sound until the full *fortissimo* is reached in bar 423. There are few such splendid climaxes as this. From the entry of the fugato, bar 431, I took the time somewhat quicker, about ♩. = 104. The orchestra must be warned never to slacken in strength in the least from here to bar 525. Each individual player should put forth all his energy in order to give with just as much force as the beginning and whole course of the fugato the F-sharps (bars 517–525), which rear up magnificently over two octaves. Following are some small clarifications: In bars 467 and 468, the flutes can be supported by the piccolo up to the first note of bar 469. From bar 480 to bar 485, first note, the second flute should play along with the first. In bars 495–498, the piccolo should play the first violin part in the higher octave; in bar 498, the second quaver in the flutes then becomes B instead of A.

Bars 425–427. The fourth horn plays the lower F's.
Bars 438–440. The fourth horn plays the lower D's and C's.
Bars 458 and 459. The fourth horn plays the lower D's.
Bar 472. The fourth horn plays the lower F.
Bar 510. The second horn plays the lower D.
Bars 514–516. The second horn plays the lower F's and D's.

Bar 525 and following bars. A gradual moderation of speed may set in here. Clarinets and bassoons naturally play the small phrases which follow without reinforcement. In bars 541 and 542 the time may be retarded still more with a simultaneous *crescendo*. At the entry of the *ff* the incomparable tension ends in a jubilating *allegro*, which in my opinion should not be taken quite so quickly as the preceding fugato, perhaps ♩. = 96–100. The woodwinds play doubled again. During the *piano* passage which precedes, the chorus should pay undivided attention to the conductor, and he for his part should keep the chorus under his eye, so that the long rest may not give opportunity for any distraction and the wonderful entry may be made with unanimous strength and precision.

Bars 563, 565, 579 and 581. The second trumpet takes the lower D's.

Bars 595 and 627. The respective metronome marks ♩ = 72 and ♩ = 60 give a satisfactory time, but it should not be allowed to drag. At the *p* in the bar before *adagio ma non troppo, ma divoto* the doubling of the woodwinds stops. Nothing can be said as to the execution of this glorious passage because words would fail to express anything. Here everything must be guided by feeling.

Bar 654. The gradually dying *fermata* should be waved off in order to give the alto singers time to take breath. But the pause thus made must be quite a short one.

Bar 655. Here the doubling of the woodwinds begins again. The metronome mark ♩. = 84 is good. The *sempre ben marcato* shows sufficiently clearly that the time is not to be taken too quickly, but this does not prevent an increase of speed in the course of the fugue. It is difficult to understand why Beethoven did not strengthen the very first note by means of the alto trombone and did not bring in this instrument until the C-sharp both here and in bar 694, where there is not even the support of the trumpet. If a good first trombone player, sure of his high notes, can be obtained, I see no reason why the first trombone should not play

in both passages. It is quite allowable too to insert melodic notes in one or two passages both for horns and trumpets, as they are certainly only omitted because they were either bad or altogether missing on the instruments of that time. The passages are:

Bar 655, upbeat, to bar 661:

2nd Trumpet

Bars 662–664:

1st and 2nd Horns

Bars 678–684:

1st Trumpet

Bars 704–708:

Trumpet

Bars 718–726. When the high A of the sopranos, which lasts for eight bars in fullest *fortissimo*, is reached, I should recommend that those singers be allowed to take breath and begin the note afresh, each when she needs to, only not at the end of a bar or on a strong beat; otherwise all will be taking breath at the same points and a series of notes will arise instead of one continuous sound. I do not remember which chorus director it was that gave me this advice, but I have always followed it with advantage.

Bar 730. Doubling of the woodwinds ceases.

Bar 758. This bar contains a still unsolved riddle, namely, the clashing of the C-sharp and the C on the first crotchet, while it is impossible to point out a mistake in any one of the parts. The melodic writing is clear. One might be led to think that the natural in the violas had been wrongly placed at the second note instead of the first. But the progression of the alto voice part would go against this, for it is perfectly natural, whereas

woh - nen,   ein____

seems to me strained. Is this anticipation of the C in the melody one of the bold anticipations which are by no means rare in Beethoven's later works? Or are we to assume a piece of carelessness on the part of the composer? I have had this passage executed as it stands, but I must confess that, in spite of all reasons to the contrary, the ear is unpleasantly struck. I therefore should not blame any one for making the corresponding corrections in the alto voice and the violas.

Bars 759–762. The second horn takes the lower F's.

Bar 763. The metronome mark ♩ = 120 gives not an *allegro non tanto*, but a *vivace*. But it is absolutely essential here to begin at a moderate speed, so as to be able to prepare for the climax at the end. I have therefore adopted only about ♩ = 96 for the beginning; the orchestra plays in softest *pianissimo* throughout, and the soloists do not need to assure us of their joy (as they unfortunately often do) in the deep chest note of conviction, but should begin with a soft and somewhat foreboding tone. And this manner should be maintained until the orchestra begins the *crescendo*, in which they also join.

Bar 810. The tempo has become somewhat animated by this time, possibly up to ♩ = 112. The *poco adagio* is then taken in such a way that a crotchet of the *adagio* corresponds approximately to the whole of one of the preceding bars. By this means the hearer obtains an impression of restfulness, but there is no dislocation of the time. The sopranos execute the turn thus

sanf - - ter

Bar 832. At this second *poco adagio* the chorus does not adopt the new time but sings the octave leap on the word "Menschen" in the previous quick time. The soloists, who have sung the

Al - le Men - schen, al - le

at an exuberant *forte*, take breath simultaneously after the last quaver and begin again *piano* on the dotted minim after the double bar; they then perform a gentle *crescendo* up to the word "Menschen." A particularly sympathetic and well graduated accentuation should be recommended to the four artists at the words "werden Brüder."

The simplification proposed by Wagner for the tenor in the following cadenza meets with my approval just as little as the alteration in the baritone solo discussed above. It is the business of the producer of the performance to choose a tenor who can sing this difficult passage as it is written, and who has enough proficiency in the art of tone colouring to subordinate his own part to that of the alto in the first bar of the figuration and not to come into independent prominence until the second bar. On the other hand it is clear that the breathing must be carefully regulated, as not one of the three upper voices will be able to sing in one breath the notes placed on the syllable "sanf-." It is both ugly and unartistic to pause for breath in the middle of one and the same syllable, so, at the sacrifice of a tie in the alto part, I have introduced a word repetition, which I illustrate in the following quotation together with some details of notation which seemed to me to be necessary.

 * A skilful singer will be able to take breath here at the repetition of the note in such a way that the audience will be unconscious of the fact.

The last *poco accelerando* and *più mosso*, which I have added to the notation, are not inconsistent with the free character of the cadenza, and permit of an execution of the whole passage unbroken by breathing. The greatest difficulty for the soprano is to avoid screaming the high B but to give it in a gentle *mf*, then to sing the syllable "-gel" with the soft accent which Beethoven evidently intended, and which is musically indispensable, although from a declamatory point of view it is unjustifiable.

An unequalled performer of this solo was Frau Emilie Herzog in Berlin.

The accompanying instruments of the orchestra should be marked *pp* instead of *p* from bar 833 onwards. Then care should be taken to see that the clarinets and the bassoon stop simultaneously with the singers at the *fermata* in bar 842. The conductor must to a certain extent breathe with the singers so that they do not stop out of necessity whilst the orchestral instruments are still holding on the note. Then after a quite short pause the *poco allegro stringendo* begins with the softest sound.

Bar 851. The woodwinds come in doubled at the *prestissimo*. It is an advantage to have two piccolos here also. In this passage of boundless jubilation the criterion for the tempo will not be the metronome mark, although this is a good one, but the intensified feelings of the conductor and the physical possibility of pronouncing the words clearly even in the fastest tempo. Enormous power, but no unrestrained noise!—This should be the object kept in view by all the performers.

Bars 878 and 879. Second and fourth horn take the lower F's. So also in bar 905.

Bar 916. The *maestoso* should be conducted in quaver-beats in such a manner that each quaver corresponds in value to the whole of one of the preceding bars. $\flat$ = 60 might well be a good metronome mark, but certainly $\downarrow$ = 60 is impossible.

The *fortissimo* should be sustained at full force and the *piano* comes in suddenly at the word "Elysium." This is very important and at the same time very difficult. Repeated practice is absolutely necessary, especially for the chorus, however excellent it may be.

The strings play the following demisemiquavers stroke for stroke in an ever increasing *crescendo*.

In the last 3/4 bar there is another strong *crescendo* in chorus and orchestra. The chorus sings the last word "-funken" shortly and sharply, and the magnificent orchestral *tutti* closes this stupendous work with one last shout of joy.

THE SYMPHONY

SINCE BEETHOVEN

Translated by H. M. Schott

Translator's Preface

Felix Weingartner's *Die Symphonie nach Beethoven*, here translated anew from the fourth and last German edition of 1926, first appeared in 1897. The author was then Kapellmeister of the Royal Opera in Berlin and musical director of the symphonic concerts of the Royal Orchestra. The mere mention of the date of its writing serves to explain the prose style. One has only to recollect the over-rich furniture and costumes of this prosperous period, not to mention the single most important criterion by which any literary work was judged in Wilhelmine Germany, namely its "profundity," its *Tiefsinnigkeit*. Even the expression of the most simple, downright obvious, almost axiomatic thoughts had to be couched in the murky vocabulary of nineteenth-century Central European philosophical jargon and to be expressed in the incredibly extended concatenations of such words which passed for sentences. To voice one's thoughts in plain, direct, straightforward terms was thus quite out of the question if one wished to be taken seriously. In Weingartner's case one therefore assumes that his style reflects his years attending lectures in philosophy at the University of Leipzig while studying simultaneously at the Conservatory.

The fiercely polemical tone of writing on music and all artistic subjects also strikes the modern reader as bizarre. Did artists and their public really become involved in such violent struggles? Were the Wagnerites and the Brahmsians drawn up in battle array with their pens and popguns ever at the ready? Yes indeed, and to a degree that often surpassed the ferocity of the political conflicts of the day. One might speculate that this phenomenon, this "transfer of aggression," like chess or go in other cultures, reflected a kind of sublimation of necessity. There was, after all, no political risk attached as a rule to the advocacy of extreme points of view in matters of art. But Imperial Germany and the Austria-Hungary of the aging Franz Josef II were by no means democratic in the sense of permitting free expression of political opinions ranging beyond the narrow limits of the accepted doctrines of the time.

Weingartner, whom most of us remember today only as a famous conductor who was among the first to record the great classical symphonies, was also a persistent and prolific if not highly successful composer. In view of some of the attitudes expressed in this book, it is interesting to recall that his long list of works includes not only eight operas but also six symphonies in the classic mold and, even more fascinating, three works denominated symphonic poems. One was based on Shakespeare's *King Lear*, another on a Böcklin painting, *The Elysian Fields (Die Gefilde der Seligen)*, while the third bore a quite generic title, *Spring (Frühling)*. To be sure, the six symphonies followed the first two of these, Weingartner meanwhile having converted from the Wagnerian faith to the Brahmsian, but the last-named symphonic poem was also the last of his orchestral works.

Weingartner's tract is of more than mere historical interest and value, however. Virtually all of his critical judgments can still find wide acceptance today, with only one major exception. The symphonic works of Franz Liszt have disappeared almost totally from the repertoire. The *Faust* symphony still enjoys an occasional revival but the *Dante* is rarely if ever performed any more. Eleven of the twelve symphonic poems count as curiosities, while *Les Préludes* makes increasingly infrequent appearances at "pop" concerts from time to time. But did not Weingartner come rather close to predicting just such a fate for the works of a man whom he along with so many others rightly characterized as "the king of artists"? Strange to tell, it is the very early and the very late piano music of Liszt which has suddenly returned to the concert hall in recent seasons, thanks to such modern virtuosi as Raymond Lewenthal and Alfred Brendel, and to the efforts of the Liszt Society in England headed by Humphrey Searle. But it seems highly doubtful that the same new breath of life can ever again be instilled in Liszt's orchestral music.

As many readers know, the versions of the Bruckner symphonies which Weingartner knew and heard were the "revised" ones which were discarded some thirty years ago in favor of those based on the composer's autograph scores. The differences involve much more than mere matters of detail. Basic structural changes and many modifications of the original instrumentation were made by the original group of Brucknerite conductors, Franz Schalk, Ferdinand Löwe and their disciples, with an occasional assist now and again from the great Artur Nikisch. This occurred during the composer's lifetime, except for the posthumously published and incomplete Ninth Symphony, first revealed in its original and only legitimate form some thirty years after Löwe's highly doctored version appeared. Just what changes Bruckner approved in the other eight we shall probably never know with certainty. Indeed, the situation has been further complicated by the fact the composer himself completely revised certain works and many passages of other compositions at various times. These revisions have, in turn, led to the publication of at least two Urtext editions, the first of which appeared during the "thousand years" between 1933 and 1945, while the second has been published since then, perhaps for extra-musical as well as artistic and scholarly reasons. Except for Eastern Europe, which strangely continues to prefer the first Urtext edition, the second Urtext version is the one generally heard today.

Be that all as it may, Weingartner's appraisal of the nine Bruckner symphonies is affected not at all. The nobility of the thematic material remains. The orchestration, with its echoes alternately of the organ loft and of Bayreuth, has its distinctive sounds. The loosely structured form, leading to "heavenly lengths" far out-stripping Schubert's worst excesses and punctuated by the grand pauses to which Weingartner refers, remains, too, no matter which version a conductor happens to select for performance.

It is impossible to imagine how Weingartner would have viewed the musical scene of today, in which the symphony in its classic form has become almost obsolete. From his book one could easily predict that his conservatism would tend to cut him off from the develop-ments which took place after his thirty-seventh birthday and the start of a new century. To him the symphonies of Mahler repre-sented the ultimate in the expansion of the form, as indeed they did. For us, to whom the *Kammersymphonie*, op. 9, of Schönberg and the even more drastically condensed orchestral works of Webern now appear nonetheless as direct descendants of Bruckner and Mahler's works, it is tempting to conjecture what Weingartner's reaction to them must have been if in fact he ever heard them. No doubt his inability to appreciate an idiom going far beyond any dissonances ever conceived of by Strauss would have prevented his perceiving the formal revolution or even reaction which they represent: the radical shrinking of the bloated, hypertrophied form used by their immediate predecessors in the Viennese symphonic tradition. It is ironic indeed that the use of a tonal language so apparently novel and daring kept the musicians of Weingartner's conservative stripe from realizing that in a formal sense, the new Vienna school was even more conservative in its way.

But the book as it stands represents a uniquely significant and still valid statement of the viewpoint of a major figure in the musical world of his day. Perhaps one might almost say "of our day," for his was a lifetime which in conventional historical terms encompassed the span from our Civil War into World War II; that is, from Berlioz' sixtieth birthday and the fiftieth of Wagner and Verdi until the twentieth of Lukas Foss. This work was surely viewed as such a statement when it was last reprinted in the Germany of the Bauhaus, Brecht and *Gebrauchsmusik*. It remains of abiding interest and perhaps even greater value to us today.

H. M. SCHOTT

Preface

It was with particular pleasure that I took the opportunity in the year 1909 to arrange for a new edition of the present study. I had long desired to do so, most of all to make a thorough revision of my comments about Brahms. In addition the material was arranged more clearly; this naturally resulted in a remodeling of the external form.

This little book originally grew out of a lecture which I presented in a number of cities. I felt that the character of a lecture, with its avoidance of an attempt at historical thoroughness, should be preserved in the new version as well. The consequent need for brevity served and still serves to relieve me of the reproach of not having mentioned so many interesting composers and so many works which deserve attention.

The changes in the present fourth edition are principally of a stylistic nature.

Vienna   FELIX WEINGARTNER
February 1926

Contents

Introduction

If on a walking tour through the Alps we had been completely absorbed in contemplating and admiring a tremendous group of mountains, whose highest snow-covered peak gleamed at us from the shimmering distance, and someone had come over to us and said, "I want to climb beyond this peak out into the blue air," then not very long ago we would justifiably have entertained doubts concerning the speaker's mental faculties. Today we may assume that the time is not distant when we shall fly over even the highest peaks in safely guided airships. But even if the ether which bathes them in light should be conquered completely, one thing is certain: the greatness of the mountains in itself will not be diminished thereby. The gallant aviator might look down at the colossus with justified pride at the moment it was gliding by at his feet. No sooner would he have passed beyond than it would rise up again before his eyes in its gigantic form and seem to call out to him, "You may fly over me with impunity but if you try to come close to me, take care that you are not dashed to pieces!"

In the face of the inexhaustible richness of forms which Beethoven materialized through his music, in the face of those expressions of a mighty world of emotion which with the selfsame power and profundity move between passion and cheeriness, between humor and rapture, it is understandable that even an artist and art critic of Wagner's high standing fell into the shortsighted and surely egoistic fallacy, too, of thinking that music had exhausted itself in Beethoven and accordingly had no choice but to dissolve itself into the *Gesamtkunstwerk* (collective work of art), that is, into Wagner himself. Without going into this fallacy further, which I have already done elsewhere, we can at least agree with Wagner to the extent of admitting with him that the musical airship which could fly us over Beethoven has not yet been invented. And if that happened, if a composer appeared who soared above him, would Beethoven become any the smaller thereby? Just as little as that group of mountains even though man's spirit of invention has found a path through the air over it. But surely the same warning which the aviator heard from the face of the mountain will resound from Beethoven's music to that genius of the future: "You may fly over me with impunity but if you try to come close to me, take care that you are not dashed to pieces!"

A great work of art can certainly be surpassed but never attained. The paradox which is contained in this sentence is only an apparent one. To take one example, is Mozart's E-flat Symphony surpassed by Beethoven's *Eroica*? Certainly. Is it matched by it? No, for it is an absolutely perfect creation and as such enjoys its own autonomous existence dependent on nothing else. If it were to be matched, then something would have to arise which was like it. But even the other symphonies of Mozart are not like it, let alone those of other masters. Perfection stands unique and alone and like the suns of the vault of heaven has its own light and its own warmth. Of it, too, one may sing, "Beautiful, thornless, full of the eternal glow of love, it can only be compared with itself." Another perfect work may surpass it in power or delicacy, force or grace, perhaps even in its display of artistic resources; it will not be dislodged thereby and will remain just as unattainable in its way as the other work in its own. Only creations which stand on a lower plane, even ones by great masters, can resemble each other, often even to the point of confusion. The flowers bloom in great profusion in the valleys; on the peaks only more isolated blossoms shoot up.

Just as with every great work there is also an aureole of isolation which floats round the head of every great artistic figure, even if in common with others his roots have drawn their strength from the soil of art. Goethe coined the saying, "Rejoice that you have two such fellows!" when he was foolishly asked to draw a comparison between himself and Schiller. It will hardly be disputed that he, who seemed to hold the universe in his hands in order to illuminate it with his clear, godlike eyes, surpassed Schiller. And still he did not match him. Why? For the simple reason that he was Goethe and Schiller was nothing other than Schiller. These seemingly closely connected poets are widely separated from each other by virtue of their natures. For that very reason the joy of having them both remains to us. However, this joy is far greater than the empty pleasure of making comparisons which sometimes may be justified in respect of less sublime figures.

The path of art does not take a straight line; the theory of evolution is applicable to it only in a limited degree. So long as an art or an art form remains in its infancy one may still speak in such terms. The course of development can be traced clearly from the Elgin Marbles preserved in London to the full flowering of Grecian sculpture. The path from the old Italian overture or *sinfonia*, the musical introduction of the opera of the times, to the symphony of Mozart and Haydn lies clearly before us, to a not inconsiderable extent in the production of these very masters, who had first to seek out the path which was to carry them onward. Before those works which have made their names immortal could be created, they wrote a vast number of symphonies which, like those of their direct predecessor C. P. E. Bach, no longer arouse lively interest. Beethoven no longer needed such preparation. When he began his creative activity, musical art had already reached a high point. With a few works he was able to come to terms with the influence Mozart and Haydn had exerted on him. Had he been claimed by a premature death, say after the completion of his Second Symphony, no one could have had an inkling of what he really was. But a wonder came to pass! A great figure in the world of politics, the First Consul of France, aroused the enthusiasm of the young musician to such a degree that he was impelled to honor him in a great tone poem and, as Athena sprang from the head of Zeus, the *Eroica* Symphony stands before us. No artist other than Beethoven has ever made such a giant stride as he did from his Second to his Third Symphony. He felt in the depths of his great soul that the ideal, I should even say the *true* life of a hero, free from the ballast of human frailty, his seminal influence and the full recognition of his worth, all begin only after his death. Thus, it is only in the first movement of his symphony that he presents the hero himself in his mighty struggle and striving, in his conquering power and in the intimate, tender stirrings of his inner life. Then, in the second, he sounds the grandiose lament for his death. In the third, the markedly brief Scherzo, he shows a picture of mankind, which from day to day is concerned only with itself, scurrying about with a joke, rushing by the sublime creature with indifference and recalling him at most with a resounding fanfare. In the last movement, the peoples of every corner of the earth assemble and amass building blocks for a fitting monument to the Hero, who has now achieved total recognition. The monument cannot be more beautiful, more sublime, than the love which is paid in tribute to his memory.

After the completion of this miraculous work, Beethoven developed an earlier sketch into the Fourth Symphony, which, actually conceived before the *Eroica*, still evidences faint links with Mozart and Haydn. But then he marched with giant strides from peak to peak until his creation was crowned and perfected by the Ninth Symphony and the last sonatas and quartets.

Despite these enormous achievements, however, Beethoven did not displace Haydn and Mozart, whose masterpieces glow with imperishable freshness at the side of his own, just as little placed in the shade as his own earlier symphonies were by the Ninth.

In science a great discovery supplements existing knowledge or clarifies and eliminates errors, until it is in turn supplemented or eliminated itself by a new discovery. There is only one truth, which we try to reach in different ways but always in the sense of approaching a mysterious goal, only to recoil again and again from barriers which are rooted in the relative intellectual powers of our nature. Once, however, a barrier has been broken, no matter how long it may have been considered impregnable, and has finally been conquered, only researchers in scientific history need be concerned with it further.

On the other hand, it is a great mistake to look upon an artistic figure who represents a high point as a barrier which has been overcome, so to speak, because other high points have come after him. Not even Wagnerian music drama, the most triumphant achievement of more recent times, has been able to displace the older forms of opera, and no one can say today whether it will not be the opera in fact which will experience a renascence in rejuvenated and sublimated form. In art there are countless truths, because each significant work and each great artist bears its own truth within itself. No one of these, however, excludes any of the others. Free as the genii of the air, they float through the ether, grouping and regrouping in a round dance as graceful as it is imposing.

The results of scientific efforts are corporeal and mortal, because each successor pushes its predecessor aside or strikes it dead. The fruits of art, however, are incorporeal and immortal. They cannot force one another from the scene because they interpenetrate. They cannot strike one another down because they are deathless. To keep to the original metaphor, but leaving aeronautical considerations aside for now, we can make the following comparison.

The objective of science can be compared to a treasure mysteriously hidden deep in a mass of mountains and in search of which innumerable tunnels from different starting points are being driven in ever deeper. Art, however, is like the profile of the peaks of this massif, where gleaming summits loom freely into the air and the beauty of one is not lessened but rather increased by that of the others. But the *Weltgeist*, the spirit of the world, which hides its countenance down below behind thick, hard-to-raise veils, up on high swings clear-eyed in joyous flight from peak to peak.

The concept of "progress," which plays an undeniable part in science and technology, is nowadays also mentioned all too eagerly with reference to art, especially to music, where it is very hard to grasp. Above all there is no avoiding the question: In what musical fields can there be said to have been progress? Today we make use of far more varied harmonic and rhythmical devices than formerly. The possibilities of combining sounds seem as little subject to limitation as those of polyphonic ingenuity. Even if we perceive progress in all this, what does it have to do with the essence of music? A composition put together with a technical skill and employing resources of which even our most audacious avant-garde composers could not conceive, would be obliterated by the few bars which introduce the canonic quartet "Mir ist so wunderbar" in *Fidelio* if such a composition did not possess that spiritual quality which radiates to us from Beethoven's music. But if it does have that quality, then the means employed are to be considered as of only secondary importance. The creator's concern will be especially to make economical use of his resources—taking the word in its broadest sense—for to say much with little, or at least not to expend greater means than are absolutely required, has always been a sign of true art, while the opposite points to vanity, which is rather closely related to bungling.

Why is it that the masterpieces of the classical period cannot age in spite of the fact that, so far as externals go, they appear in comparison with contemporary music like poor orphans next to millionaires? Why do they seem to become ever fresher, ever younger, while so much that was created much later already shows signs of age? Because no matter what their form, there inheres in them that glowing spirit which triumphantly carries them through the scrapings and howlings of the "progressive" musical monstrosities, just as the Sistine Madonna can soar above slick color effects and painters' daubs without soiling the edge of her garment.

Someone may come along someday who outdoes those works of our Classical masters—"incomprehensibly sublime works" in the fullest sense—but he will never match them, just as he in his own way will never be matched. Thus, "progress," for all its stormy blustering, must be viewed as very problematic, especially when it is most loudly proclaimed. Frequently one would like to ask those avant-garde composers towards what it is that they have progressed, in the same sense as Bismarck once asked the Conservatives in the Reichstag what it really was that they wanted to conserve. But one thing is certain: True progress does not come from without; whoever tries to construct it of external elements has gone off course.

With this introduction we can now turn to the consideration of particular figures who have since Beethoven attained positions of importance in symphonic music especially, so that from this we can draw in broad strokes a general conspectus of the course taken by the highest form of the tonal art in modern times.

Schubert, Mendelssohn and Schumann

Standing close by Beethoven, more his contemporary than his successor, one finds a miraculous musical phenomenon—Franz Schubert.

He lived out his short span on earth in Beethoven's immediate vicinity, looking up reverently at that deafened, lonely figure without being noticed by him.

In the case of Beethoven, to the extent that we are permitted to look into the workshop of his mind, we invariably find a resolute struggle to attain the ultimate musical expression of his thoughts. In Schubert's case musical ideas bubble forth as if from an unquenchable spring and are set down indiscriminately in naive joy at their very existence. His whole being was so completely steeped in music that he kept on ceaselessly producing and writing down his thoughts without sifting or polishing them.

The beautiful and sublime flowed from his pen just as effortlessly as the trivial and transitory. Even in his weaker moments there was a flowering without end. No other composer was endowed with such a richness of melodic invention. He could even dare to construct a very extended adagio, like that of the C major Quintet, out of two themes, each of which is so long that it could stand as a piece by itself. He simply strings one after the other and repeats the first with a varied accompaniment. There is no development section. So powerful is the line of his music that the art of combination, i.e. counterpoint, finds no place in it. Schubert is almost never polyphonic. His melody victoriously sweeps polyphony from the field; where the former reigns the latter becomes superfluous. What would be a fault in the case of any other composer is an advantage here. Only the over-endowed could safely dispense with one of the principal artistic resources of music. It is touching to note that Schubert still wanted to take lessons in counterpoint shortly before his death. One who could fly wished to learn to walk; a god

251

desired to take on the weight of earthly creatures. But fate would not have it thus. The gates of heaven opened and the god flew to his home for eternity.

Schubert was godlike, as Mozart had been. Both descended from their heights to mankind down below. Beethoven, the great human being, raised himself to godly height. Mozart chiseled his creations with a fine stylus of pure gold; Schubert grasps with bold but often clumsy hands at the elements themselves in order to channel them to his will. In Mozart we find the most sensitive artistic consciousness from the earliest childhood on; in Schubert, a turbulent but unerring instinct which is often unaware of its gigantic strength. Both masters were active in all branches of music. In opera, which owes masterpieces to Mozart, Schubert did not advance beyond experiments. On the other hand, in song writing he outdistanced all his predecessors and still has not been surpassed by his successors. He was the greatest musical lyricist, not only in the song but in all his music. The happy as well as the tragic aspects of Schubert are permeated by that element of melodic flow which shows him to us in the form of an inspired singer, one who allows us to feel his own sadness and joys with him, but a singer to whom it is also granted to give voice to hymns which resound out into the universe and thence back to us.

The C major Symphony! What profusion, what unbounded richness, mocking every effort at esthetic appraisal, streams out of it towards us! How great it stands there with its four monumental movements: the vigorous, forceful first, the gipsy-like, romantic second with its wonderfully mysterious horn passage (the "heavenly guest," as Schumann put it so beautifully), the splendid Scherzo and the Finale filled with the humor of the Titans! With a bold leap the last movement goes beyond all tradition, beyond every concept of the symphonic. For pages at a time it presents only figurations above rising and falling passages in thirds, then a theme whose folk-like quality has called forth headshaking among many oversensitive souls and finally, after a great number of repeated eight-measure sections, a unison on C sounded four times, and then, following forceful interjections by the orchestra, repeated twice more. It sounds as if high-spirited giants had stamped their way in and were bursting out laughing from time to time so as to shake heaven and earth. Total lack of restraint, such as no composer has dared since, characterizes this piece, which still shows as a whole and in all its parts the most perfect proportions all the same. The harmonies and structure of the C major Symphony are of lapidary simplicity and their effect is lapidary whenever it is played as befits its worth.

Language proves totally inadequate in the face of the two movements of the B minor Symphony which are left to us. Surely it is a misfortune whenever it is not granted to a great creative spirit to complete his work. In the case of this symphony I feel that it is fortunate that it remained unfinished. The first movement is of a tragic dimension such as was attained by no symphonist except Beethoven and by Schubert himself only in his songs. The second theme, played by the violoncelli, contains one of the most noble inspirations which a musician was ever given to utter. That which moved us deeply as an emotional struggle in the first movement dies away transfigured in the second. This conclusion is so satisfying that a desire for additional movements can hardly arise. One would be tempted to believe that Schubert, like Beethoven in the piano sonatas op. 109 and op. 111, wanted to end with the slow movement, if its difference in tonality from the first movement as well as the orchestrated beginning of the Scherzo did not point to the planned continuation. Even the accompaniment in Schubert often becomes a melody. Many a composer might have formed the principal theme itself out of the violin figuration with which the B minor Symphony begins. Schubert constructs the actual melody in the woodwinds and it then floats in over the violin figuration like a beautiful dark-eyed nymph over the lightly ruffled waters of a melancholy mountain lake. An image—nothing more! No comparison, such as one might print in program notes as an explanation. The B minor symphony, like all true music, has no need of such.

In a rehearsal of the C major Quintet, when the Trio of the Scherzo suddenly went off into the tragic key of B-flat minor, a famous Viennese musician is said to have cried out, "A wedding procession which stops at an open grave!" But one could just as well interpret the B-flat minor of this Trio as the onset of winter stiffness in nature, or as Banquo's ghost, or as the "mene, mene tekel" at Belshazzar's feast.* Music can inspire poetic images but it is not bound to them, because it can express more than poetry and imagery can. I make use of these sometimes because it is difficult

* [The original has "Nebuchadnezzar's."—TRANS.]

to talk about music in a non-theoretical way without occasional imagistic embellishment. It is in this sense that I should wish my poetic digressions interpreted.

Characteristic of Schubert is the boldness with which he unexpectedly modulates into remote keys in order just as unexpectedly to return again to the principal tonality. At the end of the first movement of the D minor Quartet he twice turns off suddenly into E-flat minor and navigates back to D minor with a little enharmonic change (G-sharp in place of A-flat). In the Adagio of the G major Quartet a thematic section in G minor culminates in two short, disconnected notes in the first violin and viola parts (see Example). The modulations lead to C-sharp minor and B-flat minor but the G and B-flat stubbornly persist; this amazes us today, accustomed as we are to oddities. The return to G minor then takes place within one measure.

The characteristics mentioned, of which many more could be cited, are always of a *monumental* stamp and not of mere momentary effect. The episodic, the genre style, the wearing of borrowed emotional plumage which were of importance later on are alien to Schubert. He speaks a crystal-clear language and his idiom is great, even in little pieces. The requirement so often set up, that a genius must invent new forms, has no application to Schubert. In his case the content is new, not the form, which he found ready to hand, just as did Beethoven, of whom his biographer Thayer correctly says that it was not so much his pride to find new forms for musical presentation as to surpass his contemporaries in the use of those which were already available. It is in the highly individual *content* with which he filled the existing forms without abandoning them that Schubert's genius lies.

That the genius of an artist resides in his individuality and in the way he expresses it is also evidenced in the case of Mendelssohn. He appeared as a prodigy during Beethoven's and Schubert's lifetime and remained a *Wunderkind* during his entire life. He lived to be hardly any older than Mozart, whom he resembles in so far as he was born with a fabulous command of all that is specifically musical. In Mendelssohn's works, as in those of Schubert and his predecessors, the individuality of their creator is fully and perfectly expressed. The principal difference lies only in the individualities of the masters themselves. A Raphael paints Saint Cecilia, a Jan van Huysum a little flower picture. Mastery as such must be awarded to the latter in no smaller degree than to the former. By mastery I understand the capacity to express one's individuality in the particular art completely and absolutely. To this there belongs as a very important accessory, the mastery of technical resources, which, when the above capacity is present, can and always will be attained by diligence. But underlying mastery is that great sincerity which does not give more than it can. Mendelssohn possessed this sincerity in a high degree; for this reason, even if not so great as Mozart or Schubert in his very essence, he appears to us as a figure both inwardly and outwardly complete and perfect. Thus, his compositions, too, reveal that indubitable perfection which renders any question of "how" superfluous on our part and only permits consideration of *what* this artistic figure was.

Whenever I see younger musicians turn up their noses at Mendelssohn, I want to call out to them, "Hats off, boys, when you meet a master!" One who at the age of seventeen years, when others are still groping and fumbling, wrote the Octet, a veritable model of formal perfection and sonorous treatment of stringed instruments, and the *Midsummer Night's Dream* Overture deserves the title of master throughout the ages.

After he had composed these pieces, Mendelssohn had nothing more to learn from external sources. The greatness which would have made him the equal of his predecessors was not meted out to a nature of his aristocratic, kindly, poetic and ingenious cast. To his credit, let it be said, he also did not try to assume it; at least, the works in which he did something of the sort are by now so faded that we hardly think of them when the name of Mendelssohn comes up.

Only a few years before his death, seventeen years after the creation of the Overture, he wrote the rest of the *Midsummer Night's Dream* music. Almost his entire output lies in between, and yet it seems as if the entire work had been composed at one time, so little disparity do we find. Let us, on the other hand, compare this with pairs of works of other great masters between the composition of which considerable time elapsed, say *The Flying Dutchman* with *Tristan*, Beethoven's First with his Seventh Symphony, Mozart's *Idomeneo* with *The Magic Flute*! What an enormous difference! How little Wagner succeeded in his Paris version of *Tannhäuser* in grafting upon a work of his youth the idiom of *Tristan* and the *Ring*! What an honor for him that he was not successful in this!

Mendelssohn, unlike other masters, did not go through a development, a growing out of himself. From the beginning to the end of his creative life he remained the master who had dropped from heaven, whose effortless mastery of the whole musical apparatus was to secure for him the idolatry even of those who expect more powerful stimulation from music than he was able to give.

If Mendelssohn had given his orchestral pieces in one movement the happy designation "symphonic poem" which Liszt later invented, he would probably be celebrated today as the creator of program music and would have taken his position at the beginning of the new rather than at the end of the old, so-called classical period of our art. He would then be called the "first of the moderns" rather than the "last of the classics." How much turns upon a word! The designation "overture" in fact makes no sense for *The Hebrides, Calm Sea and Prosperous Voyage* and *The Beautiful Melusine*, for an overture presupposes something to follow. These three pieces, however, introduce nothing. They came into being from scenic and poetic stimuli but are completely autonomous. One can quite justifiably describe them as symphonic poems. They differ from their successors only in that we do not need to know these stimuli in order to understand them because, in spite of the inspiration from without, music and nothing else is central to their essence. They require no explanation, not even of the titles, which while stimulating the listener's imagination could nevertheless read differently or be lacking altogether without affecting the capacity of these pieces to make an impression.

Of the two Mendelssohn symphonies which have remained fully alive, the A minor is the more significant. Here, in addition to the scenic stimulus expressed in the title—Scotland—an unexpressed poetic one as well seems to have been in the mind of the master, for he prescribes that the four movements are to be played without the customary pauses and in this, too, he is close to the modern symphonic school. By allowing the entire work to pass before us in one unbroken line, we see it take on the character of a legend of wondrous content, one of those tales which were associated with so many knightly castles in the Scottish Highlands and perhaps even today are being retold here and there. How beautiful is the principal theme of the first movement! A clarinet an octave below accompanies the gently agitated rising and falling undulations of the violins. A Scottish legend tells of a pale, transparent shadow which looks exactly like the person it accompanies and which, when it becomes visible, betokens death for that person. Could this tale have been in Mendelssohn's mind when he gave the violin melody the deep, shadowy clarinet as an accompaniment? The reminiscence of the "Mermaids' Song" from Weber's *Oberon* in the lyrical second theme appears almost intentional. This movement also contains seeds of the future. When at the end the scales in the strings roar up and down over the diminished seventh chords of the winds, does one not think that he sees the ocean stirred to fury and that the ghostly shape of the Dutchman's ship might appear at any moment? We listen to graceful and courtly play in the Scherzo. The Adagio flows by as a great song without words in its glorious, soulful cantilena. The last movements telling us of struggle and battle, is a spacious folk song of victory and sunshine. Every voice in this score sparkles with life. Nothing is forced; everything is in place. The structure is luminous, the tonal effects of admirable freshness. Mendelssohn will not die so easily as has been said. Just as the rainbow, so long as the sun shines at all, is not swept away by the strongest storm, so will beauty remain in art so long as it lives. Mendelssohn, however, bore beauty in his soul and with it his share of immortality.

Symbolizing in music begins with Mendelssohn's contemporary, Robert Schumann. Mendelssohn had only had fleeting presentiments of it, without becoming its captive. Schumann thought of himself as made up of two symbolic parts, "Florestan" and "Eusebius," corresponding to heterogeneous states of his soul, and to which he attributed now this one, now that one of his works. In his first creative period we generally perceive his symbolic purpose. He transforms the name of the sweetheart of his youth into a theme and writes variations on it. The colorful scenes of Carnival week give him the inspiration for one of the most imaginative piano works which we possess. Hoffmann's fantastic tales stimulate him to compose the *Kreisleriana*. Roundly chastised by the critics and the learned musical fraternity, he formed the "Davidsbündler" circle with like-minded friends and then made rough and tumble fun of

the "Philistines." Quite indirectly we learn that the important
F-sharp minor Sonata also owes its origin to Hoffmann and that
Schumann wished to pay tribute to Beethoven in his most beautiful
piano composition, the great C major Fantasy.

While everything in Mendelssohn strove for externalization and
he reached such maturity, at least as regards his craft, in his earliest
years that nothing more could miscarry, Schumann was incessantly
striving to put into ever new artistic forms the songs and melodies
of his gentle, romantically tinged nature. He would sit down at the
piano, for that was his world. There he found all that he needed. He
accomplished his most important work as a poet of the piano and in
his songs, many of which need not shun comparison with Schubert's.
None the less he yearned for the larger art forms. Quite early the
brilliant figure of Mendelssohn, one which operated so easily in all
musical realms, impressed itself upon him as an ideal. In his
striving to emulate Mendelssohn, to attain the same polish and
perfection of form, his own originality suffered without its being
possible to overtake his idol in this respect. A foreign element, which
he forced upon himself to a certain extent, deprives many of his
later works of the vital immediacy which delights us in his earlier
pieces. The nature of his gifts, which ripened into delicious fruits
in his smaller compositions, was later stretched and distorted to
larger dimensions without gaining in richness. It lost intimacy and
became thinner, even threadbare, because it was called upon to
give out more than it had. Schumann's productivity and its variety
were nonetheless astonishingly great even in his second creative
period. There is hardly an art form in which he did not experiment.
Since, obviously owing to his freethinking disposition, he felt an
aversion to composing oratorios on biblical texts, he selected secular
poems, even fragments from Goethe's *Faust,* for works which are
hybrids of opera and oratorio. In addition, he wrote concertos, all
manner of chamber music works, an opera and, as is almost obvious
in the case of such versatility, symphonies as well.

He succeeded best on his first try. It is the B-flat major Symphony
which may be so termed, although he had previously sketched a
Symphony in D minor which only later was put into final form as
the Fourth. Born of the spring-like happiness of his recent marriage,
this impulsive piece charms spring and happiness into our hearts.
We must love it, this B-flat major Symphony, although we cannot
conceal the fact that Schumann's weaknesses are also to be perceived in it. In his piano pieces his characteristic trait is to invent

short, very expressive themes which he knows how to vary and to work out ingeniously. But in the symphony he does not always quite manage with these themes and "themelets," even though they may have sprung from tender and beautiful emotions. If we examine his orchestral pieces closely, we find that he often resorts to repetition of individual measures and groups of measures for the purpose of spinning out the thread further, because the theme itself is too brief for this. Indeed, sometimes this theme is itself formed by repetition of one and the same phrase. His larger orchestral movements easily become monotonous through these many repetitions of notes and rhythms. One might reply that the theme of the first movement of Beethoven's Fifth Symphony is certainly briefer still than Schumann's themes. There is a substantial difference, however. In the Beethoven work, after the first appearance of this four-note theme and its single repetition, a long spun-out melody can be followed clearly right up to the second subject (entrance of the horns in E-flat major). This melody needs the original theme only for its rhythmical articulation but not for its continuation, while in Schumann *only* the repetitions of the theme keep the tonal structure in motion. It is the first movements of his symphonies which suffer most from this and in part the finales, too, which are rather conventional in many of their sections. On the other hand, his middle movements are very successful for the most part. The Larghetto of the B-flat major Symphony contains as its principal theme a melody of great intensity and on such a broad scale as is but seldom to be found. In the Adagio espressivo of the C major Symphony shines one of the most beautiful passages in Schumann's instrumental music: the twice-repeated figure in the violins which floats so perfectly up and down above the theme in the woodwinds. The main sections of the scherzi are glorious while the trios are somewhat weaker.

In the central movements Schumann's awkwardness in handling the orchestra is less apparent than in the outer movements, whose complicated structure may have demanded more technique in this respect, too, than he possessed. Almost always he works with the entire orchestral apparatus, believing he will thus achieve fullness and power. However, he overlooks the individual qualities of the various instruments; only a complete understanding and exploitation of these assures plasticity of orchestral writing. Therefore the sound produced is turgid and clumsy. The color is grey on grey. The most important voices, if one plays exactly according to his indications, cannot be heard distinctly. A true *forte* is usually just as impossible as a true *piano*. After timid and thus unsuccessful attempts to effect an improvement here, I finally decided on a ruthless process of complete reinstrumentation of certain parts. The favorable results which I achieved in respect of color, and the clarity in contrast to the murky effect of the original which was obtained, induced me to publish my experiences.*

Schumann's symphonies were composed for the piano and arranged—alas, not always well—for orchestra. But they do have genuine fire, purity and depth of feeling. Therefore it is worthwhile to exert every effort to prevent their being forgotten because of their inadequacies of orchestral technique.

Schumann as an orchestral composer appears quite monumental to us, however, in a work which owes its genesis to the poetic inspiration, so congenial to him, provided by Byron's *Manfred*. Here he is again completely himself, the visionary Romantic with a taste for the supernatural and mysterious. From this aspect of his nature he succeeded in creating that wonderful overture in which he satisfies us completely even as regards instrumentation. It is the only orchestral piece which can be ranked with his piano music of genius. Here he reveals solidity and greatness and achieves that powerful, unified line which is the hallmark of sublime creations. This is true despite the many repetitions of particular groups of measures, something which simply has to be accepted into the bargain in his case. This overture is the very type of the tragic, one-movement musical work and as such can be compared with the *Coriolanus* Overture of Beethoven and with Wagner's *A Faust Overture*.

For a long time the "melodrama," the recitation of poetry against a musical background, was considered a contemptible anomaly among doctrinaire Wagnerites—and that group included virtually everyone—principally because of Wagner's attacks on this form of art. Such an opinion does not stand up today. In any case melodrama is of a problematic, hybrid nature and its use demands taste and discretion. It would be foolish to seek to use music everywhere an opportunity to do so seemed to present itself. But there are substantial values inherent in a musical background to the word and

* F. Weingartner, *Ratschläge für Aufführungen klassischer Symphonien* (Hints on the Performance of Classical Symphonies), Vol. 2, *Schubert und Schumann*, Breitkopf & Härtel, Leipzig.

the plot. The full appreciation and exploitation of these values remains for the future. Schumann created a perfect example of this art form in his incidental music to *Manfred* after the overture, especially in the glorious "Incantation of Astarte." This scene, if well performed by the actor and the orchestra, has a profoundly moving effect. It leaves nothing to be desired, and we certainly do not want Manfred to be singing rather than speaking at this point.

Nowadays the destructive intelligence does more violence to works of art than ever. A bunch of "artistic principles"—in other words, prejudices—which are still derived in the main from a misunderstanding or thoughtless parroting of Wagner's writings, rattle around in people's heads and obstruct free creativity. Especially these days, one cannot urge too strongly the development of one's powers of considering objectively and without bias those impressions which are presented to us. It will then be far simpler to distinguish the true from the false, for everything having to do with fundamental principles in art is dead and sterile. It is always only the work or the act of genius which is alive and which gives life, no matter how they may appear.

Berlioz and Brahms

The coupling of these two names may strike one as strange. If we do not mouth the conventional, thoughtlessly repeated opinions which stamp Brahms the "guardian of conservatism" and Berlioz the "founder of modern music," there will be found (in spite of the self-evident differences which apply to great individuals) points of contact which justify this apposition, for all that each of the two masters would probably have resisted it.

Berlioz' extraordinary personality, whose greatness and far-reaching significance for music has only been recognized for a relatively short time, and still not sufficiently, came to the fore in France about the time of Beethoven's death.

The most striking of his youthful works, the *Symphonie Fantastique,* contains so much that is original that it is no wonder—considering the universal tendency to oppose what is new rather than to test its worth attentively and in a spirit of devotion—that this work was looked upon even by such outstanding musicians as Cherubini as a monstrosity: that it was not at all understood by the public; and, indeed, that the impression which it created could almost be likened to violent horror.

Berlioz achieved about the same effect at first with his later compositions as well, in spite of Liszt's tireless efforts, which obtained some recognition for him, at least in Germany. It was only long after Berlioz' death that oft-repeated performances of his works—first by Bülow, then by other conductors—brought matters to a point at which it could gradually be understood and felt that beneath the rough shell there was a sweet kernel, that behind a mass of apparently external effects there was great musical value.

If we ask how it was possible that even his major works, which are today almost universally esteemed, could have been considered for decades as effusions of a half-deranged brain, we can find three explanatory points of reference. At first encounter Berlioz' melodic invention seems dry and rather unapproachable. None of his melodies is to be compared, say, to the famous clarinet passage in the *Freischütz* Overture or to Schubert's themes, which irresistibly ingratiate themselves to the listener's ear. We believe at first that we feel coldness, almost harshness, where in truth a consuming ardor and passion seek artistic expression. Berlioz' music is like those rare human physiognomies which for the first moment strike us as unsympathetic, until on closer examination we sense to what tempests and struggles of the soul those craggy features, those deep, scar-like furrows and those strangely melancholy eyes bear witness. A further reason for its having remained uncomprehended for so long is to be sought in the unusual and grotesque boldness of its instrumentation. It is not only that Berlioz often brings in more orchestral resources than are customary, but also the use to which he puts these resources. The great demands which he makes on the capacities of the musicians, the unusually fine sense for the mixing of tone colors while still fully preserving clarity of line, give his treatment of the orchestra that characteristic coloring—never known before him, never successfully imitated after him—which has led the uncomprehending and malevolent to criticize him for inventing the instrumental effect and only then adding the music. However, even his instrumentation does not exhibit that sensuous element which, so to speak, enraptures us by purely acoustic means, as is the case with Weber's and Wagner's wonderfully bold use of the orchestra and varied employment of individual instruments. We are dazzled by Berlioz' orchestration but not intoxicated. Bright sunlight plays on light green leaves, round which breathes a clear, pure air; the deep breath of fragrant shadows in a pine forest is lacking. But his nights are alive with hideous ghostly figures which can frighten even those who believe themselves to have long since outgrown ghost stories. Finally, it was the subjects and poetic ideas chosen for his works which rendered their universal appreciation difficult, as well as the manner in which his music relates to and incorporates these subjects.

In his *Symphonie Fantastique*, which we propose to discuss first, Berlioz headed the work with a program, a statement of the poetic content about which the listener should be thinking and which characterizes each of the different movements. This procedure was not an unusual one. It has long been known that what we casually term "program music" today is in no sense an invention of latter-day composers. Rather, the effort to express definitely labeled thoughts and events through music is clearly every bit as old as music-making in our sense. We already find compositions provided with descriptive titles and commentaries by the old Netherlanders and Italians as well as by the pre-Bach German masters. Thayer in his biography of Beethoven lists a whole group of now long-forgotten compositions of the turn of the nineteenth century which were either given descriptive titles as a whole or whose individual movements bore special names, as for example: *The Naval Battle*—first movement, "The Beating of the Drums"; second movement, "Warlike Music and Marches"; third movement, "Maneuver of the Ships"; fourth movement, "Cruising Across the Waves"; fifth movement, "Cannonades"; sixth movement, "Cries of the Wounded"; seventh movement, "Victory Celebration of the Triumphant Fleet."

Great battles and politically significant events have always stimulated the imagination of contemporary musicians. Beethoven himself did not shrink from composing *Wellington's Victory*. The following program, given in Thayer, seems particularly worthy of note: "The contented pastoral life, interrupted by a thunderstorm, which, however, passes on, and the naive and loud rejoicing therefor." Who does not recognize that here we have one of the stimuli for the *Pastoral* Symphony?

Every good opera overture has its program in the libretto of the opera which follows. Spohr, in addition, supplied with his introduction to the opera *Faust* a detailed description of what the listener was to imagine. In the course of the present essay it will be stated that the program of a piece of music provided with one is not objectionable as such. Rather, it is objectionable only if the music of such a piece stands in a false relationship to the program, as will be more fully explained below, since the possibility can arise that the music can, as it were, act contrary to its own nature, thus turning into non-music and becoming incapable of giving rise to a work of art.

The *Symphonie Fantastique* of Berlioz is supposed to portray the delirium of a young artist who, in his desperation at being rejected by his beloved, has taken an overdose of opium. The dose, too weak to kill him, conjures up first pleasant, then frightful images in his mind. Berlioz really succeeded extraordinarily well in fitting this truly fantastic subject, which bears such deep contradictions within it, into a unified mold without doing violence to symphonic form or letting it degenerate into vapid tone-painting. All five movements are complete, self-contained pieces of music, highly original and significant in their conception, structure and instrumentation, requiring no further explanation to justify their existence. In the assurance of this purely musical perfection Berlioz also says that the program may be omitted whenever the symphony is performed alone (i.e. without the dramatic epilogue *Lelio*), since the work alone must be understandable to the public; only the titles of the various movements are to remain. It will not be difficult for a listener endowed with some imagination if he knows that the third movement is called "Scene in the Country," to recognize that the cantilena of the English horn at the end, accompanied by soft tympani rolls, is supposed to imitate the song of a shepherd's pipe which is interrupted by distant thunder, just as bird songs are imitated at the end of Beethoven's "Scene at the Brook." In neither case is this imitation of the sounds of nature inartistic, as it clearly arises from the completely unified basic mood of the whole work, a mood which could only spring from a spirit which absorbs the wonders of nature intensely and is highly capable of reproducing them artistically. Moreover, since in both cases the concluding measures which imitate the sounds of nature fit together musically in a totally logical way with what has gone before, they can be understood from the music alone without any program. In the case of the Berlioz piece there is even an occasion for a particularly beautiful symmetry of form. As the beginning of the movement, before the actual theme enters, consists of a duet of two shepherd's pipes (oboe and English horn), the end appears only as a variant of the beginning. Thus commencement and conclusion weave themselves into a kind of unifying frame around the delicate picture of the piece of music.

Similarly, the title "Witches' Sabbath" would have sufficed completely for the last movement, consisting of an introduction which prepares the weird atmosphere, a chorale-like section played by deep wind instruments (parody of *Dies Irae*) and a splendid fugato, culminating in a combination of the chorale with the fugue subject. The only objection one could raise is that the audience, if it knew only the title, might not be able to establish an inner connection between the first three movements and the last two. The program, which expects one to view the whole work as the depiction of an ecstatic dream, should therefore be distributed at performances without compunction, since the thoroughly musical character of this symphony ensures that the program will not mislead one into artistic subtilizations, but will only stimulate the imagination of the listener—which is also in the main the function of the title.*

As a distinct novelty in contrast to earlier symphonies, one theme runs through all five movements. In his dreams, which are presented in musical form in the symphony, the young artist is ceaselessly pursued by the image of his beloved, who appears to him in the most varied settings and forms. This theme takes the character of a melody, labeled *idée fixe* by Berlioz, which, while keeping its structure so far as the relationships of the intervals is concerned, undergoes complete changes in rhythm and expression so as to correspond to the mood to be depicted.

In the first movement the *idée fixe* appears in noble simplicity. In the second, it is embroidered with waltz-like motifs, yet remains elegant throughout. As befits the character of a "Scene in the Country," it is transformed in the third movement into a pastoral melody played by the woodwinds. In the fourth movement it appears only as a fleeting thought of the man being led to the gallows. Finally, in the last, the "Witches' Sabbath," it becomes a distorted, grotesque dance tune. The beloved has become a she-devil, who carries on uproariously with witches and other mythical beings. Berlioz did not build all the movements of this symphony out of one theme because of a lack of inventiveness; rather, the various transformations of this theme are woven into the movements, which are in other respects constructed out of their own themes.

The varying and transformation of a theme are nothing new. The most beautiful masterpieces have been created in variation form. Indeed, variation is one of the basic elements of music. But the variation of a theme from a recognizably poetic point of view—dramatic-psychological variation, I should term it—was first employed by Berlioz in this symphony and appears to be his own completely original creation. It is the same type of variation process which Liszt expanded in his symphonic poems and which Wagner

---

* In his piano arrangement of the *Symphonie Fantastique* Liszt changed the program, presenting the first three movements as natural occurrences and only the last two as dreams summoned up by the opium taken in an attempt at suicide. I do not consider this change beneficial as it unnecessarily divides the work into two parts. The sensitive listener will prefer to explain the character of the last two movements as a heightening of the exalted basic mood rather than as something quite new and added from without.

made into an intensive expressive device of his music drama. In none of Berlioz' later works was this dramatic-psychological variation technique put to such intensive use as in the *Fantastic* Symphony. He had a highly original idea, which, however, he did not exploit any more himself, leaving it rather to his successors to develop it to its full significance.

In addition to the *Symphonie Fantastique*, he later, inspired by Byron's poem and invited by Paganini to compose a piece for viola and orchestra, wrote a four-movement symphonic work, *Harold in Italy*, the value of which is hardly less than that of his first symphony. Here, too, the same melody runs through the four otherwise independent movements, but it always maintains its lyrical character without being subjected to substantial variation. After the somewhat dry first movement there follow two middle movements of miraculous delicacy. The "Pilgrims' March," with its strangely persistent bell sounds on a high B and a low C, evokes landscape moods of the most delicate charm. The "Serenade of an Abruzzi Mountaineer" is a model of free polyphony. The way in which the various themes and figurations interpenetrate freely and the way in which, despite the most artful twining of them, each one remains at every point clearly recognizable and discernible, is deserving of the greatest admiration. Here and in numerous other passages in his works, Berlioz dealt very creatively with the free combination of several melodic themes. The last movement, with its rather noisy brigand Romanticism, does not attain the high level of the middle movements, but it is refreshing in its originality and effective in its almost brutal progress to a climax.

Among the other works, in addition to the important overtures *Rob Roy*, *King Lear*, *Benvenuto Cellini* and *Roman Carnival*, we must consider the dramatic symphony *Romeo and Juliet* and the dramatic legend which already breaks into the domain of opera, *The Damnation of Faust*. In these last two works the musician of genius shows himself in strange contradiction to the "compleat artist." Obviously his innermost nature drew him to opera, but the bold symphonist and orchestrator was not yet capable of bringing to fruition the reform which it remained for Wagner to accomplish, and of building the music of the drama from the spirit of the poem, leaving the form of the opera untouched only where it does not contradict the spirit of the poem. Berlioz selected and wrote his opera texts himself according to the old formula. He dressed them up with pieces of music in his style which are among the best examples of operatic music since the classical masterpieces. He also laid his hand on great dramas, such as Shakespeare's *Romeo and Juliet* and Goethe's *Faust*, and rearranged them to suit his purposes, not for the stage, oddly enough, but for the concert hall. The purpose was the same in both cases: to find an occasion at any cost for opening a way to the outside world for the turbulent stirrings of his musical spirit—to create music and more music, the most original and beautiful of which he was capable, without considering in the process whether the form selected for the total work of art (*Gesamtkunstwerk*) had inherent artistic value. For concert purposes, which are of primary interest to us here, this yielded an aggregation of various expressive devices and forms: not altogether oratorio, opera or symphony, fragments of each and thus nothing integral. In *Romeo and Juliet* a fugato pictures the feud of the warring families, and a long orchestral recitative the intervention, warning and threats of the Prince of Verona. Brief choral and solo movements tell of the unhappy fate of the celebrated pair, of the power of love, of Queen Mab. Extended orchestral pieces depict the ball at the Capulets', the love scene and, once again, Queen Mab. This little episode, which passes so quickly in the play, is thus drawn upon twice; the tragic conflict, on the other hand, is passed over completely. A choral movement pictures the mourning of the women for Juliet's supposed death; an orchestral piece *without* singing, to which I shall refer again below, portrays the awakening and tragic end of the lovers. Finally, an operatic finale presents the flocking round of the people, Friar Laurence's sermon and the reconciliation of the feuding families.

In *The Damnation of Faust* Berlioz transplants the opening to Hungary. Why? On a trip through that country he had heard the "Rákóczi March," had subsequently orchestrated it brilliantly, and now sought an occasion to fit it into some larger work. This he found, strange to tell, in *Faust*, and to justify this interpolation the locale of the beginning had to be Hungary. He admits all this quite frankly in the preface to this work. In order to compose a "Ride to Hell," just his meat, he caused Faust, contrary to Goethe's poem (of which he otherwise made much use), to descend into hell rather than being transfigured. But this very ride to hell by Faust is such a demonic piece of music that we can hardly regret Berlioz' violence to Goethe's text.

It is to the deformation—if I may term it that—of *Romeo and Juliet* by making the subsidiary motive of Queen Mab into a major one that we owe an orchestral scherzo which is absolutely unique in its way. Among the other symphonic pieces in both these works, too, we find true miracles of highly original and characteristic music. Let me cite here the brilliant "Ball at the Capulets'," the glorious albeit somewhat spun-out "Love Scene," as well as the "Dance of the Will-o'-the-Wisps" and the "Dance of the Sylphs" in *The Damnation of Faust*. The latter work, together with the *Fantastic Symphony*, is the most significant of Berlioz' creations.

His entire career had a weighty and by no means sufficiently appreciated influence on the development of the art of music. He can be considered the founding father of the so-called modern school because of the techniques, mentioned above, of dramatic-psychological variation and the free combination of several themes and because of his ingenious inventiveness in the treatment of the orchestra, which today has reached such heights of virtuosity that the music as such is often overlooked. But it is mainly the obvious *effects* of his instrumentation which were most eagerly imitated, while no attention was paid to the masterly, transparent style of his orchestral writing. Thus his "effects" are still telling today, while the exaggerated imitations, although they startle for the moment, soon fade just because they are merely imitations, which do not spring, as did Berlioz' effects, from intrinsic artistic necessity.

Modern orchestral technique is based on Wagner, not on Berlioz. Even in instrumentation, the only field in which Berlioz, in the view of shortsighted detractors, has any claim to mastery, he has remained isolated. What links him with the old masters, however, is that he was not a programmatic musician in the current sense in spite of his attempt to give a program to one of his major works; rather, most of all in the major work in question, he was a great musician who upheld the claims of musical form with meticulous care and did not allow it fall victim to humbug. It is, indeed, the much-discussed program of the *Fantastic* Symphony which *separates* him from his so-called successors rather than placing him at the head of their ranks. He enriched music with new expressive resources; he led it on to new paths. But because he remained aware that music is noble enough to be capable of treading new paths on its own without having extraneous branches grafted onto it, he did not lose himself in clever piecemeal sound effects but created fully

integrated musical works, which are entitled to claim the standing
of classics. His fertile imagination seems all the greater to us the more
we exert ourselves to fathom its unique character by the reverent
study of what it produced. But those who would toss him on the
scrap heap in favor of contemporary figures only reveal the utter
poverty of their idols and of themselves, too.

Brahms makes it even more difficult for us than Berlioz does to
understand the unique character of his musical mind. In Berlioz,
even in his most original creations, there is much that is superficial
and theatrical. His passion turns to pathos, his expressive feelings
become sentimental and his humor grotesque. What he expresses
cannot be misunderstood, whether one be attracted or repelled by
it. In Brahms, none of this holds true; nothing lies on the surface.
The listener must dip his cup deep into the spring of the music if
he is to enjoy a refreshing drink. Berlioz wears his grief for all to
see and never tires of telling us about it. Brahms bottles his up inside
himself. But if a melancholy tone ever escapes from his breast,
then we feel that we have had an encounter with fate. While Berlioz
in his joy works himself up to oblivious ecstasy, Brahms gazes
quietly but with flashing eyes over green fields and up into the blue
heavens. Not everyone understands the brightness of these eyes.
Whoever does so even once will forget it never more.

A wonderful remark about Mozart has come down to us from
Brahms. He said, "We can no longer write so beautifully; let us at
least try to write as purely as he." That he did. His art is pure, I
should almost say limpid. Nothing specious attaches to it. In
approaching it one should not seek any ephemeral charms. It will
not tolerate weakness. It is distinguished by strength and manliness.
Above all, however, one must know how to *listen* intently. With
Brahms it is through such listening that real hearing begins.

Berlioz as well as Brahms, they both have their roots in the very
soil of music. They wish for nothing more. But Brahms is more
firmly rooted because he derives all his strength from this soil,
while Berlioz requires an external stimulus, mainly of the literary
variety. Brahms is the most "absolute" musician among the recent
masters.

Schumann, who after a brief period of interest had drawn back in
repugnance from Wagner and everything connected with him,
introduced Brahms with enthusiastic words as the future messiah
of music. His vocation already seems prefigured in Schumann's
words of promise, namely to be set up by enemies of the daring

reformer of opera as a counterweight to him, as the guardian of "absolute" music against futuristic, literary and program music. In truth Brahms was indebted even later for no little part of his fame, which came to him comparatively earlier than to other composers, to the unceasing efforts of a horde of opponents of the Bayreuth master who neglected no opportunity to play him off against Wagner. But in fact the boundary between the so-called absolute music (attributed to the symphonist in contrast to the dramatist) and other music is not at all so important as is widely believed. Music which in a certain sense could be termed "absolute," fabricated without external stimulus, formalistic note-chopping and phrase-making, probably flows more frequently from the pen of a Philistine, but because of its barren dullness it can lay no claim to our respect. In that connection it is also quite the same whether the work in question is a flirtation with "neo-classicism," with "modernism," with both of them or heaven knows what other journalistic classification of merchandise. All music on a higher plane, even without words and program, cannot disavow emotional influences on the composer; in this sense, of all our masters, none has been an absolute musician—Beethoven least of all. But then, there is something else again which is all too often overlooked by those who use the power of position, of influence or of the pen to deprecate, belittle or pass over in silence one who does not suit them and thus to further the cause of another—overlooked, therefore, by the partisans who out of blind fanaticism, or for reasons other than the objective evaluation of what is presented to them, are friendly or inimical to it and wish to shape public appreciation according to their views—namely, the power of truth, which slowly but surely conquers everywhere. The manufactured, factitious kind of success is like a flash flood caused by a furious downpour. At a spot where otherwise no water flows, it suddenly springs up, tearing away everything in its path. Sooner or later there is no trace left of it. The true, genuine type of success is like a spring which percolates out of the hidden depths of the earth. At first it flows, long unnoticed, as a thin rivulet, becomes a little brook, a stream, finally a river and flows into the sea, into infinity. However one may try to drain or stop up the spring, it gushes forth again into the light of day.

Happily it has long been clear that the zeal of the "Brahmsians" could not diminish Wagner's greatness and Brahms has assumed his rightful place in the history of art in spite of the retaliatory attacks formerly leveled at him by the "Wagnerites." Time is the most severe judge. It swallows up what is time-bound. Only what is above it cannot be touched by it.

That Brahms belongs to the unassailables is no longer in doubt today. His works force their way triumphantly even in the face of those who, if they could, would like most to shut themselves off from him. This great and simple figure, who with a noble modesty shunned any obtrusiveness, would doubtless have encountered misunderstanding, which nothing of significance can avoid, but would not have been able to engender hatred as such had it not been for two circumstances: the artificial rivalry with Wagner already mentioned, which was formerly kept up successfully but is not attempted any longer today, and the defiant comparison with Bach and Beethoven, thanks to Bülow's famous *mot* about the three B's, which was at the time rather premature, to say the least.

What was the sense of trying to make rivals out of Wagner and Brahms? Wagner lived and worked exclusively in music drama; Brahms longed for a good libretto but, probably fortunately, never found one. Can one imagine two artists who affected each other less than these two? While the one actually built his dream of an ideal festival theater but at the same time—half joyfully, half in spite of himself—conquered the stages he had formerly despised, the other lived a somewhat withdrawn, modest existence, out of which marvelous symphonic creations and profound, beautiful songs arose. Brahms felt high regard for Wagner even if no particular sympathy. Wagner took opportunities to interest himself in the compositions of his younger fellow artist. After hearing the *Variations on a Theme of Handel* he made the classic remark that the old forms are not dead so long as there is someone who is truly the master of them. Who knows whether on closer contact Brahms might not have had a stimulating influence on Wagner, just as the latter did on him to the extent that this was possible on so strong a personality as Brahms's. At least, although Wagner's impulsive nature could give way to odious remarks, which Brahms accepted in proud silence, there was no reason for open enmity and none broke out between the two masters themselves. But friends and enemies on both sides did not rest. They sneered, baited and incited until two camps had formed which spoiled both for themselves and for others their pleasure in the great creations of those two men. Decades had to elapse before the diehard "Brahmsians"—or "Brahmins," as they were jestingly termed—admitted that Wagner was nonetheless a great man, and until the rabid "Wagnerites" no longer spat when Brahms was mentioned. This was a comedy which had need of a modern Aristophanes!

I understand Bülow's awakening and growing enthusiasm for Brahms very well for I experienced it myself. But, as befitted Bülow's impulsive nature, this enthusiasm marked a change of direction rather than an enrichment. He had to lose Wagner in order to win Brahms. Let us also not forget the personal factors which naturally played an important part in the case of Bülow. Would he ever have brought himself to propagandize for Brahms as he did if the break with Wagner, so painful for him, so very regrettable for the cause of art, had not occurred? Here for once a basically noble man fell into the error, so often committed by the petty and spiteful, of furthering the renown of one artist quite immoderately in order thereby to diminish that of another. If one reads Bülow's letters of earlier times and compares with them what he said and did in the last years of his life, one can only feel regret that a spirit like his had to stand apart from Wagner's work at a time when it most had need of him. If one is moved by the struggle with which important figures have to fight their way through the indifference and ill will of their contemporaries and if this seems to lend them the glory of the martyrs, it was painful in the case of Brahms to be reminded that he was the darling of a biased party and of a famous conductor whose slightest whim was trumpeted forth as a prophetic pronouncement by his flatterers, and that the express purpose of both was to make him—a man whose own greatness was sufficient for him—their symbol in their fight against another great man.

It is in any event a great mistake to compare one figure still in process of development with another who has already reached fulfillment. Only when one views the totality of an artist's work can one come close to evaluating him properly. The fact that Bülow placed the relatively youthful Brahms in close juxtaposition to those two exalted masters, Bach and Beethoven, had to arouse the opposition of Brahms's adversaries and possibly even cause embarrassment to his friends. Surely Brahms himself was much more ambitious to write his own first symphony than one which, perhaps because of apparent similarity to Beethoven, could symbolically be termed the latter's tenth. This would-be honor was paid not only to Brahms's

First but also to Liszt's symphonies and to those of Bruckner. It was not given to Beethoven to write the Tenth Symphony. May it, however, be granted to many composers to create a first symphony which takes hold like the claw of a lion, as did Brahms's First! In none of his later symphonies did he recapture the immediacy and thrilling power of this piece, even though the Second breathes more of life's joy and the Third and Fourth reveal more intimate depths of the inner life. The first movement of the First straightaway actually reminds us of Beethoven. The feeling of awe which comes over us in many Beethoven movements—of expecting the earth to open all of a sudden and a gigantic fist to reach out at us—takes hold of us here, too. The music strikes our hearts as tough, astringent, unapproachable, at times almost ugly in sound, but full of tragic sublimity and compelling persuasion. That which the first movement denies to us the second bestows in rich measure; it is one of the most beautiful among all the symphonic slow movements which have ever been written. Here all is euphony, melody and a yielding to emotion, without any trace of the intellectual brooding from which Brahms's music, especially in slow movements, is not always entirely free. This movement is a gem of the entire symphonic literature. The third movement, which rushes by rather fleetingly, is followed by the most beautiful part of the whole work, the rather extended slow introduction to the last movement. The horn, which after the somber minor sounds in C major through the string tremolos as if the sun were breaking through a rolling morning mist, produces an extremely intense effect reminiscent of Schubert. Very moving indeed is the first quiet entry of the trombones, which Brahms wisely has kept in reserve until now. The following final section grows with irresistibly increasing animation up to the triumphant conclusion (This section's principal theme, because of its slight resemblance to Beethoven's "Ode to Joy" melody, gave rise to many foolish comments and to a very sensible, gruff reply from the composer.)

In total contrast to the First Symphony, the Second sounds an idyllic note. Sunny energy and optimism set its basic tone. Especially outstanding is the rich and colorful treatment of the orchestra. The first movement is a masterpiece from the beginning to its folk-like close. The second, slow movement, can only be appreciated sufficiently after repeated hearings. It unfolds itself to the musical sensibility slowly but fully. If I may, I should compare it to a

Dutch landscape at sunset. The eye at first is aware of nothing but sky above the endless plain; inattentively and almost wearily its glance sweeps over it. Gradually, however, a perception grows out of it, broadly, softly, and speaks to us. The minuet-like intermezzo is a delightful, graceful, playful piece, almost too slight for the content of the other three movements. The last movement brings the glowing work to a powerful close.

The last two symphonies of Brahms at first did not enjoy the great success of the first two. They even disappointed quite a few. No adagio overflowing with melody as in the First Symphony, no exultant finale as in the Second, are found in these works, which perhaps are the least extroverted of all the principal creations of the master. A lightfooted, scherzo-like intermezzo, like that of the D major Symphony—which is often applauded with shouts of "Encore!"—will also be sought in vain; instead there is a plenitude of beauties to be won, which will remain forever in the mind of one to whom they have revealed themselves fully. Who will easily forget the principal theme of the first movement of the F major Symphony, stretched out in an imposing arch, or that most tender and personal second theme? Musical thoughts like these are earthbound no more; they carry us into the realm of infinity. One must only have the capacity to let oneself be carried away, but not in banal delight over apparently ingenious external features (which so often only sauce over a poverty of invention) so as to consider a cymbal clash of greater worth than a wonderfully wrought tonal fabric formed in the depths of the heart. The second movement, so simple and yet so charmingly harmonized, the third, a song without words in the most beautiful sense, and the highly characteristic severe last movement with its quiet conclusion dying away in solemn resignation—these and the opening movement form themselves into a symphonic work which becomes ever more profound and noble the more we are able to assimilate it.

In the Fourth Symphony the two middle movements, for my taste, are of lesser value. The outer movements, however, are of absolutely monumental grandeur, especially the final movement. In this connection I mostly hear praise of the tour de force of using the old form of the passacaglia as a movement of a modern symphony. Certainly that is astounding, but for me the truly miraculous element is the extraordinary spiritual content of this piece. I cannot get away from the impression of implacable fate which imposes an ineluctable downfall on a great man or a great people. In spite of all struggle and efforts at defense, destruction is foredoomed; it approaches with inexorable steps. The conclusion of this movement seared with deeply moving tragedy is a veritable orgy of destruction, a frightful counterpart to the paroxysm of joy at the end of the last symphony of Beethoven. Could Brahms have felt prophetic here?

Four symphonies by Brahms are listed. Actually he wrote eight of them, for his concertos are also symphonies with obbligato solo instruments. Beethoven had already raised the instrumental concerto to a symphonic level. Brahms confirmed and completed this sublimation by an even richer elaboration of the orchestral part, which now plays an independent rôle and no longer that of a mere accompaniment, and by an even closer blending of the solo instruments with the body of the orchestra. His masterpiece in this genre is the Second Piano Concerto in B-flat major. The Adagio ranks with that of the First Symphony as regards the flowing melodic line. In the last movement, that magical laughter of the freest and noblest humor, one can really speak of a Beethoven-like level without mere banal phrase-making and without slighting Brahms's own individuality. Here we are led into regions where an attempt at comparison means only the pitting against one another of the highest forces. In the domains from which this piece derives the great spirits foregather, stretch out their hands meaningfully to each other and look deeply into each other's eyes—bright, filled with the view of all creation and yet so childlike—and then go their own ways again.

Let a particularly warm word be given to the Double Concerto for violin and violoncello because quite unjustifiedly it was long viewed as a stepchild of the master's muse, even by his partisans. I believe that the reason for the misunderstanding lay in deficient performances. If I hear that this difficult piece has been "presented" with one rehearsal, somewhat like a concerto of Vieuxtemps, then I know without having been there that the best of soloists—and they are the only ones who should venture this piece—cannot save the total impression of the work. Here is a loving elaboration of the orchestra part as in a symphony, requiring a perfected ensemble and balance of the orchestra and the two solo instruments which is only to be achieved through a number of painstaking rehearsals. Perfectly performed in this sense, this particularly forceful piece will not lack for success.

It cannot be denied that Brahms's creative work, perhaps more than that of any other master, is sometimes mannered; in his weaker works this can be disturbing to a certain degree. By this special mannerism of Brahms's I mean a complex of various devices for constructing a piece of music. One of these is his much favored habit of syncopation, i.e. the displacement of the bass against the rhythm of the upper voice or vice versa, so that one limps behind the other. Imagine a simple melody, for example one progressing and harmonized in quarter notes, in which the bass notes do not coincide with the corresponding melody notes but always lag an eighth note behind, so that the music takes on an odd, learned aspect without thereby gaining any inner significance. It looks rather like someone who pulls a serious face without his countenance becoming any the more expressive. Then, too, Brahms has a penchant for combining duple and triple rhythms, such as setting a line of quarter or eighth notes against triplets, a device which if used for long or frequently creates a feeling of unsteadiness. Still another of his habits is to accompany the upper voice, often even a middle voice or the bass, at the third or the sixth and then to tie the parts together in a kind of tricky syncopation. A variety of broken figures, and thematic structures, too, starting from the fifth of the triad combined with the third above and next fifth while avoiding the root, are so frequently to be found that the pattern shown in the example

has already been labeled the "Brahmsian Leitmotiv."

Whoever looks over his compositions of all types with an eye for the mannerisms cited will find the facts confirmed. Maybe he will then agree with me that these mannerisms are the reason why in Brahms there arises here and there a certain complexity which, in contrast to true simplicity, creates a feeling of monotony from which certain of his works and many sections of his works are not entirely free. While the essence of music reveals itself in great masterpieces, including those of Brahms, it is, so to speak, the conceptualization of it which appears to us in such passages. We then have, if I may say so, scientific music, a play of sounding forms and phrases, but no longer that universal language, without concepts, yet most expressive and totally comprehensible, which our great masters, including Brahms, were able and felt bound to speak. This language grips and stirs our hearts because we recognize ourselves in it with our joys and sorrows, our struggles and triumphs. Such music is artistic in contrast to artificial.

But only in very few cases are we faced with the concept of the artificial in contrast to the artistic where Brahms is concerned. A very real similarity between him and Beethoven can be found in the fact that he created only very little that was inferior and to which the above restrictive comments apply in the least. His self-discipline and self-criticism, strictly applied since his early youth, protected him from careless scribbling and from the danger of publishing what was not ready. In Max Kalbeck's biography we are told in great detail to what reworkings and often even painfully conscientious examinations he subjected his works before they took on definitive form. "The pen is not only there for writing but also for striking out," is one of his pithy sayings which every composer ought to put up as a motto over his desk. Also, those very characteristics of Brahms's music tagged as mannerisms often lend it a very personal charm. Brahms without syncopated notes would not be himself.

Like the great masters of past periods Brahms, too, turned with particular affection to chamber music and created fine works in it. The most profound and tender notes in the soul of music can best resound where there is no superficial brilliance of means to deceive us. Berlioz was too decorative in his feeling to sense a compulsion to chamber music. He needed the full orchestra.

I have already refuted elsewhere the quite foolish prejudice that Brahms's instrumentation was poor.

Berlioz and Brahms, as antipodal as they may be in most connections, still are, each in his way, living testimony to the correctness of Wagner's pronouncement that the old forms are not dead so long as there is someone who is truly the master of them. In that respect both masters are pioneers of true progress and indeed in a far higher sense than that in which tribute is generally as eagerly paid to Berlioz as it is withheld from Brahms.

Wagner's Impact on Symphonic Music

Bruckner and Some General Observations

It goes without saying that so prodigious a figure as Wagner's, although his domain is almost exclusively the music drama, has cast and still casts his rays and shadows into other areas. Two men of strong character who devoted themselves either not at all or only hesitatingly and with little success to music drama sought to make use of the overpowering effect of Wagnerian art in the areas of their own vocations and, thus, in their way to follow in the footsteps of the Bayreuth master. They were Wolf in the song and Bruckner in the symphony, the former through the introduction of the declamatory style and a richer working out of the piano accompaniment, the latter by a type of thematic development and orchestral coloration based on Wagner.

In addition to some church music and a string quintet, Bruckner wrote only symphonies, even a "Ninth," which, however, he did not complete. These symphonies show great similarities with each other. All have a ponderous solemnity which in the slow movements, without exception the most admirable, rises to impressive heights and on occasion to genuine greatness. The finales, which are far below the level of the other movements, more or less resemble free improvisations and bring out very strongly a negative characteristic of Bruckner's, the lack of a clear and systematic formal sense. The last movement of the Fifth Symphony is an exception, for, after an endless introduction, it presents a mighty and intensifying fugue which forms the high point of the work. The scherzos, often filled with sublime humor, generally have trios that remind one of Austrian folk tunes. Many more characteristics recurring equally in all nine works can be termed mannerisms to a far greater degree than Brahms's syncopations: the tendency to continual modulation, which even takes themes through many keys in the course of their sequencing; the concluding sections over an ostinato passage in the bass on the pattern of the coda of the first movement of Beethoven's Ninth Symphony; certain strangely empty-sounding places which either enter after a great building up to a climax or which bind large sections of individual movements together; thematic figures with simultaneous sounding of the same figures in retrograde motion as if they were mirroring each other; and finally the pauses, both long and short, of which Bruckner makes plentiful use. It often seems as if he had lost the thread and could think of no other way to deal with the problem than by interrupting the music so that he could start to spin something anew.

Bruckner's creative work does not make the impression that there had appeared to him in an inspired moment of conception a unified and total picture which he then had only to heighten and deepen by artistic elaboration to achieve ever greater clarity and final perfection. Rather, it is as if he waited at each step to see what his trusting, childlike, dreamy musical sense would whisper to him. When this had gradually been reduced to writing, the pieces were finally put together as best might be without troubling too much about whether everything fitted into place and without taking much time over attaining an objective view of the whole. Everything is tinged with touching idealism. The good Lord, in whom he had boundless confidence, wished him well and would see to it eventually that something tremendous came of all this. It is Bruckner's idealism which to a certain extent disarms even his adversaries, one of which I confess to being. Just think of this schoolmaster and organist from a background of poverty and without the benefit of any higher education steadfastly composing symphonies of dimensions un-heard of till then, filled with difficulties and unusual features of every sort, which were an abomination to the complacency of contemporary conductors, orchestra players, listeners and critics! Think of him, for all the utter certainty of non-recognition and failure, unswervingly keeping to his goals, departing not one step from his path, flirting neither with fashion nor with easy success! One can do nothing else but bow low before this phenomenal man, touching in his naïvety and honesty.

A musician once brought Beethoven a manuscript which he had headed with the words, "With God's help." Beneath this Beethoven wrote in his mighty hand, "Man, help thyself!" Many have learned that in the long run the dear Lord does not help when one cannot also help oneself. Even Bruckner was often left in the lurch by his deep religious feeling, for he was not always very adept at self-help.

I confess that hardly anything in modern symphonic music can cast such a spell over me as a theme or a short section from Bruckner's works. But this magic wears off more or less in the course of the work and sometimes disappears altogether. My artistic sensibility has always unerringly indicated, and will surely do so in future, that what is felt to be beautiful and great can only hold one's attention uninterruptedly if it is presented in perfected form.

It is precisely this formal element which is inseparably bound up with the essence of every art and which is unambiguously revealed in every great masterpiece, no matter to what period it belongs, that does not stand the test in Bruckner. It is not that he was looking for new forms and moved gropingly like Liszt over unaccustomed paths. Rather, it is that he stands in an uncertain relationship to the old forms. For him form as such is not the inexorable law, deeply rooted in nature, by which organisms having the power of life must build their constructs; instead, the plans of earlier symphonies are for him mere schematic designs, an instruction manual so to say, according to which he arranges and connects his often wondrous thoughts. So far as melodic invention was concerned, he was truly one of the rich. Others could bring up whole works on the crumbs which fell from his table. But the capacity to realize his ideas does not keep pace with his inventive powers. The technique is clumsy, the polyphonic texture of the voices is faulty, the structure is often broken up. The glorious themes are more like pearls strung upon a cord than linked together. That explains the fragmentary nature of his compositions, to which his propagandists always refer with farfetched and extenuating phrases, as if they felt that they bore their master's guilt. One could almost harbor the wish that Bruckner had had fewer ideas, but that the structure of his creations had been executed in a more unified and methodical manner. Thus the noblest thoughts often flutter away only because they merely cropped up without being placed in relation to each other according to their relative importance. One feels this all the more since many of his themes have the character of the Wagnerian dramatic and symbolic motifs, whose masterly, psychologically convincing working out stands before us as a shining example when we hear Bruckner's music and urges us to make comparisons. In addition, Bruckner's style contains what amounts to a demand for the systematic use and development of themes while he, on the other hand, has recourse to transitions which, even though perhaps thematically derived, stand in no organic relationship either to what has gone before or to what comes after. "Once the theme is over, the twaddle begins," a musician given to drastic opinions once said to me after the performance of a Bruckner symphony. That is a severe but not wholly unjustified judgment. If I draw on the reverence due from me to such an exalted and ambitious talent as Bruckner's and seek to harmonize my objective opinion with it, then I arrive at a simile which expresses the meaning of the opinion quoted above in a more dignified manner. Bruckner's symphonies are like the ruins of a wonderful temple which have been restored by an inexpert hand. We see mighty columns, glorious capitals and monumental beams but one part does not always accord with another and the gaps are often filled in with ordinary masonry. The eye, therefore, must content itself with the contemplation of beautiful details and forego an impression of the whole, just as the ear with Bruckner's music.

The most unified and spontaneous of the nine symphonies, relatively speaking, is the Fourth, the so-called "Romantic." The most beautiful single piece which Bruckner wrote, however, is the great Adagio in C-sharp minor from the Seventh Symphony, the elegy for Richard Wagner, the master in whom Bruckner's artistic existence had its roots. Bruckner's first supporters had indeed been Wagnerites, too, happy to have a symphonist on their side now whom they could play off against the detested Brahms. Once the frivolous nonsense which not only compares Bruckner with Beethoven and Brahms but even seeks to elevate him above them has spent itself, then Bruckner will, in my opinion, take his place in the history of art with other masters, the place amongst complete works which falls to an immense torso. But however that may be, Bruckner will not remain without influence on later symphonic writing. In opposition to polyphonic and instrumental craft, which seeks to render super-fluous the positive power of musical invention, he sets up the sincere force of his great and beautiful themes. May it now be given to younger composers to follow him in this direction.

Bruckner exercised a particularly great influence on one of the outstanding artists of recent times, Gustav Mahler. Mahler, who was his pupil, can also be considered his successor. He, too, wrote mainly symphonies, mostly of even more colossal dimensions than

Bruckner's, drawing upon extended instrumental and, on occasion, vocal resources. He also reached his "Ninth" and even an uncompleted Tenth Symphony. He is related to Bruckner through the breadth of his themes as well as through the fact that he remained a musician and wished to be nothing else, so that he abstained from programmatic experimentation. Melodies of such breadth and beauty as the beginning of the last movement of his Third Symphony or the lyrical outpourings of the violins in the Finale of his First are hardly to be found elsewhere in so-called modern music. But the successor is vastly superior to his forebear in the way in which he constructs his works. Mahler handles the technique of composition with a sovereign mastery which was denied to Bruckner. One may, without definable cause, find bizarre, even ugly elements in his works. One may be put off for a time by a sense of prolixity and surfeit, perhaps by the often insufficient self-criticism in the selection of thematic material. Still, the first four symphonies of Mahler contain, in greater abundance than the later ones, pearls and precious gems. But everything that he wrote bears the stamp of strong feeling, rich imagination and a glowing, almost fanatical enthusiasm which still compels our sympathy even where, instead of controlling it, he allows himself to be completely carried away by it.

I must digress here and speak of certain external circumstances which show up as traces of Wagner in our artistic life. I have already pointed out that Wagner made an intense expressive device in his music dramas out of the dramatic-psychological variation of a theme, as I have termed it, which Berlioz first employed in the *Fantastic* Symphony. In that connection let me warn against a blending of the musical-dramatic with the symphonic style. While referring to Wagner's *On the Application of Music to the Drama* and what he said in it on the subject, let me add that, admitting certain exceptions, a criterion of symphonic themes is their breadth and their special melodic character, while the themes for music drama must be distinguished by their pith, often by their meaningful terseness.

The musical dramatist's gift of invention is stimulated to productivity by elements other than those which act on symphonists. Actual persons and events to be presented physically upon the stage give him those formative motifs which often reveal to us in a flash the deep significance of those events more than words or any other art could do. The moods of an intimate, contemplative nature, the emotional residues of great events, whether actual or fictional, which do not require and indeed may even resist embodiment through the drama, these are what inspire a symphonist to creation. His work will be like a living-out of his being in music, whence the breadth of the themes and the truly great instrumental melodic line, rarely possible in opera. If one can call the orchestral writing of a music drama "symphonic," i.e. meaningfully constructed according to the laws established by the drama in question, then one can, if the underlying emotions are very vigorous and varied, term a symphony "dramatic." The whole world is a drama and music reveals its innermost essence to us. In this sense, music, too, is "dramatic," as we most clearly recognize in Beethoven, to whom we must always refer back if we really want to speak meaningfully about this art. One should take the "symphonic" in music drama in a concrete sense but the "dramatic" in the symphony in a meta-physical one, and carefully preserve this distinction, since confusions could have the consequence that pieces of music would arise which might seem more similar to fragments from operas than symphonies, and on the other hand, symphonic pieces which did not belong there would loom large in operas. It is an exemplary excellence of Bruckner's symphonies that their themes, although they show a relationship to Wagner, still remain genuinely symphonic.

Wagner's themes, as they are varied for dramatic purposes, have been given the name "Leitmotivs." This expression is as inappro-priate and tasteless as most of the appellations which have been bestowed on these so-called Leitmotivs. A motif which is to "lead" us on the right path through musical labyrinths, as it were, so that we do not lose the track, certainly should never vary so that it can always be recognized by us without question. Wagner's themes, however, are constantly being varied and appear in the most change-able relationships to each other, just as the stirrings of our emotional life and volition within our own souls. In their protean nature they would therefore hardly be suitable for leading the inexperienced through uncharted territory. But no doubt they become, through their variation and their interconnection (only possible because of the polyphonic nature of the music), a faithful emotional reflection of the characters on the stage. It is through this sort of thematic working out that Wagner's drama achieves its penetrating power and clarity. The Leitmotivs, with their fanciful names, and their vessels, the "guidebooks," have brought more confusion than enlightenment to the study of Wagner's art, for very often it was thought that one had studied the works sufficiently when one had discovered as many Leitmotivs as possible—just as one picks out the hidden funny figures in picture puzzles—or had learned by heart the themes listed in the guidebook. It would have been much more important to have gained enlightenment about the unfailingly melodic character of the Wagnerian music drama in spite of the declamatory style and the detailed motivic elaboration.

But particularly reprehensible is the way in which the leitmotivic method of dissection has now been carried over into music which is not constructed in Wagner's manner and even to works of the classical period, in the belief that this would benefit the public's understanding. One result of this carry-over is the use of "program booklets" customary at orchestral concerts in many cities. An introduction written by a good musician and provided with musical examples is certainly welcome, particularly in the case of new works. But it cannot be stressed strongly enough to the public that they should be read before or possibly even after the performance together with the score or a good piano arrangement, but in no event during the performance. We should apply all our energy and attention to the appreciation of a work of art. A distracted listening accompanied by hasty, superficial reading has no value; indeed, it is an offense to the work and to oneself. A stop should be put to this by all possible means, including appropriate action by teachers.*

Tune detective work, which occasionally assumes epidemic proportions, is a fruit of this crime. Having become unaccustomed to grasping a piece of music as a whole because of these dissecting guides and programs, the "connoisseurs," who have drawn their wisdom from such sources, now turn their attention when hearing new works only to the themes, which are presented to them in meagre musical examples in the more or less tastefully put together booklets. The barren pleasure of drawing comparisons is immediately stimulated. When Wagner was somewhat more contemporary, it was agreed straightaway that younger composers had to be his imitators above all before they might imitate other masters. Heaven help us if, for example, G and C were sounded in a definite rhythm.

---

* Certainly the struggle will be all the more difficult the bigger the business done by impresarios with program booklets, which also contain advertisements.

The borrowing of the two notes from the "well-worn Sword Motif" was unmistakable. Mercy on us if an ascending chromatic progression was discovered! The new theme tnus was tne "tiresome Love Motif" from *Tristan und Isolde*. Two broken fourths derived from Beckmesser's "ricocheting Pummeling Motif" and dotted triplets from Alberich's "malleable Forging Motif." Finally the whole work was decried as one "squeezed out of saintly Wagner." It is astounding with what speed a new work could be "killed off" without one's ever having come to know it. If nothing or too little was found in Wagner to throw enough suspicion on the sacrificial beast, then the theme hunters would look into Liszt and Brahms, into Berlioz to the extent that he was familiar, then into older masters, finally into Meyerbeer, operettas and street ditties. It would be a special study to put together with the help of lengthy experience the arrant nonsense which has come out of this "detective work." A "wag" has stated that the theme in the final scene of *Götterdämmerung* at Brünnhilde's words "Fühl' meine Brust auch, wie sie entbrennt" are borrowed from the ditty "Du hast die schönsten Augen"! A similarity of notes is certainly there but how long must the ears of this fortunate sleuth have been!

Today the epidemic of tune sleuthing has lost its virulence because in the sound-complexes which are now considered as the highest development of music meaningful themes do not occur and melody is quite taboo. But the appearance of works which are music in the true sense of the art can help the bacillus of this insidious disease immediately regain its virulence.

The tune detectives in their half-childish, half-spiteful pleasure at finding coincidences of note patterns forget the character of the theme, the place where it ocurs, the manner of its treatment and finally the image, quality and physiognomy of the entire work. They hear with their eyes, not with their ears. They forget that the same sequence of notes is far from being a reminiscence. Many factors must enter in before it can become such, including tempo, tonality, expression, position in the course of the whole, but above all the recognizably identical, inner need for precisely this and for no other sequence of notes, for only then do we establish the composer's inability to find the proper expression and the necessity for borrowing which derives from that. But they also overlook the fact that through the entire mood of a passage and the recalling of a similar one in the work of another composer, the feeling of a reminiscence can be produced without any identity of note pattern whatsoever. Strangely enough, these mood reminiscences are noticed much less but are really the more objectionable because they, more than an inadvertent identity of notes, indicate a composer's lack of independence. Similar note patterns occur throughout the greatest masterpieces from Bach to Wagner in great numbers, but they have never had an influence on the esteem for these masters, and it never occurred to anyone before to try to make them a measure of the value of these works.

If a composition bears the unmistakable features of its author and if it is perfect as a whole and in its parts, then a fortuitous coincidence of notes with a passage from any other work is completely devoid of significance.

I state this as clearly and definitely as possible. In the first place I do this as a protection for such composers who run the risk of doubting their own gifts because of the condemnation they receive at the hands of the tune sleuths. Secondly I do so as a warning both against and to those who, out of fear of such condemnation, forcibly eliminate any innocent coincidence of sound from the possibly highly spontaneous and worthy musical ideas which occur to them and who thereby give their works the stamp of "conscious originality." This is the worst possible approach, for it gives rise to those affected, *recherché*, tortured and bloated pieces with superficial attempts at profundity and overrefined banalities which we encounter so often today in the song as well as in the symphony and the opera. Such works can have prospects for success only if they are put together with provocative skill and are placed before the public with real business acumen. I do not believe it amiss if I term the fear of not being considered original as the evil demon which robs many of our young composers of the feeling for wholesomeness, forcefulness and sincerity. I am not afraid in the least of being reproached for having shielded clumsy plagiarism if I cry out freely and frankly: "Better an honest reminiscence than a monstrosity!" Not everyone has the strength to let the undoubtedly unpleasant effects of this pointless tune sleuthing calmly roll off his back. Not everyone is so self-assured as fearlessly to face up to the demon Fear of Unoriginality. Not everyone, finally, has the healthy self-confidence needed to shrug off this whole simplistic degeneration of the critical faculty, whenever it does not seem necessary on occasion to pronounce a few forceful words on the subject.

The Symphonic Poem

Just as Wagner influenced Bruckner through his music, so did he influence his noble friend and patron Liszt through his character as a composer-poet. Wagner characterized as the basic flaw of the "old opera" the making of an end, the drama, into a means, and a means, the music, into an end. Following this theory in his own works, he put the music in second place and assigned to it the rôle of a prime minister, to be sure, but still a character subordinate to drama, the king. Liszt had no feeling for music drama. His intelligence, however, was so great that he recognized the significance of the Wagnerian reform quite apart from the admiration which his friend's music instilled in him. Schumann, Berlioz and even Beethoven had dared to give music a poetical foundation and indeed to create it under such an influence. When the urge to speak a personal musical language had been awakened in Liszt, who at first had been active only as a virtuoso, his inclination to follow the predecessors named above was substantially strengthened by Wagner's advance, which was then becoming manifest. The thought was clearly to create in symphonic music a counterpart to music drama, making the music the servant of the poetic idea there, too. Hand in hand with this went the effort to heighten the expressive power of music so that it could be increased to what, in terms of speech, would be a literally meaningful direct clarity of expression. Since this, however, did not just happen by itself, and music remained music in spite of all attempts which were made on it—but, on the other hand, raised itself forthwith to the required capacity for the clearest expression as soon as the word in the vocal sense was added to it, whether in song or opera—the further consequence ensued that Liszt had to attempt to prop up his compositions indirectly with words. The program, to the extent that it had been used at all, had served earlier composers, even Berlioz in the *Fantastic* Symphony, as an emotional stimulus. With Liszt it became the governing essential, the manifest poetic subject which was his sole point of departure, that which alone determined the structure of the work, and for the sake of which he broke down musical form in an improvisatory manner.

To be sure, he had once, but only once, had a predecessor in this in the person of Berlioz, namely in the next to last orchestral movement in the dramatic symphony *Romeo and Juliet*, entitled "Romeo at the Tomb of the Capulets—Invocation—Juliet's Awakening—Joyous Ecstasy and the First Effects of the Poison—Death Agony and Farewell of the Lovers." Berlioz attempted there to reproduce in clear form the details of the dramatic action through melodic fragments, accents, chord progressions and expressive figurations, so that one might believe oneself capable of following the dramatic action in every measure of the music. However, the impression which this composition makes, even in the best of performances, is a completely confusing one—indeed (my reverence for Berlioz does not keep me from saying so) downright laughable at times. The reason for this is that here music has been set a task which it is not capable of performing. Were it not for the fact that a hint about the action of the drama is provided by the title (as well as by the explanatory note referring to the capricious rewriting of Shakespeare by a famous actor),* we would be at a total loss vis-à-vis this strange composition. The feeling of being at a loss continues even when we know what we are supposed to imagine.

* TRANSLATOR'S FOOTNOTE: The reference is to Berlioz' acknowledgment that his *Romeo and Juliet* was based on the "acting version" by David Garrick which was the basis of the French translation used in contemporary performances with which he was familiar. Garrick's version, one of many made by producers and actors from the seventeenth century until relatively recent times—today we tolerate cuts but no rewriting!—has the play conclude with the death of the lovers, eliminating Friar Laurence's sermon and the reconciliation of the families. (An interesting parallel can be drawn between this truncated version of *Romeo and Juliet* and the customary elimination in earlier days of the final sextet in Mozart's *Don Giovanni*, which thus ended as the stone guest dragged Don Juan off to hell.)

Garrick's version may be studied in the *Romeo and Juliet* volume of the series *A New Variorum Edition of Shakespeare*, prepared by Horace Howard Furness (Philadelphia, 1871; Dover reprint, 1963), p. 395.

But Berlioz, although apparently stimulated to write his symphony in the first instance by French performances of the play "avec le dénouement de Garrick," nevertheless composed a final movement with triple chorus as well as orchestra and explains this in his preface to his dramatic symphony:

"This final scene of the reconciliation of the two families belongs solely to the domain of opera or oratorio. Since Shakespeare's time it has never been played in any theater. However, it is too beautiful, too musical, and crowns too well a work of this nature for the composer to be able to dream of treating it otherwise."

But we really must be amazed at how clear and precise the words of the title seem in contrast to the music, which, as soon as it abandons the melodic line of its beginning, seems like someone who, having suffered a stroke, wishes to speak but cannot.

Here we have reached the point at which the true nature, the true mission of music reveals itself in all its splendor. Here we see that it is an art which never can speak to us in conceptual terms because above and beyond all concepts it shows us the innermost and essential life of the world in a highly refined image. However, we also see at this point that music is stripped of its majesty when an artist requires it to explain events to us in the way words do. Music is demeaned and robbed of both the sensitive as well as the infinitely meaningful and unique quality of its nature if it is bound slavishly to a program, measure by measure, episode by episode. Music certainly can reproduce the mood, the emotional situation which an event produces in us, but it cannot depict the event itself. That pertains to the art of poetry and, in other ways, to painting and sculpture. If nevertheless music undertakes to perform this task so incompatible with it, then we experience something similar to hearing a person trying to speak in a language which is foreign to him. It is well known that the result is not only incomprehensible but even funny. In such cases music has entered into the false relationship to the program previously noted, and ceases at such a point to be music. This was felt by Berlioz himself when, foreseeing the ineffectiveness and basic instability of the next to last orchestral movement in *Romeo and Juliet*, he apparently turned against the public, in reality against himself, and in the following terms recommended omitting the piece altogether:

"The public has no imagination. Thus, pieces which appeal only to the imagination have no public. The following instrumental scene finds itself in this position and I urge that it always be omitted except when this symphony is performed before a select audience to whom the fifth act of Shakespeare's tragedy in Garrick's version is fully familiar and whose poetic feeling is on a very high level. This will be the case once in a hundred times. Furthermore it presents enormous difficulties to the conductor who wishes to perform it. Accordingly let there be a moment's pause after 'Juliet's Funeral' and then begin with the last movement" (Breitkopf & Härtel score of *Romeo and Juliet*, page 165).

This note, as well as the fact that Berlioz admits that the *Fantastic* Symphony, too, can dispense with its program, reveals his true relationship to music more penetratingly than the longest essays of those who want to make him into the founding father of a degenerate tendency.

Whoever cannot do otherwise may picture something concrete—let us term it an "event"—in his imagination while listening to a piece of music. This will not substantially diminish his capacity to absorb it, for a good piece of music rests on much firmer, much deeper foundations and speaks to us with much more force than the imagining of that "event." It tells of things from the uttermost depths, of which that "event" is only a likeness, a mere image. The piece unveils its secret for us and makes it transparent, whence the powerful significance of music in drama. But the reverse—taking the "event," be it physical or emotional in nature, dramatic or philosophical in content, as a subject and attempting to express in music not merely its general effect on our emotions but the whole succession of occurrences within it—this is first of all a foolish undertaking, because only words, and in certain isolated cases a painter's or sculptor's rendering, possess the ability to do so (thus the artist is mistaken in the choice of his medium), but in addition, it is an objectionable undertaking, because music, the idiom of the very spirit of the world, thereby is forced into a service beneath its dignity and suffers from a mode of expression at odds with its exalted character.

Musicians will dispute certain details of Schopenhauer's superb elucidation of the nature of music, but the totality of his conception will never lose its significance.

Although the fragment of *Romeo and Juliet* discussed above fore-shadows the manner of his creative activity, Liszt nevertheless produced works of considerably greater, indeed of truly great worth, to the extent that he was successful in finding for many of his compositions an artistic form which permitted the work in question, while keeping to its program, still to appear as self-contained and not in conflict with the nature of music. In *Mazeppa* a wild movement, rising to a frenzy, pictures the death-ride of the hero; a short recitative-like andante, his collapse; the following march, introduced by trumpet fanfares and growing to a triumphant climax, his exaltation and coronation. Here two independent compositions are linked together by a short transition into a single whole. The construction of the tone poem *Orpheus* grows out of a grand crescendo, leading through several sections to a high point and dying away softly and ever more faintly in a diminuendo, all in accordance with the long program which can be summed up as follows:

"Orpheus strikes the golden strings of his lyre. The whole of nature listens reverently to the wondrous sounds. With noble strides the god passes before us, delighting the world by his appearance and his playing. The tones of his lyre grow fainter; the heavenly figure is seen farther and farther away. Finally it vanishes from our sight altogether."

The comparison with the prelude to *Lohengrin* is obvious, for it, too, could be based on such a program. But it is just this comparison which shows Wagner's vast superiority over Liszt. While Wagner constructs his piece with absolutely overwhelming logic, with expression, instrumentation, figuration, melody and polyphony building up, step by step, till the climax takes our very breath away, Liszt has to resort to repetitions and sequences and thereby achieves only a superficial effect in spite of the noble themes. Nevertheless *Orpheus* can be considered one of Liszt's best works.

If we heard *Mazeppa* and *Orpheus* without any titles, we would doubtless hear in the first a painful and stormy mood which falls into despair and then rises up again victoriously, and in the second we would feel the presence of a sovereign gentleness which comes upon the scene and then floats away—all this without our necessarily having to think of Mazeppa or Orpheus. As already noted once before, our imagination is powerfully stimulated by the title, not bound to it in submission, because the works cited are imbued with positive musical force and because they owe their inception to musical feeling and creativity, not merely to a clever urge to illustrate. This type of program music I can defend; its opposite, however, a formless improvisation on some underlying concrete ideas, this I must condemn. When Liszt attempts in his symphonic poem *Die Ideale* (The Ideals) to interpret musically successive fragments of Schiller's poem, then to weld this interpretation together into a unit, and writes over the individual pieces of music the portions of the poem which he would like imagined at the relevant places, so that in fact only those armed with the score can know just what they are supposed to think at that moment, then the more faithfully the music tries to follow the conceptual content of the poem, the more abjectly will it fail. Compare this with the Overture to the first version of *Fidelio*, actually the first *Leonore* Overture, always referred to incorrectly as the second. It is far from having the value of the great one but is a proper overture to an opera because various important elements of the action to come are discernibly presented in it: Florestan's imprisonment, Leonore's courageous setting out to free her husband, her seeking and searching, their meeting and the struggle with Pizzarro, the victory, a brief reflection on the horrors they have lived through, their grateful feelings towards God and finally the jubilation of the happily reunited couple. Despite Beethoven's quite programmatic treatment of this work, how well he understood how to maintain its symphonic character and form! How well he was able to achieve the greatest lucidity with resources which lie within the limitations of music, a fact which in itself alone ensures its lucidity! Let us recall the powerful sudden entrance of C minor at a point at which one expects the usual reprise of the first section in C major, a feature which is lacking in the great *Leonore* Overture. This is supposed to picture the moment of greatest danger, the confrontation of Leonore with Pizzarro. How straightforwardly and without any violent jolt he then interweaves the motives from the opera at the passage where Pizzarro recoils from Leonore's pistol! I should like to point to this very overture as a model of the extent to which a program can be combined with music without doing violence to its nature. It is for me the most perfect symphonic poem which exists and as such the best introduction to the opera *Fidelio*. The great Overture is not suitable for this because it grows beyond the bounds of the theatrical, existing as a unique tone poem in itself alone and carrying us off into joyous heights of the greatest happiness, from which it is impossible to return at once to the confinement of the prison courtyard. To degrade this Overture, however, to the status of an intermezzo after the first act or the dungeon scene, or even, as happened in Munich, an exit march for the audience after the performance, that is an abuse which only leads one to wonder at the tastelessness with which it was defended and the obstinacy with which it is adhered to.

Liszt's symphonic poems *Hamlet*, *Prometheus* and *Héroïde Funèbre* suffer from a deficiency of musical invention. The *Mountain Symphony* (*Ce qu'on entend sur la montagne*), which begins with so much genuine feeling and ardor, loses its effectiveness because of a disregard of form which amounts to a total lack of plan. *Die Hunnenschlacht* (The Battle of the Huns) forms a counterpart to *Mazeppa* and is possibly superior to it in musical worth. It is an energetic piece for which Liszt fortunately provided no program, but which he explained adequately through a reference to Kaulbach's colossal painting.

The graceful *Les Préludes* hardly requires any clarification; nor does *Hungaria*, a Hungarian rhapsody in the grand manner. *Tasso* presents a delightful middle movement in F-sharp major and a rather noisy but uncommonly effective final climax, so that the opening, which suffers from formlessness, can be taken into the bargain.

It is quite noteworthy that Liszt gave the best that he had to offer in those two works which come closer to symphonic form than all of his symphonic poems, namely in the two great symphonies based on Goethe's *Faust* and Dante's *Divine Comedy*. The *Faust* Symphony, as its title promises, presents three character portraits, Faust, Gretchen and Mephistopheles. The first movement is the weakest despite its splendid themes. The fragmentary type of development, the great length, the unfortunate literal repetition of the whole introduction in the middle of the piece, appear to justify the desire for sensible cuts and condensations.* The second movement is very poetic, distinguished by a wonderfully simple and spun out principal theme. It is certainly not music congenial to Goethe's noble creation which we hear. Rather, it is a portrait of a beautiful, intelligent society lady costumed as Gretchen. She plays "he loves me, he loves me not" with cultivated daisies and not with the wild flower. But the great melodic charm, the colorful and perfumed instrumentation and not least of all the homogeneous character of this piece, so unusual in Liszt, give it the stamp of particular charm. The last movement is indeed highly original, a coruscating orchestral scherzo of diabolical pungency and ferocity. For all its goodness, Liszt's nature had much sarcasm in it. In this Finale he displays himself fully in this sense. It is astonishing with what art he has here used and developed the dramatic-psychological variation of a theme invented by Berlioz. Mephistopheles is "the spirit which always denies" and his operative principle is that "all that is produced is worthy of decay." Thus, Liszt has given him no theme of his own, but instead constructs the entire movement out of caricatures of earlier themes, namely those relating to Faust. Only the most crass lack of understanding could raise the reproach of a lack of musical invention against Liszt here. If our old masters

* I have already done this in performance.

created great movements out of themes of a few measures by their manifold variations of them, why should similar procedures be denied to a composer when a poetic thought is the driving impulse and the artist, like Liszt in this instance, works on completely musical lines so that the elucidation of the poetic element remains secondary? Is not musical inventiveness a great part of such a variation of themes for purposes of characterization—and perhaps hardly any less inventiveness than the earlier masters must have possessed? Moreover, I cannot agree with Wagner, who rejects dramatic-psychological variation—to use my expression—which is such a necessary technique in music drama, as a farfetched effect in the symphony. The sudden entrance of the minor mode in Beethoven's original *Leonore* Overture mentioned above is certainly already such a variation of the theme otherwise occurring in the major. Just as this variation technique in music drama is determined by the action, so, too, it must conform in the symphony to the laws of symphonic form. These laws allow the imagination of the composer such wide leeway in works with and without specific and definite titles as is available to nature, which can create innumerable individuals within the same form, each different from the other. If, indeed, someone were to ask me for the rule of this form, I should have to answer him in Hans Sachs's words, "You establish it yourself and then you follow it." Yes, this following, this relentless conformance to this self-imposed rule, this refraining from deviation before everything is clear and in place, this tireless, patient working until what gradually emerges matches the inspiration although the labor is not apparent—that is what finally leads to the perfection of a work of art. It is no merit to depart from the usual form without reaching a fixed goal. It is senseless to term sticking to form as reactionary. The "revolutionaries" forget that with their invectives against form they finally become the same sort of Philistines as the pseudo-Classicists once were with their fear of the possibility of innovation. Everything is a matter of what the whole work has to say to us. If it says something clearly and plainly, sincerely and without reserve, in a language which permits rejection or approval but no strained interpretation, then content and form will stand together as equals, then it will be a masterpiece. Experiments, however, whose problematic inferiority must be touched up with pompous programs and which in addition try to arouse an impression that it has been the artistic "purpose" that the entire work should limp along formlessly in confusion—such attempts cannot pretend to such an honorable estate. In many of his works Liszt, in spite of the beauty of individual parts, did not go beyond the experimental stage. In some, however, and especially here in the "Mephistopheles" movement of his *Faust* Symphony, he reveals to us that, in spite of his wanderings down programmatic and poetic blind alleys, he possessed a deep understanding of the true nature of music. When the infernal devilish spirit has grown to the height of its power, there appears the principal theme of the "Gretchen" movement in its original, pristine beauty, as if floating on transfigured clouds. The power of the devil in shattered by it and sinks away into nothingness. The poet could even permit Gretchen to turn into a criminal; the musician keeps her a sublime, bright figure. Powerful trombones ring through the dying chords from hell. A male chorus quietly begins to sing Goethe's sublime words of the *chorus mysticus*, "Everything transitory is but an image," and a tenor voice continues in the clearly recognizable notes of the Gretchen theme, "The eternal feminine draws us ever onward." One can identify this tenor voice with Goethe's Doctor Marianus and think of Gretchen as being transfigured into the Mater Gloriosa. One is also reminded of Faust's words as he sees Gretchen's image in the vanishing cloud:

> Like the soul's own beauty the lovely form ascends;
> Without dissolving, it rises on into the ether
> And draws the best of my heart up with it.

So it is that in major musical works golden threads spun out of the very sunshine, lightly, gently uniting music and the poetry which called it into being, ennoble both arts and fetter neither of them.

Just as outstanding in its way as the *Faust* Symphony is the tone poem on Dante's *Divine Comedy*, with its deeply moving portrayal of the tortures of the eternally damned, the melancholy and alluring so-called "Francesca" episode and the "Purgatorio," which rises gradually to ever higher spheres of pure feeling. Liszt attached no program to the *Faust* Symphony; he could and should have refrained from having one written by Richard Pohl for the *Dante* Symphony and prefaced to the score. The terms "Inferno" and "Purgatorio" are familiar to every educated person and the music tells us quite enough. Nor do we need at all to think of Francesca and Paolo during the middle section of the first movement in order to grasp and appreciate the particular beauty of this *intermezzo lirico*.

Mannerisms can be pointed out in Liszt at least to the same degree as in Bruckner: breaking off when the flow of the music cannot be maintained in a steady stream—which has a characterizing effect only in rare instances, merely a disturbing one in most—the habit of accompanying slow melodies at first with a few, usually arpeggiated chords and then going on monodically so as to add on a tonally higher sequence; the lack of polyphony of any sort unless a fugato is struck up—the two fugatos in the *Faust* and *Dante* Symphonies are of great quality, let me not fail to add—the myriad literal repetitions; the mainly triumphant conclusions with a strong preference for the brilliant key of C major; the often painfully noisy employment of percussion instruments; and, finally, the effort to construct essentially different parts of one work out of the same theme, an attempt which even with all the composer's skill in transformation still evokes the feeling of monotony and ultimately of boredom.

Against these faults stand as virtues the beauty—in part energetic, in part ingratiating—of many of Liszt's themes, and above all the firm feeling that, like Bruckner, he never wrote for the sake of superficial success; that he went his way with the deepest inner conviction that he was, in his way, a pioneer of a new art, just as Wagner was in his; that when with proud resignation he uttered the words, "I can wait," he firmly believed that later generations would redress the injustice done him in his lifetime. This is a belief which has been fulfilled in part and will be so even more, unless all indications are deceptive, if even only a small number of his works, but these few all the more securely, establish their place in the changing taste of changing times. As I was fortunate enough to have had friendly relations with Liszt to the extent that the difference in our ages allowed, it is impossible for me to conclude these observations without recalling his great personality. It has long been a part of recorded history how this great man worked tirelessly to aid artists intellectually congenial to him to spread the fame of their works. He gave genius and talent in every field a helping hand, supported young artists in word and deed, and in all this never undertook anything for his own benefit, in fact often neglected the advancement of his own creative works for the sake of others. I believe that no one, even those to whom his works are unsympathetic, will want to deprive him of the gleaming crown which unselfishness and the noblest love have set upon his head for all time. In his human relations Liszt was the king of artists!

In recent years numerous composers of various nations have created symphonic works which in part have sprung from the soil of classic form and in part owe their existence to a poetic subject—which, however, does not always connect them with typical program music. Let me take, for example, the *Vltava* (Moldau) of Smetana, which is so delightful in its originality and instrumentation that neither the loose structural connection of its sections nor their imagistic titles trouble one. The music speaks from its own heart and all accessory matters are of secondary importance.

One of these works lifts its head ever higher, the *Symphonie Pathétique* of Tchaikovsky. The earlier creations of this master were like dramas full of striking effects, rich in suspenseful, occasionally brutal situations, and whose value sometimes was not on a level with the forceful impression which they were able to produce. But the last of his symphonies, the *Pathétique*, combines purity and power of feeling with truly tragic beauty and perfection of form to such a degree that its place of honor in the front rank of post-classical symphonies is assured. However, it must not be senti-mentalized, as many a "podium rubato virtuoso" would have it, for that makes the symphony unbearable, like many other pieces which suffer this fate.

Just as Gustav Mahler was the successor of Bruckner, so, too, Richard Strauss, the most sensational modern composer, can be considered as Liszt's successor, little as this might be inferred from his first, very solidly wrought orchestral compositions, founded on a thoroughly formal musical basis: a symphony and a four-movement suite entitled *Aus Italien* (From Italy). Initiated by the composer Alexander Ritter into the formulae and mysteries of the modern school, he soon belonged to the guild of so-called progress and in the course of the years raised himself to the rank of its undisputed leader. The series of symphonic poems which he has written to date at first showed a development of the talent for thematic combination and orchestral technique which seemed to make nothing further appear impossible. The astonishment at the infernal sounds which more and more openly roared, groaned, scraped, squeaked and moaned in his compositions gradually yielded to a prurient expecta-tion as to what a new work could bring out by way of the as yet unheard and unprecedented. Just as Hans von Bülow contrived his conducting and behavior in the concert hall in his last years so as to make one ever curious to see what would happen next, so did Strauss with respect to his composing. And he succeeded in keeping the public in suspense. In fact, he did not disappoint these expectations for a long time. An intensification even took place when he provided his wild, raging, colorful orchestral fantasies with vocal parts and by the use of contemporary plays transferred them to the opera house. This type of sound production is more justified in that setting than in symphonic music, because the powerfully realistic species of Wagnerian music drama cultivated by Strauss requires powerfully realistic sound which no one has been able to produce as well as Strauss. Listeners grew unaccustomed to expect fine-sounding music from Strauss and half curiously, half indifferently, let the most daring dissonances flow by so as thankfully to prick up their ears when, after an interminable, often painful uproar, a melody or a few euphonious harmonic progressions were heard—only to disappear again soon, as though they felt out of place in their environment. Strauss knew and still knows very well how to evaluate and prepare the effects of these interruptions, just as he prepares his closing sections, which he usually forms on melodic lines so as to make the contrast with what has gone before doubly impressive. Strauss knows how to grip the mob. His gifts are combined with a sure sense for hitting on what must arouse interest at the moment. He possesses an unfailing instinct for sensing the secret, as yet unavowed needs of the public and for satisfying them with amazing speed so as to appear as a leader when in fact he is being led. Just now he is turning quite ostentatiously to a kind of simplicity, because the longing for this is unmistakable. But true simplicity cannot be had to order and certainly least of all when one has formerly and just as ostentatiously turned one's back on it.

The strong sensual appeal of Wagner's music has called forth an excitation of musical feeling and an exuberance of taste which caused the great ethical elements in Wagner to be overlooked completely, so that we have clung all the more to external features, such as strident brilliance of orchestration, epicurean splendor or grotesque eccentricity of harmony and melodic lines of not very exalted eroticism. Moreover, it was believed that from Wagner's bold procedures one could derive the license for reckless arbitrariness of every sort. Once stimulated by the glow of Wagner's musical idiom, alongside which Liszt's coruscating formlessness was also tolerated gradually as a kind of kindred phenomenon, people became increasingly submissive to the thrall of that seductive, anarchic twofold charm which appeared all the stronger the more ephemeral it was in reality. If Strauss had continued on the course he had taken in his first orchestral compositions, he would presumably have had increasing difficulty in establishing himself the more he gained in inner greatness. Thus he achieved his first success when he created with an inspired hand *Don Juan*, a piece in which, thanks to his thorough symphonic schooling, he avoided the rhapsodic elements predominant in Liszt, so that the piece flows along in much more of a pleasing, uninterrupted stream than Liszt's symphonic poems. He heightened his creative powers in *Tod und Verklärung* (Death and Transfiguration), a piece of great passionate intensity, effective in its originality and structure, sincere and genuine in its feeling, except for its closing section, which is more pompous than transfigured.

He attained a still higher level—of success, too—in *Till Eulenspiegels Lustige Streiche* (Till Eulenspiegel's Merry Pranks). Here he offers something of himself. Roguishness is not foreign to Strauss, for he knows how to poke fun not only at others but also at himself. Many of the monstrous features in his later compositions, at which the admiring initiates languishingly rolled their eyes while less believing souls crossed themselves as though the devil had appeared to them in person, may be bold experiments which one might well offer to a public which has already learned to believe in the name of the author. Strauss may thus have been the first to rub his hands in secret delight at the amazement of the former as well as at the disgust of the latter.

Eulenspiegel has nothing to do with this, however. It is a brilliant orchestral scherzo which I do not consider program music. On the occasion of the *première*, Strauss, confident of the musical character of this piece, declined tastefully and—when I recall certain Eulenspiegel anecdotes—tactfully, to add a program. We would receive a completely definite impression from this piece even if it were performed without a title, and in such a connection we would not have to think of Eulenspiegel at all.

Lengthy introductions were prefaced to Strauss's later compositions. The orchestral apparatus which he conscripted became ever more complex, and ever more frenzied the manifold fullness of sound which this mass of instruments produced. The forces employed stood in an inverse relationship to the intrinsic worth, and the ninth of his tone poems, the *Alpensymphonie* (Alpine Symphony), presented a decidedly weak, almost cliché-ridden swan song of the program music species. If Strauss wanted to play Richard II, the musical world, wading in the sanguinary swamp of atonality, by degrees appeared fit for a Richard III and ready to relegate the "pioneering" Richard II to obsolescence even in his lifetime. The deviation from the lofty paths of art, first for idealistic and later for selfish motives, has taken a fearful toll. In today's period of brutalization of artistic feeling there remains only the expectation of a total collapse of all that enlightened minds have held to be great and beautiful, and the hope that a few courageous souls will be brought to their senses and to a vivid awareness of true creative power by just this collapse. The bright genius of music which speaks to us in Beethoven's works has veiled its head. We are faced with its dark antagonist, a demon which is only waiting to swallow us up altogether, something in which, however, he will not succeed.

Epilogue

There is no lack of artists who, in the face of the seemingly total exhaustion of our available musical apparatus in many modern works, and in an effort nonetheless to leave open the possibility of progress, lay hands on this musical apparatus, particularly on our tonal system of scales, by declaring it outmoded and in need of modernization. This modernization is supposed to occur in part by the use of exotic scale patterns, in part by the introduction of quarter tones or third tones. It is known, of course, that on occasion composers have drawn on the ecclesiastical modes current in earlier centuries so as to give one of their pieces a special stamp. The greatest example of this is the glorious Adagio in Beethoven's A minor Quartet. Exotic scales, whose characteristic features as a rule are the omission of an important scale step (the leading tone, the third or the fifth) as well as diminished and augmented intervals, can be of charming effect, but only for a brief time and in shorter movements. Used for too long, they involve the danger of fatigue since, no matter how they may be constituted, they resemble each other so much in structure and feeling that the ear cannot discern substantial differences between them. But they certainly produce, without exception, a mood of uniform melancholy, which can then be freely interpreted as Norwegian, Spanish, Slavic or Oriental, but which turns to boredom when it persists too long. Neither the exotic nor the antique modes can achieve more than episodic value.

One can hardly raise the objection to a still greater diminution in the size of scale steps than is now provided by the semitone, i.e. to the introduction of third and quarter tones, that the human ear would not become accustomed to them. Our hearing has become used to so much that with time it might even be enabled clearly to distinguish such small intervals and not to regard them any more as false. The objection lies deeper. I believe that it inheres in the nature of every art to overcome a resistance which lies within itself. The sculptor has to present the soft, living forms of the human body in hard marble. A human figure made of pliable wax has no artistic value. Colors as such do not glow but nevertheless the painter must produce light with them just as he has to create the illusion of depth on a flat surface. A picture actually presented in three dimensions with real light is a panorama or stage setting, not a painting. In poetry the contradiction arises that out of the word, which is merely a transmitter of prosaic thoughts, thus largely practical in its nature, there grow worlds filled with wondrously actual life and convincing to one's imagination. Finally, the musician has the task of conjuring up flowing and subtly changing forms out of scanty and awkward material. Only twelve semitones are available and each is separated from the other by a very perceptible gap. After twelve leaps over these gaps one again arrives at a point above or below that of the beginning. From there the leaps go on as if one were moving up and down over rods arranged in spirals and set at rather great distances each from the other. If one smudges the intervals, as on a violin for example, then it is not music but an unarticulated howling which results. The introduction of reduced intervals would only contribute to a progress towards such howling, from which our semitone music is at times already not too far removed.

To deprive art of its resistance is to destroy it.

We should be clear about one thing: that the emergence of the new and the great depends not on material external factors but on the culture of the entire people as well as on that of the individual person! What the individual is worth is expressed in his works, and what a people is worth, in the way in which it accepts the works.

The artist cannot remain apart from the bustle of the world. It is from life that he must receive his ideological views, his stimuli and the guiding principle of his own dynamics. Will our present-day existence, nervous, hasty, and tense to the utmost, permit in the midst of all such hurry and bustle the formation within a human spirit of that degree of contemplation and concentration from which can flow great works of art which do not bear the stamp of current fashion? Will there be a return—without a reactionary movement— to that sublimity without false solemnity, that grace without frivolity, that power and appeal of spirit which were the distinctions of our great masters, on the basis of today's mode of living and sentiments? In our age of technology and mercantilism, is an art still possible which stands above its time and thereby above all time? And if this really comes to pass, will a generation grow up which is able to appreciate this art? It is impossible to answer this. Moreover, the composers now coming to the fore should not concern themselves too much with these questions. Let them rather strive first of all to create within themselves a soil on which a pure art can bloom, one which serves no other end than its own beauty for its own sake. Feel, think, experience in the great manner (this is what I should like to call out to those who sense the divine gift of talent within them) and keep your souls as pure from all that is base as our masters did, for then you will bring forth what is right, and just as you do so, it will be good! If you cannot do that, then heap Ossa on Pelion, write for a thousand trombones and twice a hundred thousand tympani, and a monstrosity will emerge. Mere brilliance of workmanship alone will not do the trick. Naturalness, direct and forceful sincerity, that is what we need. Write down straightaway what lies in your hearts and speak out as unambiguously as possible what must be said! That will be a picture of your own self, an utterance of your being and in each instance something integral and genuine. But in addition have the courage to remain what you are if success does not present itself as quickly as you believe yourselves entitled to hope. Moreover, do not believe that a new Ninth Symphony or *Nibelungen* tetralogy must always emerge. It is granted only to a few to walk upon the heights of humanity and such superhumanity cannot be learned, cannot be constructed. It must come to us as the rarest endowment, as the most precious gift from another realm. "From which?" you ask, thirsting for knowledge. Well, from that realm which only he would deny who has never felt a breath from it steal over him. Be it a little song or a great symphony that you compose, it will only be a masterwork if that same motto suits it which the great Beethoven was entitled to write on the score of his *Missa Solemnis*:

From the heart—may it go to the heart.

A CATALOGUE OF SELECTED DOVER BOOKS
IN ALL FIELDS OF INTEREST

A CATALOGUE OF SELECTED DOVER BOOKS
IN ALL FIELDS OF INTEREST

WHAT IS SCIENCE?, *N. Campbell*
The role of experiment and measurement, the function of mathematics, the nature of scientific laws, the difference between laws and theories, the limitations of science, and many similarly provocative topics are treated clearly and without technicalities by an eminent scientist. "Still an excellent introduction to scientific philosophy," H. Margenau in *Physics Today*. "A first-rate primer . . . deserves a wide audience," *Scientific American*. 192pp. 5⅜ x 8.
S43   Paperbound $1.25

THE NATURE OF LIGHT AND COLOUR IN THE OPEN AIR, *M. Minnaert*
Why are shadows sometimes blue, sometimes green, or other colors depending on the light and surroundings? What causes mirages? Why do multiple suns and moons appear in the sky? Professor Minnaert explains these unusual phenomena and hundreds of others in simple, easy-to-understand terms based on optical laws and the properties of light and color. No mathematics is required but artists, scientists, students, and everyone fascinated by these "tricks" of nature will find thousands of useful and amazing pieces of information. Hundreds of observational experiments are suggested which require no special equipment. 200 illustrations; 42 photos. xvi + 362pp. 5⅜ x 8.
T196   Paperbound $2.00

THE STRANGE STORY OF THE QUANTUM, AN ACCOUNT FOR THE GENERAL READER OF THE GROWTH OF IDEAS UNDERLYING OUR PRESENT ATOMIC KNOWLEDGE, *B. Hoffmann*
Presents lucidly and expertly, with barest amount of mathematics, the problems and theories which led to modern quantum physics. Dr. Hoffmann begins with the closing years of the 19th century, when certain trifling discrepancies were noticed, and with illuminating analogies and examples takes you through the brilliant concepts of Planck, Einstein, Pauli, Broglie, Bohr, Schroedinger, Heisenberg, Dirac, Sommerfeld, Feynman, etc. This edition includes a new, long postscript carrying the story through 1958. "Of the books attempting an account of the history and contents of our modern atomic physics which have come to my attention, this is the best," H. Margenau, Yale University, in *American Journal of Physics*. 32 tables and line illustrations. Index. 275pp. 5⅜ x 8.
T518   Paperbound $2.00

GREAT IDEAS OF MODERN MATHEMATICS: THEIR NATURE AND USE, *Jagjit Singh*
Reader with only high school math will understand main mathematical ideas of modern physics, astronomy, genetics, psychology, evolution, etc. better than many who use them as tools, but comprehend little of their basic structure. Author uses his wide knowledge of non-mathematical fields in brilliant exposition of differential equations, matrices, group theory, logic, statistics, problems of mathematical foundations, imaginary numbers, vectors, etc. Original publication. 2 appendixes. 2 indexes. 65 ills. 322pp. 5⅜ x 8.
T587   Paperbound $2.00

A Short Account of the History of Mathematics,
W. W. Rouse Ball
Last previous edition (1908) hailed by mathematicians and laymen for lucid overview of math as living science, for understandable presentation of individual contributions of great mathematicians. Treats lives, discoveries of every important school and figure from Egypt, Phoenicia to late nineteenth century. Greek schools of Ionia, Cyzicus, Alexandria, Byzantium, Pythagoras; primitive arithmetic; Middle Ages and Renaissance, including European and Asiatic contributions; modern math of Descartes, Pascal, Wallis, Huygens, Newton, Euler, Lambert, Laplace, scores more. More emphasis on historical development, exposition of ideas than other books on subject. Non-technical, readable text can be followed with no more preparation than high-school algebra. Index. 544pp. 5⅜ x 8.   Paperbound $2.25

Great Ideas and Theories of Modern Cosmology, *Jagjit Singh*
Companion volume to author's popular "Great Ideas of Modern Mathematics" (Dover, $2.00). The best non-technical survey of post-Einstein attempts to answer perhaps unanswerable questions of origin, age of Universe, possibility of life on other worlds, etc. Fundamental theories of cosmology and cosmogony recounted, explained, evaluated in light of most recent data: Einstein's concepts of relativity, space-time; Milne's a priori world-system; astrophysical theories of Jeans, Eddington; Hoyle's "continuous creation;" contributions of dozens more scientists. A faithful, comprehensive critical summary of complex material presented in an extremely well-written text intended for laymen. Original publication. Index. xii + 276pp. 5⅜ x 8½.   Paperbound $2.00

The Restless Universe, *Max Born*
A remarkably lucid account by a Nobel Laureate of recent theories of wave mechanics, behavior of gases, electrons and ions, waves and particles, electronic structure of the atom, nuclear physics, and similar topics. "Much more thorough and deeper than most attempts . . . easy and delightful," *Chemical and Engineering News.* Special feature: 7 animated sequences of 60 figures each showing such phenomena as gas molecules in motion, the scattering of alpha particles, etc. 11 full-page plates of photographs. Total of nearly 600 illustrations. 351pp. 6⅛ x 9¼.   Paperbound $2.00

Planets, Stars and Galaxies: Descriptive Astronomy for Beginners,
A. E. Fanning
What causes the progression of the seasons? Phases of the moon? The Aurora Borealis? How much does the sun weigh? What are the chances of life on our sister planets? Absorbing introduction to astronomy, incorporating the latest discoveries and theories: the solar wind, the surface temperature of Venus, pock-marked face of Mars, quasars, and much more. Places you on the frontiers of one of the most vital sciences of our time. Revised (1966). Introduction by Donald H. Menzel, Harvard University. References. Index. 45 illustrations. 189pp. 5¼ x 8¼.   Paperbound $1.50

Great Ideas in Information Theory, Language and Cybernetics,
Jagjit Singh
Non-mathematical, but profound study of information, language, the codes used by men and machines to communicate, the principles of analog and digital computers, work of McCulloch, Pitts, von Neumann, Turing, and Uttley, correspondences between intricate mechanical network of "thinking machines" and more intricate neurophysiological mechanism of human brain. Indexes. 118 figures. 50 tables. ix + 338pp. 5⅜ x 8½.   Paperbound $2.00

THE MUSIC OF THE SPHERES: THE MATERIAL UNIVERSE — FROM ATOM TO QUASAR, SIMPLY EXPLAINED, *Guy Murchie*
Vast compendium of fact, modern concept and theory, observed and calculated data, historical background guides intelligent layman through the material universe. Brilliant exposition of earth's construction, explanations for moon's craters, atmospheric components of Venus and Mars (with data from recent fly-by's), sun spots, sequences of star birth and death, neighboring galaxies, contributions of Galileo, Tycho Brahe, Kepler, etc.; and (Vol. 2) construction of the atom (describing newly discovered sigma and xi subatomic particles), theories of sound, color and light, space and time, including relativity theory, quantum theory, wave theory, probability theory, work of Newton, Maxwell, Faraday, Einstein, de Broglie, etc. "Best presentation yet offered to the intelligent general reader," *Saturday Review.* Revised (1967). Index. 319 illustrations by the author. Total of xx + 644pp. 5⅜ x 8½.
Vol. 1 Paperbound $2.00, Vol. 2 Paperbound $2.00,
The set $4.00

FOUR LECTURES ON RELATIVITY AND SPACE, *Charles Proteus Steinmetz*
Lecture series, given by great mathematician and electrical engineer, generally considered one of the best popular-level expositions of special and general relativity theories and related questions. Steinmetz translates complex mathematical reasoning into language accessible to laymen through analogy, example and comparison. Among topics covered are relativity of motion, location, time; of mass; acceleration; 4-dimensional time-space; geometry of the gravitational field; curvature and bending of space; non-Euclidean geometry. Index. 40 illustrations. x + 142pp. 5⅜ x 8½.
Paperbound $1.35

HOW TO KNOW THE WILD FLOWERS, *Mrs. William Starr Dana*
Classic nature book that has introduced thousands to wonders of American wild flowers. Color-season principle of organization is easy to use, even by those with no botanical training, and the genial, refreshing discussions of history, folklore, uses of over 1,000 native and escape flowers, foliage plants are informative as well as fun to read. Over 170 full-page plates, collected from several editions, may be colored in to make permanent records of finds. Revised to conform with 1950 edition of Gray's Manual of Botany. xlii + 438pp. 5⅜ x 8½.
Paperbound $2.00

MANUAL OF THE TREES OF NORTH AMERICA, *Charles Sprague Sargent*
Still unsurpassed as most comprehensive, reliable study of North American tree characteristics, precise locations and distribution. By dean of American dendrologists. Every tree native to U.S., Canada, Alaska; 185 genera, 717 species, described in detail—leaves, flowers, fruit, winterbuds, bark, wood, growth habits, etc. plus discussion of varieties and local variants, immaturity variations. Over 100 keys, including unusual 11-page analytical key to genera, aid in identification. 783 clear illustrations of flowers, fruit, leaves. An unmatched permanent reference work for all nature lovers. Second enlarged (1926) edition. Synopsis of families. Analytical key to genera. Glossary of technical terms. Index. 783 illustrations, 1 map. Total of 982pp. 5⅜ x 8.
Vol. 1 Paperbound $2.25, Vol. 2 Paperbound $2.25,
The set $4.50

FABLES OF AESOP,
according to Sir Roger L'Estrange, with 50 drawings by Alexander Calder
Republication of rare 1931 Paris edition (limited to 665 copies) of 200 fables
by Aesop in the 1692 L'Estrange translation. Illustrated with 50 highly
imaginative, witty and occasionally ribald line drawings by the inventor of
"mobiles" and "stabiles." "Fifty wonderfully inventive Alexander Calder
drawings, impertinent as any of the artist's wire sculptures, make a delightful,
modern counterpoint to the thoroughly moral tales," *Saturday Review*. 124pp.
6½ x 9¼. Paperbound $1.25

DRAWINGS OF REMBRANDT
One of the earliest and best collections of Rembrandt drawings—the Lippmann-
Hofstede de Groot facsimiles (1888)—is here reproduced in entirety. Collection
contains 550 faithfully reproduced drawings in inks, chalks, and silverpoint;
some, hasty sketches recorded on a handy scrap of paper; others, studies for
well-known oil paintings. Edited, with scholarly commentary by Seymour
Slive, Harvard University. "In large matters of appearance, size (9 x 12-inch
page), paper color and weight, uniformity of plate texture, typography and
printing, these two volumes could scarcely be improved," *Arts and Architecture*.
"Altogether commendable . . . among the year's best," *New York Times*.
Editor's introduction, notes. 3 indexes, 2 concordances. Total of lxxix +
552pp. 9⅛ x 12¼. Two volume set, paperbound $6.00
Two volume set, clothbound $12.50

THE EARLY WORK OF AUBREY BEARDSLEY
Together with *The Later Work*, the standard source for the most important
Beardsley drawings. Edited by John Lane, *Early Work* contains 157 full-page
plates including Burne-Jones style work, the *Morte d'Arthur* series, cover
designs and illustrations from *The Studio* and other magazines, theatre
posters, "Kiss of Judas," "Seigfried," portraits of himself, Emile Zola, and
Verdi, and illustrations for Wilde's play *Salome*. 2 color plates. Introduction
by H. C. Marillier. xii + 175pp. 8⅛ x 11. Paperbound $2.50
Clothbound $8.50

THE LATER WORK OF AUBREY BEARDSLEY
Edited by John Lane, collection contains 174 full-page plates including
Savoy and *Yellow Book* illustrations, book plates, "The Wagnerites," "La
Dame aux Camellias," selections from *Lysistrata*, illustrations to *Das Rhein-
gold, Venus and Tannhauser*, and the "Rape of the Lock" series. 2 color
plates. xiv + 174pp. 8⅛ x 11. Paperbound $2.50
Clothbound $8.50

Prices subject to change without notice.

Available at your book dealer or write for free catalogue to Dept. Adsci,
Dover Publications, Inc., 180 Varick St., N.Y., N.Y. 10014. Dover publishes more
than 150 books each year on science, elementary and advanced mathematics,
biology, music, art, literary history, social sciences and other areas.